Praise for *Rusted Off* by Gabri

'A sympathetic and insightful account of the lives of the people in a struggling and troubled country town.' Prime Minister's Literary Awards judges

'Chan has produced a clear-eyed, honest and necessary decryption key for the times in which we live.' Rick Morton, *Australian*

'The Australian political book of the year because it sets about reporting the remarkable political times we live in in the way the story needs to be reported: from the ground up, with empathy and intellect.' Katharine Murphy's Book of the Year 2018, *Guardian*

'The definitive account of life on the other side of the city-country divide. Written with a soft heart and a hard head, this is one of the most important books about Australia today.' George Megalogenis

'*Rusted Off* strives to see the good in the contemporary Australian condition, rural and urban, but equally tell the story of national transition that has left us divided, resentful and less secure than earlier generations.' *Sydney Morning Herald*

'Chan is a very good journalist, trained to get at the particulars of what she is reporting and to enrich her account by seeking out contextual factors. Chan's account of the political history is skilfully interwoven with narratives tracking the lives of individuals from her community.' Jane Goodall, *Inside Story*

Also by Gabrielle Chan

Rusted Off: Why country Australia is fed up

WHY YOU SHOULD GIVE A F*CK ABOUT FARMING

(BECAUSE YOU EAT)

GABRIELLE CHAN

VINTAGE BOOKS
Australia

VINTAGE

UK | USA | Canada | Ireland | Australia
India | New Zealand | South Africa | China

Vintage is part of the Penguin Random House group of companies
whose addresses can be found at global.penguinrandomhouse.com

First published by Vintage in 2021

Cover photography: Tomato dissection, from plant to ketchup,
by Maren Caruso, courtesy of Getty Images
Cover design by James Rendall © Penguin Random House Australia Pty Ltd
Internal design by Midland Typesetters, Australia
Typeset in Minion Pro by Midland Typesetters

Printed and bound in Australia by Griffin Press, part of Ovato, an accredited
ISO AS/NZS 14001 Environmental Management Systems printer

A catalogue record for this
book is available from the
National Library of Australia

ISBN 978 1 76089 933 2

penguin.com.au

CONTENTS

For Henry and Lily and all
my grandchildren to follow

INTRODUCTION

If you had told me thirty years ago that I would be moved to write a book in my fifty-fifth year about farming, I would have said you were barking mad. I literally didn't give a stuff about farming. I was an inner-city journalist who grew up in the middle of Sydney. Farmers were 'out there' *she gestures* – a long way away from any substantial action worth knowing about. Farmers were the remnants of a quaint occupation that Australia used to rely on. Something about a sheep's back. I knew they grew wheat and beef. What I did not think about was the connection with the bread in the toaster or the steak in the fridge. Sure, farmers were rolled out any time we wanted to make a statement about Australian identity, but I didn't know any. They just weren't relevant to us, the vast majority in the city. We talked about them when there was another drought, though I can't remember seeing them on television much – maybe the farmer look-alike in the Sydney Olympic opening ceremony riding a horse, but that was about it. Farming had nothing to do with my life and that was fine by me.

And then I met The Farmer. I suppose you could fall in love with someone and hate their occupation. I didn't; I became thoroughly fascinated by The Farmer's job. As a committed eater, who wouldn't love a food grower? But, as you can imagine, I had some preconceptions. My journalism started under the Hawke–Keating Labor government of the 1980s and my political writing started in the 1990s, at the beginning of the recession Australia had to have. Long-standing industries were being decimated. The death of the manufacturing industry was showing me in practice concepts like structural unemployment and inflation, which had previously been just theories in Year 12 economics. I didn't, however, take much notice of the structural adjustments going on in farming. I was vaguely aware of agriculture, but it didn't intrude into what I used to think were the exciting parts of politics, like leadership spills or factional intrigue.

It just gets so much more personal when your livelihood depends on it. The Farmer's mixed broadacre farm is a commercial-sized operation in southern New South Wales, which primarily grows sheep and wheat. It is a family farm, bought four generations ago when the large squatter blocks were carved up during one of the land reform periods. The squatters had taken it from the Wiradjuri people, who have lived here for tens of thousands of years. The descendants of those first inhabitants continue to live here and the traces their ancestors left on the land are unobtrusive but unmistakeable.

The way Indigenous people fed themselves, the way they survived and thrived, was underpinned by their system of encouraging the foods they prized, and sculpting land for their long-term use. Landscape was embedded in foundational and spiritual beliefs, while intimately woven with life-giving food. The people's mark was left on the terrain, but land was considered neither separate nor outside of the people.

I was grafted onto a farming culture that has European roots; whose development was based on an industrial model from the get-go. The colonial leaders' first job was to feed the settlement, then to export the excess to help feed England, the mother country. Farmers were encouraged and protected in Australia, as they still are in many countries. Land was bestowed, stolen or bought, its bounty was for taking and its capacity considered infinite. Like a rubber band, we thought it could stretch without breaking because that was the economic imperative. To feed people.

So it wasn't my plan to transplant myself from a city to a country culture on a mid-sized traditional farm, but life has a habit of getting in the way of plans. To be clear, I am a journalist, not a farmer. And I do want to make that clear – the farm enterprise belongs to The Farmer. I don't have an agricultural degree. I am not like a lot of women who are farmers in their own right, yet only recently recognised. Hell, I don't even do the books. It's not my thing. I don't work the farm day to day because I write.

We did try to work together when the kids were little, but it didn't turn out very well. Early in our marriage, The Farmer suggested I climb up a rickety ladder into an old concrete silo to shovel out some mouldy wheat in the bottom so he could refill it. He suggested that, because the ladder was rickety, and a little bit rusty, TBH, it would be better for me, as a lighter person, to do it. I did not want to appear a scaredy-cat or a shirker, the worst thing you can be around here, so I climbed in. I was asked to move the grain out of the tiny opening about a foot up from the base of the silo. It was a stinky operation and The Farmer soon discovered what it was to be married to an annoying newspaper journalist. As he stood outside the tiny opening, shovelling the grain away from the silo, my live commentary involved a soliloquy on the inefficiency of the system, the stupidity of old flat-bottom silos, ten things he could do to improve the operation, the danger of mould to an allergy sufferer like me, and scattergun questioning on how much else of his infrastructure was this outdated. I could only hear mumbling, punctuated by 'Jesus Christ' and promises to do it himself next time.

Suffice to say, we are very independent-minded people. I don't run The Farmer's operation and he doesn't write my books. But somewhere in the last twenty-five years of living on a farm, and increasingly reporting on rural issues, I started to question the economic agenda that was set in train by the Hawke–Keating and Howard governments in those pivotal decades. Australia, like many countries around the world, was outsourcing what it could not do for the cheapest possible price. But how was this going to work for food?

I decided to look at this farming caper that I had been living alongside for all these years. I wanted to understand how it came to be, and I discovered that by pulling a thread on a farm, I was quickly taken to foundational philosophical questions about the way we live and how we want to organise our communities, and society as a whole. Farming remains as central to the questions of humanity and our future as it ever was. We just don't think about it that much because we think we have solved that food problem a long time ago and there are far more urgent questions to get on with.

I wanted to know one simple thing. Why you should care about farming. Or indeed whether you should. Because maybe I would find that we don't need to care; that food will be made in laboratories by big processors, a range of versions of Soylent Green, either in liquid or solid. And then we could just lock up large swathes of landscapes to return to wilderness, to somehow capture carbon and reverse species loss and renew waterways without human management.

In my investigations, I was forced to strip away the white noise and return to the basics. What is this act called farming and where does it lead? I thought about many issues, beginning with this: every person and animal needs food to live. How food is grown and where it comes from are choices for every individual and country to make.

Think about how this currently happens in Australia. At its most basic, farmers use soil and water to grow crops and raise animals. In the act of growing, farmers must look after landscapes. Australian farmers manage up to 60 per cent of the country's land mass and account for up to 70 per cent of its diverted fresh-water extractions.[1] So we all have a stake in farmers doing their job well.

The acts of choosing a farming system for a place, growing food and selling it are like trying to weave a large tapestry. They require care, dexterity, a range of skills, and if one thread comes loose, things can start to unravel. Farmers feed us, look after the landscape (or not), punch above their weight for exports and contribute to, or ameliorate, climate change. They play a crucial role in the social infrastructure of many rural communities.

Farming both contributes to and is endangered by the biggest existential threats of our time: climate change, water shortages, soil loss, energy production, natural disasters, zoonotic diseases, population displacement and geopolitical trade wars.

That means we need governments to get the policy settings right. Yet no Australian political party is doing serious thinking about how to knit together food, farming and environmental policies to continue feeding the population while mitigating climate change and biodiversity loss. We remain caught in old ways of thinking about farming that hark back to 1788. But the growing market pressure on environmental, health and animal welfare issues mean farming cannot be business as usual.

For a brief moment, at the height of panic over the COVID-19 pandemic in 2020, we got a glimpse of what it's like to live without basic ingredients on the shelves. Bread, pasta, rice, meat and canned goods disappeared from supermarkets. Small local food producers were overwhelmed as people wanted to source food from elsewhere. Food prices rose and global supply chains could not cope with demand. After years of market-centric structural change, national production capacity was left wanting, and not just in food chains. Face masks, medical equipment and hand sanitiser were the first priorities, but there was a flicker of discussion about food security.

The Australian government and national farming advocates reacted with campaigns to snuff out any conversation about holes in our food system. Nothing to see here, they said. Yet this was a live opportunity to look around the world and realise why so many countries consider farming and natural resources to be in their *national strategic interest*.

As I write, Australia has no national food policy, no national drought policy, a Hunger Games-style water policy, a cursory climate policy and no vision for how land management and environmental assets should fit with farming and food security in a warming climate.

Nor are there any state or national strategies or guiding principles to govern the competition between our limited high-quality, food-production land and residential development, mining and energy interests. Conservation, agriculture and land management are dominated by two loud clubs. One says, lock it all up. The other says, it's my domain and I can do what I like. I'm interested in a more nuanced approach.

I wanted to think about key questions. What do we want to

farm? If we concentrate on a few big exports – say beef and wheat – what diversity do we lose along the way? Do we want shorter supply chains for some critical assets in case of future epidemics? Who do we want to do the farming? Do we want to maintain a balance of big corporations at scale, smaller and mid-sized family farmers, including Indigenous land owners, as well as micro growers? Do we want our land and water owned and managed by 800 companies or 80,000 companies and families? Do we want to put all our environmental and food eggs in those 800 baskets? How do we want to look after the land and water that we rely on for farming in a changing climate? We all need to care about those questions.

As someone who lives and draws an income from food production, I wanted to think about the whole bloody thing, to consider the chain that leads from the soil all the way to the eaters, because as a country we need to understand how farming fits as one piece in one big landscape puzzle. And I wanted to examine themes that resonate around the globe to know where the trends are and what we can expect in the future.

This book is also a response to the contradictory policies around food-growing. Here are some messages from governments and eaters to farmers. We want clean, green food to feed the world. We want scale because we want cheap food. We want family farmers. We want the mums and dads. We want big global capital. We want lots to export to help our balance of payments. We want resilience. We want farmers to stand on their own two feet. We want to pay no subsidies. We want farming to be like any other business. We want farmers to use the latest technology. We want them to look after the environment. We want farmers to look after native habitat for declining species. And now we want them to sequester carbon to turn around both their own emissions and some of the rest of the population's emissions. I think that just about covers it.

My discovery process has not been linear. Like a beagle on the scent of a bunny, it has zigzagged – through time and disciplines; from science to philosophy to politics to culture and back again. It's been maddening, confusing and confronting. It accounts for the challenges of farming but also challenges the way we farm. Many times I've thought I have bitten off more than I could chew because the act of farming and its ramifications seem so simple but are so complex.

Since these are such complex systems, I can only act as a guide of sorts, to describe my various windows into the food-growing chain. My view will be different to others because a view depends on where you are standing. It cannot be exhaustive but I hope it sheds a light on some important changes that are going on in our food system, and where the cracks are appearing. I believe it is an urgent conversation. Australian farming is changing rapidly. If you look across this landscape in coming years and you don't like some of what you see, you can't say you weren't warned.

Indeed, that's where you come in. Eaters will be the ultimate arbiter of where and how food is grown and how the land is cared for. There are many more eaters than farmers, and we all vote. We all have a stake in the future of food and farming. I am going to show you why.

Chapter 1

ON THE BIG PICTURE

Most people come at food production as eaters and not growers. I think it's important to connect what we eat to who grows it and how it is grown. Responsibility flows between the producer and the eater and back again. Food, like voting, has strong cultural links. When I think of my food culture, I think first of my beloved Australian grandmother, who had a meal for every night of the week. Sunday was roast lamb, roast potato, carrots, parsnip and soggy cauliflower. From there, she ranged through a predictable menu, which I adored. There were crumbed cutlets with peas and mashed potatoes. There was what she called 'sour cream stew' – a beef stew with carrots, sour cream added at the end, and served on rice. I suspect it was an Aussie version of the Hungarian stew. Another favourite was cauliflower cheese with a steak. There was of course spaghetti bolognaise; that came with a classic iceberg salad, tomato wedges and shallots or red onion.

Meat was a given, potatoes and peas were fresh and shelled, boiled with a sprig of mint. Sometimes she would branch out, with a silverside, or tripe with white sauce, though we weren't gone on tripe so she tended to save it for when her grandchildren weren't eating. Curry was also on the menu, but it was her version – with apple and sultanas; blander and sweeter than our home-cooked Singapore curries. We hoovered it up all the same.

Dinner was served like clockwork at 6 pm, after my grandfather had (most nights) returned from work and the pub, and would be over by 6.30, but not before dessert when we grandchildren were there, which was usually ice cream with a baked pudding of some sort: bread and butter pudding, rice pudding, baked custard. There were pikelets in a tin on the fridge, and cheese and Saos for anyone who needed them later. That was usually my grandfather, who'd insist on 'small for me' at dinner, before announcing he was still hungry after the plates had been washed up and put away.

Food was procured by my grandmother on her daily walk 'down the road' in Sydney's beachside Coogee in its pre-hip days. The supermarket was first – there, she picked up only what she needed that day. Then the butcher, who knew us all by name. Then, if she wanted something slightly exotic, she might go to Con's fruit and veg shop. But if it was standard potatoes, peas, cauliflower and tomatoes, it would be Mr Ed, who had a fruit barrow on the corner of the main road, which she saved until last. He put the veggies in a paper bag and swung it around a couple of times with both hands to close the top, so the bag had little pig's ears.

In my Singapore grandparents' household, it was my Chinese grandfather who did a lot of the cooking because he ran the well-respected Polar Cafe in Singapore until his retirement. He also went shopping daily, but he went to the wet markets, taking my father to help carry the goods home. Theirs was a protein-rich diet, a legacy of a living through wartime Singapore, where protein was the holy grail. He told me once that his seven children had grown tall because of all the meat they ate.

Everything in the household centred around the dining room table. When my family visited from Australia, we three children were instructed to take as few clothes as possible. Instead, we packed food into our oversized luggage; beautiful Australian food my grandparents could not buy in Singapore. We would call it 'produce' now, but food is food. There was stone fruit, tins of sockeye salmon and roasted salted pumpkin seeds. We'd even take novelty stuff like wine bladders, which had just hit the market in Australia. The first night in Singapore was spent catching up, with longnecks of beer for the grown-ups, and pumpkin seed shells being dealt around the laminex table like mahjong tiles. It was glorious sucking the salty outer layer, before splitting the shell between your teeth, pushing back the skin and delicately extracting the seed without breaking it. I'd practise for hours.

In our own home in suburban Sydney, the fusion of a Singaporean-Chinese father and an Anglo-Celtic mother mashed together these two food cultures. Lots of wok business, stir-fried anything, including spam, curries and fried rice, and whatever could be bought in bulk. Dad once brought home a huge bag of carrots, which he proceeded to boil and freeze. We ate them forever. Budget and volume were the key factors and when the bulk supermarkets turned up in the late 1970s, he was a regular visitor. Cases of Nutri-Grain and boxes of tinned mushrooms (I don't recommend them) were stacked in the laundry if they'd been on special.

After my parents split, my stepmother arrived and introduced us to lots of new food. Beef Wellington blew our minds, and avocados were like gold, to match the shag pile. Watermelon salads, scooped into little balls, SERVED IN THE WATERMELON! Clearly anything was possible. The diet was incredibly meat-heavy. It was not, and still is not, unusual to have four shared dishes, three different meats and one vege.

Those meals seem a long way away from the stuff most of us eat today. I am not glorifying them. As much as I still love a roast, I wouldn't want one every day, as The Farmer mostly had, growing up on a sheep farm. His childhood meals were a window to country Australian culture. Rolled oats for breakfast, scones for morning tea and a roast lamb for lunch. Dinners were steaks, mash, peas, pancakes with the leftover lamb, macaroni cheese, *Women's Weekly* curry, shepherd's pie as well as golden syrup puddings, baked puddings, bread and butter puddings in the same enamel baking dishes my grandmother used.

I share those stories because the food system is so much more than the stuff that ends up on your plate. Food is simple. We can't live very long without it. Our health depends directly on its volume and quality. Wars are fought over food and its lack. Think of any revolution and it usually starts with famine or shortage.

Food is also complex. On a daily basis, it creates space for human connections and, increasingly, it speaks to our identity. We obsess over what we are prepared to eat and what we won't eat. Many of us now use food as a marker for our values: carnivore, vegan, vegetarian, pescatarian, gluten-free, paleo. We eat based on price, or our wish to mitigate climate change, or to have an effect on land regeneration, local producers or the price of milk. Yet so many of us take the supply of our food for granted, particularly in a high-producing country like Australia.

The modern food system is vast, taking in animals and humans, their cultures, their governments, the natural resources of soil and water and the climate, global supply chains. The interactions between all of these elements would create a flow chart that circles and then scatters, like a mob of lambs. While these are global themes, they lie at the heart of our strategic national interests and are particularly central to the future of country Australia.

At the same time, just like eaters, farmers are fracturing into tribes. We often talk about multigenerational farmers because it seems to matter to us that there is a historical lineage – notwithstanding the much longer line of generations of Indigenous people who were driven off their land. Indigenous Australians practised light agriculture and land management in a way that respected the natural world's connections. We now have to feed a much bigger population but there are elements of this Indigenous legacy we could draw on. We have been too slow to acknowledge this.

We also have to understand identity plays a big role in motivating people who want to farm. Growing up on a landscape can send deep roots into a place and make someone value a landscape much more than its market value. That does not necessarily mean the custodian looks after it any better. We have to acknowledge that.

All children begin life as little David Attenboroughs, chasing lady beetles and knowing the best places to find the turtles and hunt for tadpoles and look out for water rats. And many people I know who are born and work on the land always have that connection to nature and place. But, even if they pursue a career on the land, others might have that view of the world drummed out of them at university, particularly in an agricultural degree. The rules of the economy, the policies laid down by our governments, are set on turning little David Attenboroughs into *Farmer economicus* – maximising economic profit as a food producer.

Those are the only signals food producers get right now, and a farmer needs to feed their family. *Farmer economicus* is the model farmer, in control of their domain, sovereign over the lands within their boundary fences. The idea of nature as man's dominion goes back a long way in the western canon. Back to the sixteenth century and Francis Bacon and his vision of new science. Back to Genesis, which set out man's dominion over nature. The farm images crept in with the King James version. 'Let Us make man in Our image, according to Our likeness; let them have dominion over the fish of the sea, over the fowl of the air, and over the cattle, over all the earth and over every creeping thing that creepeth upon the earth.'

Far be it from me to dispute the Bible, but the climate is telling us otherwise. The era of maximising returns while using animals and landscape at will is over. And if you don't believe the science, you might take heed of the mighty market.

Financial liberalisation pursued since the 1980s has and will continue to change the nature of farming, what food is grown and how it is grown, and that will have material effects on food supply into the future. Governments and large agribusiness constantly tell farmers to grow more food but rarely focus on the range, quality or health outcomes of the food grown, or the production impact of pushing the landscape or its inhabitants (human and otherwise) to produce food en masse for the lowest possible price.

No doubt, all that production has fed a lot of people and pulled a portion out of poverty. But the world currently wastes one-third of all food grown, while two billion adults are overweight. Another 690 million are going hungry.[1] The food system is out of whack.

And while the price of food is historically low in richer countries, the price of conventional farm inputs is rising. As a result, the only way most farmers can increase their pay packet is to increase the amount they grow by doing more with less. This is particularly true for mid-sized growers who produce bulk commodities rather than supplying niche farmers markets and premium food retailers.

The focus on growing more has made agribusiness input companies and food processors rich, but keeps many farmers chasing their tails, which can result in their land condition going backwards. Buy more land, buy more machinery, take on more debt, require more inputs and then buy more land. Ad infinitum.

The looming problem is that the price of food is not sufficient for land and waterways to be cared for properly, even though land and water care become ever more critical as the climate changes. Added to these environmental challenges are the clear structural changes in farming. Post-invasion, Australian farms have swung between very large operations owned by squatters to smaller family farms encouraged by government land acts to increase food production for export. Australian governments, big agribusiness and many farming advocates have been singing the productivity song for a long time. These messages accelerated in the financial deregulation of the 1980s. Get big or get out. Produce more with less. Buy bigger machinery. Grow more tonnes. Trade in futures. Trade in water. Get rid of your collectives, cooperatives and single-desk trading platforms. Anything legal goes.

A lightbulb moment for me was realising that deregulation is a misnomer. Farming wasn't so much deregulated as it was *re*regulated – to favour the interests of investors, traders, private equity and banking. As a result, many farmers can make more money out of trading water than they can growing food. That is a problem.

In the process, mid-sized farmers are hollowing out. Foodie-focused farmers markets favour small, niche producers who know the names of their sheep and can turn up on weekends to talk to their customers. That is harder with a flock of 5000, let alone 50,000. At the same time, large consumer markets, the big supermarkets, favour cheap food at scale such as that produced by large corporates or corporatised families.

Historically, in the last century Big Agribusiness, Big Capital and Big Food have left much of the food-growing to family farmers because that's the risky bit. Now they have discovered that growing food at scale can add another link in their vertically integrated chain.

Global superannuation funds, private equity firms, banks, large corporatised families and state-owned agribusinesses are buying as well as leasing farm land because it is a safe haven in an unpredictable world and demand for food is rising. Along with low interest rates, demand is driving the current Australian rural land boom, and it is driving a fundamental change in who's farming food and how it's farmed, particularly on irrigated land. Still, when most Australians think of farming they think of a mid-sized family farmer. We know this because the large food companies sashaying into agriculture still put pictures of Mr and Mrs McDonald in overalls on their tomato cans. They don't use a picture of the chief executive officer of a private equity firm in a suit. Is that because they're aware the population would likely prefer a more democratised landscape?

Multinational corporations have both contributed to the increase in global food production and profited from it by producing herbicides, pesticides, tractors, spray rigs, fuels, oils and parts. Multinationals have also dominated commodity trading and food manufacturing, some since colonial trading days. In the nineteenth century, governments intervened through land reforms to ensure the business of growing food was dominated by small to medium-sized family farmers. Those small-business people essentially owned their jobs and maybe employed a few others. Technology has been progressing, but there are still so many jobs that can only be done by a human. A robot can't do the delicate work of picking cherries. A robot can't shear a sheep well.

The economics of farming is, therefore, transforming our food-growing industry and the landscape into something else. Despite those government interventions, decades of deregulation mean Australian farming no longer consists mainly of small to medium family farms. Australia has scale and size, and the land is still relatively cheap by global standards, even though the soils aren't as fertile as in other farming countries. Australia has an open water market, which makes water a tradeable commodity that sells to the highest bidder. That works really well for big investors with access to specialised knowledge and cash.

So what do we want farming to be? The headline answer, if you ask the major farming advocacy body, is in dollars. The National Farmers' Federation (NFF) in combination with the federal government want Australian agriculture to be a $100 billion industry by 2030. That means adding another $40 billion worth of value from 2021.

The $100 billion plan comes with an aspiration to grow sustainably in a changing climate. Food production is a significant source of greenhouse gases (around 13 per cent of emissions in Australia) but land management can also be a carbon sink. Soil erosion is happening at a much faster rate than soil formation – ten to twenty times faster for no-till farming and up to 100 times faster for conventional tillage, according to the Intergovernmental Panel on Climate Change (IPCC).[2]

The way we farm can create better environmental outcomes but the current food price is holding a portion of farmers back from making bigger shifts. In the end, someone has to pay for impacts that travel far beyond the boundary fence – the farmer, or the eater via the price of food, or both. The NFF's plan would see 5 per cent of farm income come from payments for environmental services provided by the farmer. It wants to measure natural capital, or the environmental assets in any given ecosystem, to get a scientific measure of whether it is rising or falling. This would be a big shift in Australian policy, which I will come to in 'On natural value'.

For most Australian eaters, our food culture has long been separated from the land and the people who grow food. Who eats the wheat or the beef and how she eats it is neither here nor there to most farmers. This is not to say that farmers are not proud of what they produce. It is simply to reiterate that volume is the only way most can make money, and once they get the cheque, they prepare for the next harvest.

Originally, volume came from land size. The more land you had, the more food you could grow. Technology improved and horses were replaced by tractors. A wing of humans and scythes was replaced by headers. After the Second World War, American agronomist Norman Borlaug worked on initiatives to increase crop yields, with the aim of feeding the world – a movement that came to be known as the Green Revolution. More food could then be grown without more land. Borlaug won a Nobel Peace Prize in 1970 for his role in fighting global hunger. He was also interested in yield to ensure what we would now call sustainable development.[3] Improving yield was a way of taking the pressure off the natural world; it was a way to sustain us with a food system that served humans while keeping the natural world in balance.

Fast forward to the twenty-first century. Combine the biggering of food production with ongoing environmental degradation, and the policy signals become vital. As larger and larger companies control bigger parcels of land, the impacts of their farming on the environment will also be at scale, for good or ill. That will have ramifications for our landscape. So do we want to keep going in this direction of bigger landholders? And putting aside their size, do we care if farmers look after the landscape or are we only concerned with cheap food? Would we be prepared to pay for that stewardship in the price of our food or our tax dollars?

Whether it is an Australian Indigenous burn, the introduction and culling of pests like foxes, mice and rabbits, growing a sustainable crop, preserving land for a national park, or the wholesale clearing of Amazon forests for more cattle, we must accept that humans shape landscape, to a greater or lesser extent, for better or for worse. These are value judgements, usually ordained by governments. We have come to this point in the cycle of nature and economics because government has mostly directed land use. In Australia, we have focused solely on growing more and more to earn export income. Given that governments have much of the control over the direction of land use, we need to work out whether export is the key reason to drive farming. We need to decide what successful farming and landscape management looks like and what we are prepared to trade off in the process of growing food.

If governments want to feed a nation and have viable regional populations and cities that are less crowded, we have to come to an accommodation on how we live on land and use it in the Anthropocene. It is not enough to say, 'I live in a city, it's up to someone else.' If you eat, you have a stake in how and where food is grown. You have a stake in who grows it, how it gets to you and who profits. Equally, as a farmer it's not enough to say, 'I am the owner of my land and it's nobody's business whether I rip and tear.' A land manager's actions have consequences. We have to ask, 'What is the best way to farm for our local places?'

The good news is that Australians have created a lot of innovative natural resource management programs, which have brought together formerly warring tribes like the green movement and the farmer groups. The bad news is that in the past decades, small-minded politicians have sought to snuff out the legacy of the previous governments. We don't back good ideas for the long term and then we wonder why evidence-based policies don't work. We have killed more clever policy institutes than I've had hot breakfasts: the National Water Commission, Land and Water Australia and the National Climate Change Adaptation Research Facility, to name a few. All were doing good work to try to synthesise and build the foundations for some connected policy solutions for managing our very tricky and ancient land mass. As a smart land management expert once told me, 'We're trying to add more storeys to a tall building using bricks and timber from the lower floors.'

We are very task-oriented creatures until we're pushed off course. The COVID crisis should be forcing a rethink of communities and the foundations on which our systems of exchange are built, not least around food. If your anxiety rose when you experienced a row of empty shelves at the supermarket during the pandemic, we need to talk about where that food comes from.

You see, though I have lived on the farm for a quarter of a century, I discovered I am still steeped in the mindset that food always comes from a supermarket. Trips there were my formative childhood experience. I still make a distinction between the food I buy from the supermarket and the stuff we grow on the farm. This is in spite of the fact that farming is not a side dish for us. It underwrites our life. It pays the bills.

The staple, historic Australian commodities that The Farmer grows are delivered in bulk, the wheat measured in tonnes when it lands in the local delivery terminal. It is not hand milled and lovingly baked into your daily bread in a farmhouse oven. Our lambs are delivered to a buyers' market. We don't process those animals into retail packs and cart them around as chops to weekend markets. We don't spend our days dressed in rugged, sexy farm hipster wear, spruiking our story on Instagram. We are price takers. There are no artisans around here.

Not that I wouldn't love to be an artisan. Like half of the world, I did try to bake sourdough during lockdown, until the supermarkets ran out of yeast and flour. We have silos full of wheat but I had no mill, so I bought some spelt flour from the chemist. My first attempts were pathetic. I quickly ploughed through the 1 kg flour bags so I ordered a 25 kg sack. When it turned up, it was covered in German. The bag of wholemeal had flown all the way from Germany due to the shortage in Australia, the fifth-biggest wheat-growing country in the world. It had made its way onto a wheat farm. I shrivelled at my stupidity. It was time to buy a home grain mill.

My sourdough craze didn't last long – one of my main problems was a leaky oven that struggled to come to a high enough temperature. But it did set me thinking about our separating what we grow and what we eat – even farmers. I had mentally filed the wheat that filled our silos as a commodity, opting for the convenience of ready-milled, stale inert flour. Not choosing our own product made absolutely no sense.

But that is the modern mindset: food is something you get from a supermarket. And it has created one of the biggest duopolies in the Australian economy. Number one is Woolworths and number two is Coles and they have around a third each of the total market. It is passing strange that as people who built our modern economy eating home-grown lamb chops and wheat bread, we seem unable to think strategically about what we want from the food system and the people who supply us with that food.

Essentially, we must find a way to knit together the need to grow and supply food with how we manage landscape. Australia needs a national master plan for its land and food; we need to know how we are to protect our sacred places and unique species for their longevity, and that of the environment and our rural communities.

Responsibility for food, farming and landscape is shared by a number of local, state and federal government ministers and departments, particularly agriculture, environment, health and home affairs. The imperative to get it right impacts our kitchen tables, the nation, the globe. Because it is everybody's responsibility, it is nobody's responsibility.

I am convinced that the job at hand for these ministers and departments, or concerned citizens, is to imagine a food, land and water system that walks the path between wild utopia and human reality. We need to devise a plan that looks at the country as a whole and determines for our population projections of how much food is necessary to sustain ourselves into the future and how diverse our food system should be – in what it produces, in who produces it and where they live. This plan would identify and protect the best food-production land and intertwine with the national reserve system that maps conservation areas across the country. It would identify high-value conservation areas and prime agricultural land as no-go zones for developments like housing and mining. It might point to partial development areas and open slather sites. It might map out areas designed for clever future housing that would not impinge on limited high-quality food-production land.

In supply, a food plan would be both local and global, with short, stout chains into our local communities and regions, and then longer freight lines that share our substantial production capacity with the world but particularly with our near neighbours. The priority is a realistic food price that covers the requirements of a healthy ecosystem and the humans who provide their labour to bring the food to your plate. It would acknowledge, rather than deny, our reliance for food security on many different imported components, from the fuel, machinery and inputs to widgets. It would identify our weaknesses. It would be robust and transparent enough to link to a natural capital account so we could measure the outcomes of food production on our natural world and keep building smarter choices. It would measure the nutrition of the food so eaters could reward healthful food systems and encourage wholefood eating in a world that suffers from both obesity and undernourishment.

And while we are at it, why curb our ambition? We rely on land for so many different things and, as the climate changes, those uses are going to change. Our national plan might also include suitable sites for carbon sequestration projects and renewable energy. It would consider a transparent water policy and a visionary soil policy, with its capacity to balance our carbon budget. Finally, this national backyard plan would be afforded the status of the defence portfolio. That would make it of primary importance in both the cabinet, the budget and the nation.

Such a food, land and water plan is, surely, a no-brainer.

Chapter 2

ON HISTORY

Oral McGuire was named after pioneer of US television evangelism Oral Roberts. McGuire is one of eleven children, and once you take into account his parents' brothers and his sisters' children, grand-children and great-grandchildren, there are 105 in his family. If you add up all the generations alive, and all the other surnames, you get to about 5000 people, all part of McGuire's extended family. So, he tells his kids, if they come from the Western Australian wheatbelt, they are our mob. The Ballardong Noongar mob.

His mother nailed Oral's name because preachers are story-tellers and Oral is descended from a long line of storytellers. He also chairs the Noongar Land Enterprise Group (NLE), represent-ing eight Noongar family groups who have acquired land through the Indigenous Land and Sea Corporation (ILSC) in the past two decades.

When the ILSC had the chance to acquire country, Oral gave the real estate agent strict instructions. Oral told him, 'If you look at the land and think, there's no way it would be good for sheep or cropping, that's the sort of country that we want.'

'It's pretty rugged country,' he tells me.

Noongar Boodja (country) takes in 200,000 square kilometres of southwest Western Australia. Its fifteen different languages and dialects make up the Noongar nation, the biggest Indigenous cultural block in Australia. The businesses in the NLE cooperative cover 20,000 hectares and the family groups plan to pursue ethical and appropriate partnerships within their traditional kinship laws/lores. The NLE cooperative model allows them to share common knowledge across marketing and commercial opportunities while maintaining a diversity of different products. As representatives of an ancient culture, they want to bring their story to the world through food and medicine produced on their land, as both traditional custodians and property owners.

'Being able to use stories and storytelling and language in a songline or Dreaming-story context helps us understand the marketability of what we are doing, but also take advantage of much of the bush produce and much of history of knowledge and connection to country, and a lot of native species endemic on our properties,' says Oral. 'This is very much a cultural expression. We are committed to healing country so therefore [are] developing initiatives [that are] culturally appropriate, commercially viable, focused on environment and cultural values.'

The land they found had been cleared of most of its vegetation. Over-farmed, over-fertilised, over-cropped and over-grazed. The spirit of the land itself had been damaged, he says. 'We knew it felt right, we knew it was on our country. For 150 years, they had Noongars going to this country, but only to the front, where the shearing shed was. Beyond that, Noongars had not walked on this land for 150 years. People didn't know, people had been disconnected from the heritage and culture that existed there.

'My younger brother and I felt good on this land that was now our property. We knew it was connected to the river. The country had this magnificent, solid presence, and energy from magnificent granite, these big boulders. We knew there was something there. Now we know this is a ceremonial ground on the hill directly behind the house. It's been recognised for state significance for the heritage we have on this place. We didn't know it was there when we first came here, but now it has been confirmed by ourselves and other cultural leaders.

'We got this place and realised it was more than a block of land. It had more than a good sense about it, it was actually sacred land and it was handed back to us. I knew, and I know now I was led by the spirit of my old people. Particularly my old men.'

So they decided to plant a million trees. They had never heard of carbon farming, or the technicality of biodiversity mixes, or environmental management. 'All we knew was that our land was not well, which [meant we had been] irresponsible in a way as custodians. We felt an absolute strong urge and responsibility to heal our country.'

Indigenous food production and land management have recently broken into Australia's mainstream consciousness in a way that has not happened in white settlement history. Bill Gammage's *The Biggest Estate on Earth* and Bruce Pascoe's *Dark Emu* are two of the best-known recent books that paint a picture of the Australian continent through early explorer documents, eyewitness accounts and landscape images. There are many more. Non-Indigenous Australians can now consider a First Nations people who may have lived in a more managed landscape. It is a departure from the hunter-gatherer stories that most of us learnt at school. These authors somehow broke through the crusty old explorer tropes to present a different picture – from Sir Thomas Mitchell's description of grass piled into hayricks to the Brewarrina fish traps. Sometimes changes of attitudes require a change in focus. Just as Australia's worst-ever bushfires of 2019–20 opened the way for a conversation about Indigenous fire management, Gammage and Pascoe are the more visible authors who have opened the way for a deeper conversation about Indigenous food and land management techniques. Says McGuire: 'Those books articulated what we've always thought and known anyway. There's a great opportunity right now, no question. There's a significant market out there for pretty much everything. Whether it's COVID or global warming or climate change elements, people want to see far more appropriate and ethical behaviours around food production and the management of land and our natural resources.'

At the centre of the Noongar project are traditional owners' commercial enterprises, focused on bush foods and medicines. McGuire describes bush products as a multi-billion-dollar industry, in which a negligible 1 per cent of Aboriginal people all around the world are involved. The Noongar project seeks to address the imbalance and take advantage of those sorts of opportunities because Aboriginal knowledge is the foundation of that industry.

McGuire is deeply aware of the opportunities his generation have had because his parents had none. They were trapped in what he describes as the 0.4 per cent of Indigenous peoples' history: dispossession of lands and waters, depopulation through incarceration and massacres, slave labour and discriminating employment and assimilation policies. His parents' experience negated the other 99.6 per cent of First Nations history of pre-European settlement, with its sophisticated systems of governance, land management practices, sustainable harvesting of natural resources and relationships between First Nations as well as in international trade and commerce.

'We have never ceded our rights to our traditional and tribal lands, and *terra nullius* is well and truly gone. However, I must say we still struggle with the challenges of policy and politics and the way our issues and opportunities are created. There's a mindset still that reflects *terra nullius* – that Aboriginal people are subordinate to a more progressive non-Aboriginal community and society. We battle with these things.'

In conversation, McGuire's frustration is evident – with the system, with land management and the creeping desertification of some farming country. Our people represent a first, he says; we were doing the things thousands of years ago humans have only now become renowned for doing. He warns that the threat of land degradation is only a few years away and that if something is not done to improve land management, not only will food production decline but so will rural towns that depend on that industry.

There is an urgency to his words, as he channels his frustration over the crushing weight of recent history into energy: 'As it did with COVID, nature will make decisions for us. It will destroy structures and icons . . . They won't last, like Uluru, Juukan Gorge, those beautiful landscapes. I want people to stop treating us like children. We are the wisdom holders and we are the carers of everything. Allow us to be reinstated.'

The NLE families are working with an Aboriginal apiarist, who is training ten Noongar people in the art of beekeeping. They are also working with scientists on a floral mapping analysis of their country, and a chemical analysis of their honey, to add some scientific understanding to their cultural understanding of their food products. If the honey is up to scratch, they hope to break into the food-as-medicine market – one of the fastest expanding sectors in food.

'When the boat sailed up, my old people standing on the hill were without doubt amongst the most healthy people on Earth at the time. The fools on the piece of wood were . . . physically, psychologically destroyed; people chained up. Far out, man, they were probably the most unhealthy people on the Earth at that moment in time.'

The legacy of invasion, the relatively new entry of the NLE into the ever-rising agricultural real estate market, and a particular amount of red tape for Indigenous land businesses, make the average farmer's struggles over red tape look laughable. The NLE is a startup business hoping to rebuild, brick by brick, a fusion of traditional and modern cultures. In many ways it has one hand tied behind its back. Sure, the group was gifted their land. But when it comes to Indigenous land management, all the things non-Indigenous business owners take for granted disappear. For example, there are caveats on government-purchased land. There is no access to commercial finance to develop businesses. All decisions have to go through a board. Economic pursuits are not paramount but have to make way for social and cultural heritage aims. These types of businesses are welfare dependent, not by choice, and therefore cannot pay wages to employ people.

'People think we Indigenous people get land and it's all easy and not accountable in appropriate ways, and that we are under-skilled and lack the capacity to do the farming that other farmers do, the "traditional farming" that you mob call it.

'Aboriginal land doesn't get ownership. It doesn't belong to me personally, it belongs to the corporation, and there are lots of governance and compliance issues around us as a corporation. We can't go, like the farmer next door to us, to get credit through the bank to raise finance and capital to do the things we really want to do. We are bound through the caveats to always go back through the ILSC and the government and always be cap in hand to someone to help us do the things we want to do.

'We can't pay wages. No one can be employed unless we get approvals to employ. Unless we get approvals from our "chief protector". Essentially, we end up being welfare dependent. We are trying to break that nexus. We are trying to push the government and the ILSC to support Aboriginal people to generate our own enterprises and maintain ourselves through commercialising the enterprises we want to do, even if it's down to the cultural aspects.'

The NLE's ambition is to recreate the Noongar economy, and that can happen through land management and food production. McGuire is also part of another group of Noongar leaders who set up the Noongar Chamber of Commerce and Industry (NCCI), signified by a small stone, or 'booya', landing in the water. The booya was used as a trading currency, and Noongar today use the word when they are talking about money. They want to recreate the Indigenous native grass grainbelt, which is described in *Dark Emu* and other histories. 'We are encouraging whitefellas to do the same,' McGuire says. A 2015 report from the government's agricultural research unit, the Rural Industries Research and Development Corporation, on native grasses found 'the high value potential of exploring Australian native grasses for food markets'.[1]

Only 14 of the 9000 or so species of plants in the southwest of Western Australia are currently exploited; the NLE has identified a market for a portion of these species, as well as for grain. McGuire has planted 70 hectares of native species mix, which can be developed not only as a native fodder feed system for future livestock but also as a place where people could forage, based on Noongar cultural principles. The group wants to develop bush produce that covers pharmaceuticals, botanicals and cosmeceuticals, with both a cosmetic and pharmaceutical effect. The products have complex benefits, which McGuire says reflects the more holistic approach of Indigenous culture. 'Ngooka' as the word for honey is so much more as a concept. 'Country' does not cut it when it comes to boodja. It is hard for non-Indigenous people to understand the complexity of Indigenous thinking, he says. He is confident that Aboriginal people will become powerful again. 'Cultural authority will come out on top. When we speak the way we do, that language resonates with this land, nothing resonates like our original languages.'

Since the NLE returned to country, half the place has returned to trees. McGuire is a former professional firefighter and they have reintroduced cultural burning methods to the country. He is comfortable with using cool burning as a traditional Indigenous tool, but he has big concerns with incendiary burns from planes and helicopters as often practised by state authorities. It annihilates their boodja. He wants to change that practice.

'When you stand in country amongst your trees, as a traditional owner, I think as a human, in fact, there's a spirit in the fire. There's a spirit in the way you are practising your land management and you connect to the country, you connect to the fire itself. It's a great emotional and a spiritual activity to get involved in.

'I believe environmental values sit under cultural values, so when traditional owners take country back and they do it in the right spirit within the cultural lores and environmental values, country gets looked after. Because it's not just the land aspects and the soils and the trees and plants. It's everything – the biota, the ecology, the hydrology, everything within cultural responsibilities and custodial responsibility in terms of our cultural values ensures the environment is returned – and *we* are healed.'

Australian white culture has not been very good at melding food and land management in an articulate way and mostly has excelled at ignoring how First Nations cultures did so. We talk about either food production or the environment, but the fusion of a system of land management relating to both has not been successfully implanted in the public mind. An example: the federal Coalition has merged the agriculture, water and environment ministries. It is the right move to think of those pieces as part of the whole. However, I suspect it was for the wrong reason – so the Nationals could ensure agriculture grabbed environment in a political headlock. There are many histories of agriculture in our libraries but sometimes you have to attack a problem in a different way. I could learn a lot from studying the development of agriculture and the stump-jump plough, but as an enthusiastic eater I started at the other end. Food is the door into agriculture for most non-farming people and I was convinced it had the potential to help me work out how to explain why we need to think more strategically about farming.

The search sent me back to touchstones in an admittedly thin genre. For me, the definitive food history of Australia is an exhaustive encyclopaedia called *One Continuous Picnic* by former *Sydney Morning Herald* journalist Michael Symons, written in 1982. Symons had been reporting on the rising tide of waste in Sydney's beautiful harbour, getting more and more downcast about the state of the environment and the world. He was producing exposés about large polluters and packaging industries pushing campaigns against 'litterers', making the problems about the litterer rather than the companies that make the packaging. He was getting dispirited.

Then a simple dinner with a few friends lifted him. The reconnection, the excellent lamb and a few hours of conversing became the turning point for a lifestyle change and a move for a few years to

Tuscany. Enjoying the experience of seasonal food among a peasant culture who lived close to their soil, he watched as they tended their vegetable patches and cooked food within its season. Symons' thesis is that Australia is the only continent that has not supported a truly agrarian society, and our food culture is poorer for it.

'Our land missed that fertile period of settled agriculture and cooking. There has never been the agrarian interplay between society and soil that created the great traditional cuisines as we know them. Almost no food has been grown by the person who eats it; almost no food has been preserved in the home; and indeed very little preparation is now done by a family cook. This is the uncultivated continent. Our history is without peasants.'[2]

So, we are an industrial nation and that is how we feed ourselves. For the average city dweller, such as I was until I moved out of Sydney, farming is the antithesis of the modern lifestyle. Perhaps that's been the case since the arrival of the First Fleet. Symons suggests that of the thousands of people who landed, 'It is often said that only one was a farmer, although this undoubtedly undervalued the widespread pastoral and horticultural knowledge of the day.' Certainly, we can't discount the role of the English enclosures, where big farmers fenced off commons used by peasant farmers for a subsistence living. Those laws, which made 'fat sheep and lean people', pushed people out of the country into city slums to work in factories. Some of them would have been transported to Australia. Given the mission of the first voyage, many soldiers and urban poor were transported. As Symons points out, these were 'two model groups of consumers'.

Any attempts at vegetable gardens were raided, even those deliberately planted on Garden Island in order that, supposedly, they'd be safe from marauding, hungry convicts and soldiers. When the situation became dire, Governor Phillip sent the *Sirius* back to Cape Town to stock up. Many accounts describe the madness that descended on the colony with near-starvation. All the while, Oral McGuire's forebears were comfortably living off the country.

Hunger was Australia's 'first democratic experience', wrote Robert Hughes in *The Fatal Shore*. Food was the first and obvious obsession in the colony. It caused much angst that the hierarchy of convicts and military was not reflected in the rations, apart from half a pint per day of near undrinkable 'vile Rio spirits' for the soldiers. Salted beef was more prized than fresh fish, even if, next to a harbour full of seafood, the prisoners could get five times as much fish as part of their ration. Culture dies hard when it comes to food.

The first merino sheep arrived in 1797, the happy combination of wool on its back and meat on its bones providing a stable export for the motherland and food for hungry mouths. As the colony developed, world trade also took hold in portable products like tea, coffee and sugar. Enter the commodity. Tinned meat arrived in 1820 and things got more portable and more preserved from there.

Early colonial governments encouraged people to come over the seas to develop large-scale agriculture, such as it was then, pushing Indigenous people off their land to grow staple Western trade crops. Infrastructure was provided for that purpose, underwriting white settlement of inland areas. 'In agrarian societies, industrialisation broke up the extended family,' writes Symons. 'In Australia, it worked the other way, reuniting the nuclear family in a country of lonely itinerants.'

There were differences of opinion over how that might happen. There was tension from the beginning between big farmers and the small family settlers, and it has reverberated in white Australia ever since. Some activists, like Caroline Chisholm, tried to promote the idea of the small settler and women's place within that model, while government encouraged larger farms to create more volume. It sounds familiar.

The story of the small settler was a 'very sad one – pathetic is perhaps the proper description', wrote C. J. King in his 1948 study of the first fifty years of New South Wales agriculture. They were the 'victims not alone of the elements and of a peculiarly harsh and forbidding country, but of monopolists who had preyed on their defencelessness'.[3]

In comparing Australia to North America, Symons describes the difference between small- and large-frontier colonialists. Native Americans cooked and cultivated maize, potatoes, sweet potato, haricot beans and many other plant foods, plus roast turkey, roasted peanuts, clam chowder and lobster. Symons suggests that later North American colonies in the Appalachians were 'largely self-sufficient and only peripherally connected to the market economy'. Or as the American historian Carter Goodrich wrote in the *Economic Record* in 1928: 'The United States owes its individualism largely to its small man's frontier; I think it is not fanciful to suggest that Australia owes much of its collectivism to the fact that its frontier was hospitable to the large man instead.'[4]

That is, the Australian frontier was populated by workers servicing large squatters' blocks rather than greater populations of small-business holders. These large holdings were not only the norm but the spark for land reform, including the Robertson Land Acts of 1861, which provided for the legal purchase and occupation of Crown lands, and were designed to give the working class a chance at owning land.

'It could be argued,' says Symons, 'that opening up the country required a form of peasant living, but most arrivals settled in towns and were fed by massive imports of food, and squatters kept down the number of smallholdings. Certainly, we neglected the vital task of assimilating Indigenous plants and animals into something resembling an environmentally appropriate agriculture or cuisine.

This country became the world's earliest truly urban nation, in which many of us could no longer even recognise a tomato plant.'

In Wendell Berry's landmark 1977 essay 'The Unsettling of America' he lamented the ramping up of large-scale farming to the detriment of people who knew their small place and 'husbanded' the land with affection. But he also makes an important distinction in that essay that does not contrast so much between large and small as rather between exploiter and nurturer.

'Whereas the exploiter asks of a piece of land only how much and how quickly it can be made to produce, the nurturer asks a question that is much more complex and difficult: What is its carrying capacity? (That is: How much can be taken from it without diminishing it? What can it produce *dependably* for an indefinite time?).'[5]

Symons noticed similar trends happening in Australia – of the large displacing the small. He reminded me that the Democratic Labor Party and its spiritual leader, the conservative commentator Bob Santamaria, tried for years to get people on to small farms. It didn't work.

When systems fail us, we often turn to the fundamentals for comfort. Oral McGuire and the Noongar mob seek to return to land, to restore themselves and their country. COVID sent many of us to the kitchen to bake bread – a tradition that had long disappeared from most Australian households in favour of a soft, sliced, nutritionally empty loaf. People frustrated by politics revert to the most basic pleasure, gathering neighbours to eat and talk about how to carve a better system of representation. Climate change, water usage, farm size, soil loss, productive land loss to mining, energy and residential spread, rising emissions, how we feed ourselves and with what – all of these things require sitting down at the kitchen table because farming and our rural landscapes are changing quickly. Perhaps doing so is a first step in addressing the tensions that now plague food and farming in our landscape. Pull up a chair.

Chapter 3

ON RISK

Strip away modernity. Unlearn everything you know about the complexity of your average day. The ordinary interaction, the workaday worries, the pinging of your phone, the relentless roll of the inbox. You are left with the human condition. Our most basic needs, as the American psychologist Abraham Maslow noted, are the physiological needs: food and water, sufficient rest, clothing, shelter, health and reproduction. Humans have been driven by these needs forever. We have been controlling and weaponising and hoarding them for just as long because, whether you're the hunter-gatherer, the grower, the shopper or the corporate titan, you cannot forget these needs, even if you do outsource some of them to Uber.

In Australia and much of the developed world, we often forget that food and water are central to the human story. Food is so plentiful, so present, it is not even secondary. It is incidental. It is a hurried meal at the end of the work day. It is a snack grabbed in the car for a long drive. It is a drive-through coffee, the stuff that puts the cherry on the cake of a celebration, a commiseration, a birth, a death, a deal. It now comes in a powder form, protein powder, the sort of prototype Soylent Green.

Still, we are nothing if not contradictory. So we fetishise food. We post pretty meals on social media. It is not uncommon for humans to sit down to watch *MasterChef* in lounges next to pristine, state-of-the-art kitchens that are rarely used for anything other than heating up a takeaway, or perhaps assembling a home meal delivery subscription, the biggest food trend of the decade.

Yet in 2020, when we saw the shelves stripped empty in a COVID panic, how quickly the instinct to protect those basic needs kicked in. Those of us in developed countries were transported back through history, to the many moments of scarcity, as if living past lives or responding to genetic memories. A shard of glass reflected the food deficits happening across the world and, suddenly, in some parts of our own country. In a flash, the basics became important. The impermanence of gathering food was underlined.

We were exposed as humans. The growing political uncertainty, topped by pandemic, has left us in a state of constant alert. For Australians, bushfires and disease have created twin peaks of existential dread.

When it comes to food, I cannot help but have a foot in the macro and the micro camp. As 2020 began, I was surveying the broader political and rural landscape but also living with the planting of the next crop and the travails of sheep in a wet season. I see nutritional poverty in small towns but I also see the holes at a national and international level. Rather than start from your dinner table, it may be more useful to think of food in the global strategic context. Given the current world is about uncertainty and how to make it more secure, personally and globally, let me start with risk.

To talk about the risks in food and farming is to be the Eeyore of the industry. You feel like the spoiler, the pessimist, the Cassandra, a prophet of doom and disaster. There is an undeniable pressure to talk up farming in public. Yet there are some real issues around risk that Australia needs to think about as food growers in one of the least subsidised and most variable climates head further into the anthropogenic era.

Again, it's not as if the work has not been done. The reports are there. Numbers have been crunched. Projections have been made. Still, governments place the work in the bottom drawer. Exhibit A: the CSIRO's 2019 Australian National Outlook (ANO) report, headed by economist Ken Henry and businessman David Thodey, which underlines Australia's luck, both bestowed and made.[1] That work highlighted a fortunate country with good employment opportunities, liveability, decent public services and rich biodiversity. But for all these assets, according to the report, Australia stands at a crossroads of two different futures: an 'outlook vision' or a 'slow decline'.

In 'slow decline', Australia drifts into the future with weak economic growth, investment and education outcomes. The economy is increasingly vulnerable to external shocks. Productivity and wage growth are relatively low.

In the 'outlook vision', Australia reaches its full potential. Economic growth remains strong and inclusive as Australian companies use technology to place productivity on a more globally competitive footing, which creates more export-facing industries. Improved educational outcomes provide skills to compete in this technology-enabled workforce.

Climate change and the environment are listed in the report as one of six challenges facing Australia (and the world). Farming is critical to this challenge. Others include the rise of Asia, technological change, social cohesion, trust in institutions and demographics.

'How well Australia manages these global and national challenges will have a significant effect on its future economic, environmental and social well-being.'[2]

The report urges five key shifts involving land, industry, urban areas, energy and culture. One of the important messages is that the way we manage land and integrate food production on that land is *central* to where we go as a country. It is not some quaint cottage industry that's in gentle decline.

The authors urge a land shift that will create 'a profitable and sustainable mosaic of food, fibre and fuel production, carbon sequestration and biodiversity'.[3] That requires deep thinking. While the ANO warns against the dangers of picking winners, food manufacturing and agriculture are listed as key growth areas when thinking about the national outlook.

Food sector manufacturing is important because of the volume of food production and our location in Asia. The opportunities centre on two areas. The first is the provenance story of food, boosted by technologies like biosensors and blockchain to show the journey from paddock to plate, and the integrity of the food. The second is to focus on food nutrients and quality to get more out of what we grow.

Australia has a chance to capitalise on food growing because 'the world's population and its demand for food are growing fast, but the world's arable land is not'.[4] ANO said more efficient and advanced agricultural techniques are required to get the most out of the world's land resources. The authors named things like genomic technologies, which can help develop crops that are resistant to root diseases and tolerant of subsoil constraints, drought conditions, frost and high temperatures. Precision farming and water-resource management are other growth areas, made possible by high-performance Earth-observation data analytics and space-enabled ground sensor networks to help relieve drought pressure while increasing agricultural yield.

This bullish attitude around the saviour qualities of technology and selling food into a booming and wealthy Asia – reminiscent of the NFF's goal to grow agriculture to a $100 billion industry – is always tempered by the reality of growing food in the most arid continent on Earth. The ANO report lays out those challenges clearly and they are significant. Climate change is the overwhelming factor but it is coupled with stagnant or declining productivity due to the drop in agricultural research and development investment from state and federal governments. (The decline in agricultural research funding is an ongoing theme, expanded in 'On soil'.)

Distance, small populations and complex supply chains mean that farmers are some of the 'least digitally and technologically enabled sectors'.[5] ANO argues that technology as well as research and development will improve productivity, though its authors acknowledged a significant challenge is maintaining population. 'The issue is how to broaden and accelerate those gains across the rural economy, while retaining rural community vitality.'[6] Never mind the old Coalition slogan 'jobs and growth'. Productivity gains, in the form of technology for food producers, are essentially jobless growth. This is a red flag for rural communities and rarely talked about by governments. Politicians are good about making motherhood statements about the importance of rural communities and family farmers, but their statements are at odds with their policies, which encourage bigger scale with an emphasis on technology.

For ANO, productivity is the sacred cow, not profitability. This argument – that, because food prices are falling and costs are rising, making a living for farmers is about increasing productivity – is troublesome in my opinion. Implicit in the productivity obsession is that input sellers and food processors and retailers get to keep increasing their prices, but the farmer does not. This is my problem with the argument. What's more, an increased yield may not increase the profit. Profits are a function of the yield minus the costs. Yet farming's social culture rewards the best yield. We all know when the neighbour has grown a bumper crop, we just don't know how much they spent to get it and whether it paid off. (Farmers never get to see each other's balance sheets.)

Still, who am I to argue with economists. ANO modelled both 'slow decline' and the 'outlook vision' to 2060, and without productivity, profitability slowly declines to half the current rate.[7]

The report makes a critical point about land management: 'To be strongly profitable, agriculture needs both productivity growth and ecosystem health.'[8] Global action to sequester carbon is already seeing a dollar value placed on capturing carbon: 'With growing recognition of the risks to productivity and profitability from the environment, there is much the finance and insurance sectors can do to support farmers in sustaining production and push production frontiers in an uncertain and changing environment.'[9]

It is up to governments or industry advocates to design policies that assist the twin goals of *profitable* productivity growth and ecosystem health. I would go a step further and say the goal should be healthy landscapes that produce healthy food sustainably for a living wage for thriving communities. The NFF's 2030 roadmap outlines an industry plan for 5 per cent of farmer income to come from providing environmental improvements or 'ecosystem services' within the next decade. The market for such ecosystem services includes governments and companies looking to pay for sequestration or to offset their emissions. The ANO suggests that carbon could be sequestered on 30 million hectares of current marginal farming country. That means marginal land that is already farmed could be planted with mixed species to sequester carbon. ANO recommends an optimal mix of plantings could see Australia reach zero net emissions by 2050, but three things must happen to make that possible.

First, effective global action on climate change that accepts carbon farming as one of the many essential pathways. That has already begun to happen in Australia.

Second, a need for continued research and development, investment and the development of infrastructure, such as plant nurseries and distribution channels for plantations or new technologies for establishing carbon plantations. That has yet to happen as of 2021.

Third, Australia ensures that the on-farm and landscape-wide benefits from this form of carbon farming result in a broader range of income to rural communities and benefit the natural environment. That is not in sight.

Such change would require the intensified use of prime farming land to grow more food to make up for the loss of production on marginal country. The other question is about what Australia wants. Let's assume global pressure continues to push laggard countries towards action. If we continue on a high emissions path without crimping energy and transport emissions, it will require greater offsetting in projects like carbon sequestration. That will mean an examination of how we use land and will see drawdown projects competing with farm production.

Alternatively, lowering emissions in agriculture, as well as other high-emitting sectors like energy and transport, will allow more space for, and social licence for, farming. Or, as the roadmap puts it, 'more land for farming or forestry in the future'. *Attention farmers:* that means we could make best use of our farming and landscape management if other sectors like energy and transport were also doing their bit on emissions reduction.

Modern farming is about managing risk. Farmers seek to balance a range of economic, social and environmental risks. How farmers and land managers react to those risks will have an impact on the broader population – in emissions, in food prices and in food security. The impacts of climate risk on agriculture will be felt across nations and the globe. The non-farm parts of the nation cannot pretend they don't have a dog in this race.

My obsession with risk arose from thinking about food production in the context of climate change, stretched global supply chains, pre-COVID tensions around the US–China trading relationship, Australia's role in that relationship, and its related geographic spills into the Pacific.

Then the pandemic hit. Empty shelves sparked a debate around Australian food security. Agriculture minister David Littleproud reassured us: 'People shouldn't panic, we have an abundant supply of top-quality fresh food produced from all parts of the country that ensures that there will be plenty of food on the table . . . We can take great comfort from the fact that this lucky country produces enough food to guarantee we will continue to enjoy the best produced products anywhere in the world.'[10]

Littleproud's was the standard response which, together with the NFF, always homes in on Australia's large volume of food exports (more than half of its agricultural produce). The Australian Bureau of Agricultural and Resource Economics and Sciences (ABARES) quickly produced a report to scotch the idea Australia is not a food-secure nation. It said Australia imports only about one-tenth of its food, mostly processed products like frozen vegetables, seafood products, and beverages, as well as out-of-season fresh produce.

This is to take a very literal view of food. The tuna in the can. The milk in the TetraPak. The grain in the silo. And we do have grain in the silo. But there are many inputs on most farms and many of *them* are imported. They include vehicles, machinery; a tonne of chemicals, including fertilisers, herbicides, pesticides and veterinary products; all manner of widgets, including parts, pumps, pipes and other paraphernalia. And fuel. Australia imports 90 per cent of its fuel. You can't put a crop in without fuel.

The total amount spent on agricultural chemicals in Australia in 2017 was $1.8 billion. Since the early 2000s, spending on agricultural chemicals has risen faster than any other farm cost, an increase of around 45 per cent. Two very large companies dominate the Australian ag chemical market – Bayer and the Australian-owned Nufarm: together they hold 90 per cent of the market.[11] In 2017, imports accounted for 59 per cent of the Australian chemical market, which is up from 33 per cent in the prior decade.

That is because Australian manufacturers have been shutting down, outsourcing or leaving Australian shores. It used to be that Australia would import the active ingredient and mix up the rest in domestic factories. But we don't do much local manufacturing now. Particular countries are more important than others in supplying agricultural inputs. China, the US, New Zealand and Malaysia supply more than 70 per cent of all our imported products. Germany, the Netherlands, Vietnam and Korea are all responsible for a smaller portion of the inputs. The country that provides most of what we need to grow food is China. It is responsible for about a fifth of all inputs into agri-food exports. So not only does China buy a lot of our exports, it is also responsible for making the inputs we need to grow those exports. To distil this further, we use a proportion of imported stuff to grow food, and then sell that food in Australia or ship it out as the raw commodity so others can turn it into the final product.

Australia's reliance on other countries in this context gives the lie to food sovereignty and blows a hole in ABARES' subsequent trumpeting of food security in the 2020 COVID panic. And that is a worldwide trend. China dominates the market for importing the materials that are used for their own exports. Gone are the days when you produced every part of your exported products. Australian farmers are but one link in a 'global value chain'. No country is food secure because every country is now part of a long chain of dependencies. To pretend otherwise is dishonest.

The last time the government looked closely at food resilience was in 2012. Under the leadership of public governance expert Stephen Bartos, the 'Resilience in the Australian Food Supply Chain' report was produced, commissioned after the Queensland floods of November 2010.

The report outlined just how complex the global supply chain has become. It pointed out that the increasing links in the chain between different systems, and the reliance on technology, for example, makes the food supply chain vulnerable to 'cyber attack, computer viruses, industrial espionage by cyber means and other sources of system breakdown'.[12]

We used to get our fresh produce closer by. Stretching supply chains has not only given us abundant food that requires more processing or storage to keep it fresh, but it's made us more vulnerable to natural disasters. A resilient network is a network that can bounce back from surprises. A diverse food network, which includes small and large suppliers, long and short supply chains with broadly scattered processing, manufacturing and skills, is a more resilient network. As Bartos concluded, 'a more concentrated network is less resilient than a dispersed one'.[13]

Bartos identified the trend towards pre-prepared meals. In 2013, when he was writing, the Australian ready-meals market was already valued at just over $850 million. In 2019 it had grown to $1.14 billion, and it's projected to be worth $1.58 billion by 2024.[14] The lack of understanding of basic cooking skills has a material impact on the resilience of the food supply in times of national disaster, a fact we saw on display in 2020, with a marked rise of supermarket-driven cooking shows before the nightly news, to instruct and inspire the harassed working parent.

As the report pointed out: 'Australia is a net exporter of food. This does not necessarily mean that Australia is self-sufficient in food supply. Global supply networks are increasingly important in the Australian food sector and many types of foods or inputs to food are imported. Many ingredients, additives and packaging materials that are inputs to domestic production are only made overseas and Australia relies on imports for some important foodstuffs (such as canned fish and infant formula).'[15]

While the Bartos report found that the Australian food supply chain had been, in the past, resilient in the face of localised or regional crises such as the Queensland floods, there was a big qualifier: 'Where the Australian food supply chain is potentially vulnerable is in large-scale events (such as a human or animal pandemic, or a national fuel shortage), or combinations of events that affect multiple links of the food supply chain at the same time (such as widespread electricity outages combined with floods or fires).'[16]

Sounds like 2020, doesn't it? In the event of crisis, Bartos warned, the food industry would 'exhibit limited willingness' to contribute to broader community welfare objectives, because food companies do not see their role as being responsible for feeding the population in disaster.[17] Anything beyond commercial or shareholder interests is seen as not their problem but 'matters for government'.[18] That is, don't rely on the benevolence of food companies if there's a pandemic. A company's duty is to its owners, and why would we expect anything else from profit-making organisations?

The worrying thing in the report was that certain levels of government expected commercial food companies to step up in the event of crises: 'There was also reportedly an expectation in some quarters (mainly among lower-level officials) that in a disaster, food companies would distribute food free of charge. Although food businesses frequently do donate generously, it should not be expected as a matter of course – it would affect the viability of those businesses and their ability themselves to recover.'[19] The government also had 'a limited understanding of the practical limits of the food industry's capacity to maintain supply in the event of a crisis'.[20] To expect the industry to operate as a charity is daft, particularly given that our laissez-faire political representatives long ago bought into the idea that self-interest rules. Yet here is the government actively thinking that large food companies would step in like Jesus Christ with the fishes and loaves.

As predicted, food companies did not distribute free food in the pandemic. But the major food charity supplier Foodbank reported that almost a third of Australians experiencing food insecurity in 2020 (28 per cent) had never experienced it before.[21] Vulnerable people who were already using charities for food sources – such as the unemployed, the homeless, those with mental illness, single parents and low-income workers – were made more food insecure. And Foodbank identified two new groups of people who lacked food security: casual workers, who were often young people, and international students. Demand for weekly food relief in Australia doubled from 15 per cent to 31 per cent from 2019 to 2020.

Given that we are locked into the global supply chain, and scientists predict more pandemics and climate disasters in the future, governments face a clear message – get organised or be confronted by major panics. Logically, multinational corporations are even less likely to help, because they will simply cut off the particular region to contain any risks or losses. Bartos discovered as much.

The Bartos report recommendations were both national and granular. He wanted to see a detailed understanding of food services providers at a regional level, given the local pub often becomes the focal point in disasters in smaller towns. He wanted an examination of how the Australian Defence Force and AusAID could play a role in national supply chains. And he wanted an analysis of food stockpiles, which are challenged by dates on food labelling. Many people don't know that the 'best before' date is different to the 'use by' date. The 'best before' date relates to the food's marketability whereas the 'use by' date means the date after which food should not be eaten for safety reasons.

The report urged the testing of a 'pantry list' concept, where food suppliers encourage households to stock more staples (which is ironic since the suppliers themselves don't). It called for the monitoring of risks of the overseas ownership of food manufacturing, given the risk of closures in emergencies. As far as I can discover, some state governments recommend householders keep an emergency pantry list. But the federal government has not yet moved on the report's recommendations.

I expected people involved in agriculture to be thinking about national food strategy. But in spite of farmers' association with Hanrahan's aphorism 'we will all be rooned', many are optimists. They have to be. The more I researched, the more it seemed to be that the people involved in risk, such as those in defence, those who spend their lives thinking about existential threats to the human race, are the ones thinking about resilience around food, water and natural resources. Soldiers are trained to scan the horizon for threats. Journalists are trained to prod and check for weaknesses in the national architecture. Critical risk managers are trained to think of future hazards and how they might impact society.

People like Dr Paul Barnes, Senior Fellow at the Australian Strategic Policy Institute (ASPI) and former head of ASPI's risk and resilience program. He trained as an environmental scientist and was a corporate risk manager for the Queensland Department of Primary Industries, so he understands landscape and environment and its intersection with food production. He has worked in academic roles in emergency and disaster management, as well as diverse roles such as reviewing open-source counterterrorism capabilities among Asia-Pacific Economic Cooperation (APEC) members.

When a disgruntled farm employee placed needles in punnets of strawberries, it caused a national scare and a brief conversation about food defence. Barnes is frustrated that federal governments rarely discuss national security in terms of food. 'I would like to see a discussion about much broader notions that cover approaches to the security of agriculture – not only invasive pests or plant and animal disease – but as part of a wider idea of "environmental security". Disruptions that can impact the nation state can range from physical invasion to a whole range of cyber-criminal activity or disruptions to the capability to produce food. They would all impact the way we live into the future.'

Risk is, by definition, about exposure, and the potential for loss or unexpected disruption, all of which are affected by uncertainty. An existing or emergent threat might not be planned for adequately if the threat is deemed low. Barnes worries that governments have not historically planned well for low-likelihood disruptions. 'A problem in the modern world, and in history, is that the importance of preventing surprises is often overlooked or discounted.'

He argues that Donald Horne is still on the money – that Australia has been lucky with its relative abundance of resources. We have learnt how to farm in a more adaptive way, but Horne's conclusion that Australia is sleepwalking into the future still holds because governments have been less successful at adequately merging expert advice on issues requiring national-level decision making. Landscape management in a changing climate is one area that benefits from joined-up thinking as it can impinge on choices for food production and food producers.

The obvious example is the bushfires that swept through eastern states from August 2019 to February 2020. Part of the issue was the machinery of government. States have responsibility for disaster management but the Commonwealth was ill-prepared for fire on a national scale. Fire authorities, including the Bushfire and Natural Hazards Cooperative Research Centre, had been warning state governments there was an above-average fire threat due to hot and dry conditions.[22] Either the Commonwealth didn't take enough notice or it was not a priority at the time.

'Who could have predicted that we would have this ongoing supercharged bushfire season?' says Barnes. 'Well, quite a few people did . . . these are not black swan events, they are grey swan events, as I would call them. They have a known probability.' He cites the rise of zoonotic diseases. Many emergent international disease researchers had been writing about the dangers of diseases in wet markets infecting humans for a long time.

When Barnes thinks about agricultural and environmental security, he thinks about food-chain resilience, ecosystem resilience and water. 'I think the way in which we manage water, let alone the value we attest to it, needs to be significantly improved,' he says. 'If you manage a natural asset as if it's just a commodity and an economic phenomenon, it doesn't make sense from a national betterment, or a national security, or environmental security perspective. Water is rather scarce in this country even though we are impacted by flooding regularly. I don't think we have thought through the full scope of what we are doing when we sell the rights to water to domestic owners or international interests. We need to ensure we manage our water – and other components of environmental security – in ways that are more fully protective of Australia's longer-term interests.'

The thing that would worry a risk manager is the lack of diversity in the advice, and the lack of understanding of interdependencies between environment, food production capacity and other strategic interests. Overlay this limited thinking with a short attention span in politics, and the conditions become difficult for government to focus on. Barnes feared that the focus on food supply chains in March 2020, and the environmental threats from the black summer bushfires, had already dissipated a short time after the crises. After a couple more months, any talk of food supply resilience was over. The modern political and media cycle focuses on what is important today.

If Barnes were in charge of the world, or could at least influence the government, he would put together a group of senior – deputy level – public servants from across relevant departments like food, environment, defence and other portfolios to help assess emerging 'hybrid' threats. This wouldn't remove the expertise from the departments, but it would put the thinkers charged with anticipating national critical disruptions in the same room rather than having them siloed in their various institutional castles.

So where does that leave us? It leaves us with some farmers, defence experts, public policy types and the occasional journalist thinking about the holes, but with no clear agenda from government. Some great policy work has been done, with episodes of deep thinking to identify the weaknesses. The next step – the political bit – often fails because governments can't seem to enunciate the challenges to the voters or they ignore evidence-based recommendations all together. As a result, actually putting concrete policy in place is difficult.

And yet risk is the main game in the farming sector. From the moment farmers plant a crop or birth their livestock, risk lingers like a death's head at the feast. Climate change, global price fluctuations, input shortages, weather events, climate disasters, technical breakdowns, just-in-time supply chains, perishability issues and muscled-up supermarkets are just some of the things that stand in the way of a smooth transition from paddock to plate. These are all outside the farmer's control. Add to them the things a farmer can control, including business skills, agronomic knowledge, independent benchmarking and organisation, and it makes for a heady mix.

We know this. Most of the facts and figures in this chapter are from government-initiated or commissioned material. Yet we fail to follow through. When I spoke to Stephen Bartos in April 2020, at close to the apex of the first supermarket panic, he was hopeful of change. 'The good thing is that, coming out of COVID, I'm sure this is going to be more of a priority.' Except more than a year on, nothing has changed.

Chapter 4

ON FARMING CULTURE

One of my father-in-law's sayings was 'People can't survive doing each other's washing forever'. This preference for producing things over providing services is a value judgement that cannot be underestimated when approaching farming culture. Scratch a farmer, from the micro grower to the family operation to the big producer, and you will find at some level they are proud of what they grow because food is essential. Historically, the production of food has driven farming culture's sense of self-worth. Service industries are not regarded with the same import, notwithstanding their dominant place in the modern economy.

We often talk about the act of growing food in economic terms. But it is important to pick apart the culture to understand how change can happen. The reality is, the culture is a messy confluence of business and family.

Family farms still make up the majority of businesses in agriculture, though the high-value end is heading towards the corporatised model. If family farms continue to look after land, we need to understand how they respond in a rapidly changing world to both climate change and landscape use.

I think of the average mid-sized farmer as a mix of worker and capitalist. The farmer who works in the paddock – as opposed to the Pitt Street or Collins Street farmer – is caught between these two worlds. Worker and boss. You can see this in rural towns, where class is ingrained, something I wrote about in my last book, *Rusted Off*. The Australian non-Indigenous farmer gets a certain status from holding land – an idea that was passed on by his English forebears. The smaller the community, the greater the status.

The farmer chooses where to identify on our political spectrum, which in Australia splits between worker (historically Labor) and capital (historically Liberal and/or National). Mostly, farmers choose to identify with capital. Farmers, no matter their scale, choose being the boss. That is plain in voting patterns, where farmers largely default to parties that favour the big end of town. That identity goes back to the shearers' strikes and beyond.

The confusion between worker and capital is why farmers have, historically, supported and developed various strains of agrarian socialism. There is a gut feeling in some quarters that farmers are being done over, to the point of paranoia in some individuals. That creates a default to the government fix, in the same way workers have historically favoured big government intervention. If there is a drought, governments must act, usually with funding. But the capitalist comes out in the average farmer when it comes to regulation. 'Don't tell me what I can do on my land.' Hence the old adage that farmers like to privatise the profits and socialise the losses.

Yet all the political resistance that I've seen in the past two decades has been against the various constraints on small to medium farmers brought about by globalisation and big capital.

Think about the resistance to the water trading system and its imbalances (see 'On water' and 'On disruption'), or the influx of global superannuation companies (see 'On the middle'), or even the creeping competition from big mining companies on agricultural land and the effect of their political donations on the traditional farmers' political party, the National Party. These are all characterised, fairly or not, as morality tales. David against Goliath.

These familiar battlelines can be seen around the world, for it was globalisation that sparked the foundation in 1993 of the international peasants' movement, La Via Campesina, as a direct repudiation of 'neoliberal' policies of the 1980s and early '90s. The movement was designed to help local communities take back control of their food and the natural resources required to grow the food, including the water and the seeds. The campaign is best reflected in La Via Campesina's definition of food sovereignty. 'Food sovereignty is the right of peoples to healthy and culturally appropriate food produced through sustainable methods and their right to define their own food and agriculture systems . . . Food sovereignty prioritises local food production and consumption, giving a country the right to protect its local producers from cheap imports and to control its production.'[1]

Yet I would wager that Australian farmers don't see themselves as peasants, though they often joke about it – the OED definition refers to a 'a poor smallholder or agricultural labourer of low social status (chiefly in historical use or with reference to subsistence farming in poorer countries)'.

The complex nature of farming allows it to represent itself differently at different times. Sometimes farmers are the battlers. Sometimes farmers are the cutting-edge businesspeople. Sometimes farmers are Luddites. Sometimes farmers are rich. Sometimes farmers are poor. Sometimes farmers are the salt of the earth.

Sometimes farmers are pillagers of the earth. Sometimes farmers are the best environmental stewards. Sometimes they are the worst. I could have written diversity out of this story and chosen the stereotype to suit my argument. But the truth is you can find them all among farmers.

These are observations at the macro level. Zoom into the family farm at the micro and you will recognise every family you have known, with every relationship dynamic available in the human spectrum, from parents to children to grandchildren. To mangle Tolstoy, every happy farming family is alike, but every unhappy farming family is unhappy in its own way.

I met Lyn Sykes many years ago. She was born in our town, moved away, married and became a midwife. Her public face is as an Australian pioneer in farm succession, having worked for decades in mediation of family businesses. Sykes has observed a wide range of cultures in the thirty years she has gathered farm families together to talk about how assets will be managed or passed on. She sees her job as holding up a mirror to the family unit to recognise its undercurrents. 'People remember me as that big sheila who always talks about divorce.'

She describes farmers as people who are task-focused, with challenging levels of communication, which often means they are neglectful of others. She has seen low levels of self-awareness, inclusion, equity and diversity in farm families. 'Anyone who is a little different is marginalised,' Sykes says, though she thinks that is changing. 'Top marks for an artist surviving in ag.'

Sykes usually starts a meeting with a genogram to map out the family relationships. 'If the family tells me they have a son living in London, my normal response is, "Is your son gay?"' Some ask how she knew. 'Because squillions of others have a gay son living in London. That's a reasonable example of marginalisation.'

Being different in a small community stands out. Doing things differently in the farming portion of a small community stands out more. Doing things differently as a member of an extended family business can be even harder. In Sykes' experience, family culture is the biggest influence on the capacity to run a successful business and hand it to the next generation. Her favourite example is the many new farming daughters-in-law who are criticised for the way they peg washing on the line.

'I find older women very critical of younger women. It is the same in Ireland. The pegs must be in line, you have to match the pegs and your smalls – in my case, your larges – have to be on the inside. Who gives a rat's arse?'

Hanging washing might seem incidental but farm families can be fiercely critical of their own, or of newcomers. Doing things differently, whether it is pegging your undies, or taking up a different farming system, or supporting a different political candidate, is a *big deal*.

'If you're doing ag differently to your neighbours, you need to be aware they will be challenged by that, and the way to change that is not by attacking what they are doing but to keep doing what it is that you're doing.'

Sykes says criticism is often interpreted in the following way. '"If what I'm doing is not okay, then I must be not okay. Once I decide I'm not okay, I have only two choices. I will attack you or your position, or I will defend my own." What happens when people are offered an alternative view is they either become aggressive or defensive.'

I always recall Sykes' reflections when I think of how the nation might examine the way we manage land and food production in a changing climate. If we want something different, then local, state and federal governments and even metro voters have to bear the culture in mind. People from a conservative culture who are required to change by regulation, economic or environmental necessity need to have space. 'It needs to be safe to fail,' says Sykes.

In approaching any crucial conversation in farming culture and particularly in succession, she considers three components. 'Whenever you are having a crucial conversation, remember it is (one) emotional, (two) people will have different opinions and (three) the stakes are high.'

For Sykes, attacking another generation without offering engagement or an alternative path will blow up a successful plan to hand on to the next generation. Her advice could equally apply to politicians trying to muster support for agricultural policy change or even political representatives seeking to appeal to rural voters. Attacking an industry without offering engagement or alternative paths would be a way to blow up your election campaign.

Sykes was struck by the many farmers she encountered who suffered low self-esteem. While most of us have bouts of low self-esteem, she detected an incontrovertible pattern in agriculture. I suspect that's because mostly farmers work alone. Like any solitary career – writers included – they spend a lot of time with their own thoughts.

'They grow up in isolation, are generally away from parents quite young, go to the same school as their parents, mix with a narrow group of people and their self-esteem reflects that. When something happens that doesn't fit within that narrow view, their resilience is limited. When the climate means they can't do what they do it becomes clear how narrow that is.'

Such a state makes people vulnerable to any suggestion they are doing stuff the wrong way. 'You shouldn't use those chemicals the way you trained at college or university.' 'You shouldn't plough that field in the way your father did.' 'You shouldn't keep livestock. But I will keep eating steaks.'

Isolation also means collaboration among farmers is not the natural default position. 'Farmers just aren't collaborative individuals,' says Kate Burke, who grew up on a big family farm in Victoria. She attained an agriculture science degree, a PhD in agronomy and plant breeding, and lots of practical experience. They gave her a different perspective. She didn't have the opportunity to return to work on her family farm, so she went to work for Warakirri Asset Management, a large corporate agriculture business. You will hear more from Burke in 'On corporatisation'.

She says she can't stand the victim mentality of some farmers, having heard enough of that rhetoric as a child – that the world is stuffed and it's everybody else's fault. She says the reality is that two-thirds of farmers make reasonable choices and do relatively well. And the rest? 'Farmers fail to realise they are sitting on an asset that gives them a choice [to sell it]. At least they have that choice. Our cultural conditioning in the country is to be the victim and that has really impacted our ability to manage.'

When she talks to farmers' groups about practical risk management, they usually mention the market and climate and all the 'reactionary stuff' that is top of mind. In some ways, to worry about these is human nature. But her question is always, 'What is it that you can control as a farmer?' The businesses that really leap ahead, she says, are the ones that have the skill set to take control of their own destiny rather than the ones that become caught up in structural issues they can't control, or who don't have the capacity to take responsibility for their own decisions. And that capacity comes down to the culture of their family and their district.

Claire and Brendan Booth both come from farming families but they struck out on their own a decade ago. They have a farming business in Geurie, just east of Dubbo in New South Wales, which was acquired with savings and debt. Based on the Macquarie River, with the help of irrigation they grow around 20 per cent of Australia's processed sweetcorn, and graze livestock. They have built up their farm to a medium to large business. That is, one with assets under $20 million and turnover under $5 million.

Like lots of modern farmers, Booth has her fingers in many pies. She is a lawyer, who, like Sykes, specialises in succession, and as the 2017 Nuffield scholar she focused on farming culture. The Nuffield Scholarship is an industry-sponsored program that, in its own words, 'awards primary producers with a life-changing scholarship to travel and study an agricultural topic of choice'. It gives young people who are passionate about farming (or fishing) a chance to study in a subject area of their choice. Many farming leaders are Nuffield alumni.

Booth wanted to use the scholarship to ask why farmers saw themselves as primary producers and not business people. One of her findings was that farmers don't really 'get their rocks off making money as much as growing things for people to eat and wear'. That is reflected in low financial literacy levels, something she has to deal with in sorting out farmers' wills and tax structures.

I love talking to Booth because she is always thinking ahead of the game, planning to the nth degree how their business needs to change and what the markets are doing. She understands intimately the farming culture and is also aware that land-based farming is being challenged by lab-produced foods, by social licence issues and market demand for more environmentally sensitive production. '[Farming has] got to change, and thinking it won't change is naïve.'

She is already considering farming in 2030 and beyond. So the big question for me is how the culture copes with change, and what it looks like. She paints a picture of the Booths' 2030 selves owing less money. She jokes that they'll have a whole lot of 'serviceable' but old equipment lying around because they are betting on the fact that in 2030 there won't be a big market for used stuff. Plus, Brendan is a diesel mechanic. 'I think the only people making money out of big new equipment are companies like John Deere, and then people are slaves to paying them off,' she says.

She's thinking about the next iteration of the Murray-Darling Basin Plan and she expects there will be less water available, given the climate modelling for the next fifty years. 'Less water . . . will change the types of crops people grow and how they grow them.' She expects floodplain harvesting to be non-existent by 2050, which is partly why the Booths have not used floodplain water. She wants to get future-ready.

They are thinking of a world where farmers are bigger energy providers, so the Booths have set a target of being 100 per cent renewable. This will replace the $200–$300,000 diesel bill they currently pay for powering bores. Renewable power will meet their own needs and others', in a separate system to the national grid, using batteries. That power may drive the existing food-growing system or it may drive a closed lab or glasshouse food-production system. They haven't figured that out yet.

The Booths have spent their first ten years securing water to remove that risk in a climate-focused farming business. They see the next decade spent working to replace current diesel energy costs with renewables. They are preparing to use hydrogen for tractors and renewable energy for water pumping and other energy needs. That will allow them to service a food market that wants clean, green produce. They are lucky to be in the New South Wales government's designated Renewable Energy Zone, which is planned to deliver more renewable energy into the grid. They are already surrounded by seven major solar farms, completed or in construction.

'Ultimately, if people have water and energy and they want to grow food, they will find a way to do it. It can get overwhelming when you think of what is coming in the next ten years in agriculture . . . We have to stop spending all this energy jumping around trying to be clever and strategic and trying to figure what we are going to be. In fact, we just have to provide food.'

While Booth is no fan of subsidies, she does believe the US is smart to link food to social security through the 2018 Farm Bill, though she acknowledges the US doesn't do social security well. The US Farm Bill is an umbrella bill which covers everything from food-production support to farm finance to forestry and energy systems to nutrition assistance for those on low incomes. So you might get coalitions in the five-yearly farming reviews between those who would advocate on public health grounds and those who would advocate for particular farm systems. While you can argue about the wisdom of the Farm Bill's individual policies, you cannot argue with the interconnected nature of all of those areas.

Here, Booth goes to a familiar conversation in farming. That is, the negative perception of farmers in some non-farming minds. (Farm culture is defensive; consider the title of this book.) 'The US is valuing food as a public good. As an irrigator in Geurie, we are somehow water thieves; we are an extractive industry; we rape and pillage and we use all these chemicals that give people cancer.' The reality, says Booth, is their valley only extracts 19,000 megalitres of an allowable 30,000 megalitres, after which they cut back their own allocations. 'We manage sustainably.' They have increased soil organic carbon levels from 0.7 to 3.7 per cent in a nine-year period, and their corn uses biological insecticides that allow lady beetles to thrive. That corn takes four hours to get from harvest to the can. It is a healthy, shelf-stable food available for three to four years without preservatives. And it costs $1.80 a can.

'Do you still want to tell me I'm a bad person on Twitter? Can they just come and have a cuppa on a Sunday afternoon and spend a bit of time understanding that I care about the planet?'

You might have noticed by now that the farmers in this chapter are women. If I think about the change agents in agriculture, many of them are women. They are so often the ones trying to dissect the culture, trying to connect with the eater and slowly to change agriculture by changing the world around them – whether it's local, national or even global. Their conversations are more quietly frank and they are particularly observant and articulate about the culture of agriculture.

I noticed Emma Germano when she was doing her Nuffield Scholarship in 2014. Germano travelled the world to look at export opportunities for Australian fruit and vegetable growers, after she got frustrated with watching her father take any price for their cauliflowers. She discovered the issues for Australian farmers – succession-planning, water security, urban encroachment, agri-politics and world food markets – were common to many other countries.

Emma's family has farmed in Mirboo North in Victoria's Gippsland region for three generations. Her grandfather came out from Italy with nothing and after her father and his brother split the farm, her dad took it on, growing vegetables and raising livestock. It is clear from our conversation that Emma's parents instilled in her a particularly passionate view about the landscape and animal welfare. 'Every tree on the farm is Dad's favourite tree,' she says.

She went off and did her own thing for a while, learnt how to run a restaurant business and look after staff. But that thing for land was still buried deep within her.

Like many younger farmers, when she came back, she wanted everything in spreadsheets. She wanted to know the return on every dollar. 'All the farmers are making bad decisions,' she told her parents. She lectured her dad, telling him as only a young adult can tell a parent, 'You don't know, you're too emotionally attached to the place.' And then, when they very nearly did lose the farm, Emma stood in the drizzle and the wind at the top of a hill on the day of the auction, where she could see the whole damn place. She had pre-approval from the bank to bid. She either bought that piece of land or let it go. For the same price, she could buy many other properties or businesses. Was that the very best farm, or business, or very best opportunity available?

'It had nothing to do with it. This is our farm. My dad grew the trees. My grandfather came out with nothing and I want to keep it in the family because I can. Nothing rational about it. If they weren't emotionally connected, there would be no farming in Australia.'

Actually, though, the wheel is swinging around again to mega-farming, like the squatter blocks of old. Now it is corporate farming. But Germano argues that a problem with farm advocacy, at a public level and with government, is that it often acts as if all farmers are corporate farmers. (Since our interview, she has become president of the Victorian Farmers Federation.)

'We do it in the setting that everyone is going to have a $50 million turnover, and everyone is consolidating and taking over the other farms, and everyone is in ag tech, and it's simply not true. It's not a true reflection of who the farmers are in Australia.'

Nevertheless, she brought all the textbook business ideas to the farm. She set about trying to remove risk. While she swore she would never grow cauliflowers like her dad, she struck a deal with a wholesaler to grow them on contract. The wholesaler pushed her to grow them all year round to make use of the land.

'So I sent her a picture after 80 millimetres of rain and the washed topsoil. Because it's her crop; there's no risk to me. But that's the other thing when you're a farmer – you care about it in any case. She said, "Are we harvesting today?" I said, "Of course not, we can't get onto the paddock." And she said, "Well, when will we be able to get onto the paddock?" And I heard my father's voice. "When it's dry." I know it's a dick of an answer, but it's also the answer.'

The knowledge of how land reacts under many different circumstances started to mess with her head. The management of land is a dance. Sometimes you lead and sometimes the land leads. This is the daily challenge facing farmers. The way they respond to those challenges may be innate, the stuff of personal attitude, cultural history or inherent temperament.

As we talk, Germano touches on these fundamental questions I have been struggling with in my reporting of rural politics. *How* do we live on the land? How do we mitigate climate change and share the cost? How do we *include* the full cost, the environmental, the human and the economic cost, in the price of food? All humans make trade-offs with the environment to live and work.

Germano's great frustration is that public debate on agriculture goes around in circles. Indeed, it has become so narrow that people fear talking about trigger words. In both farming and non-farming audiences, trigger words include 'greenies', 'glyphosate', 'irrigate' or even 'regenerative farming'.

She wonders out loud how we cut through public life without getting lambasted. Not so long ago, she accepted an invitation to speak about agriculture at a metropolitan Greens branch. She worried it might be a set-up, but she went along anyway, and she says the members were very generous and gracious. She asked what they wanted to know about. It was this: why don't farmers vote for the Greens, given they have so much in common?

She tried to explain that she was on board with the 'let's look after the earth' thing, but that if farmers voted for the Greens, 'We would be out of business.'

She was asked about no-till farming, a common way for farmers to reduce their impact and soil loss by not ploughing land: most conventional Australian broadacre farmers have put the plough away to stem the loss of topsoil and retain moisture. The trade-off is that paddocks are sprayed with the herbicide Roundup. That means the seed can be 'direct drilled' into the paddock, stopping the loss of carbon dioxide. This is called no-till farming. Producing the same yield for crops like wheat, legumes, barley and oilseeds without using some herbicide is currently not possible, though increasing numbers of farmers are producing crops without them. Returning to the plough is also not an option if we want to retain topsoil. Germano used no-till farming as an example of the disconnection between the reality of farming and the public debate. If glyphosate is banned, many farmers may go back to the plough, or use a worse chemical that nobody has heard of, and we are no further ahead. Alternative farming methods and technology are developing, but they mean less yield. That means farmers will need to find income from other sources, which will require trade-offs from both farmers, eaters and governments.

Germano argues that metropolitan people want to change the way farmers manage land without curtailing their own high-consumption lifestyles. There were a couple of golden retrievers in the Greens meeting, living cosseted lives, contributing to carbon emissions. A study by UCLA geography professor Gregory Okin found that 163 million US dogs and cats were responsible for 25 to 30 per cent of the environmental impact of meat consumption in the US. If those pets lived in a country of their own, their fluffy nation would rank fifth in global meat consumption, Okin calculated, behind Russia, Brazil, the US and China.[2]

'These two golden retrievers, with the lights on and heater running for them . . . you want to tell me what to do on my farm while your labs are nice and warm? This is what you don't get about the trade-offs.'

Germano represents a younger generation of farmers who are all too aware of the need to connect farming culture with the eater. She has watched farmers increase their debt levels to fund their own growth while forgetting to connect with the person who will buy their product.

'Does the average person down the street know how much Australian agriculture contributes to Australia? No! They don't care. It's not their problem. I think it's a missed opportunity that everyone seems scared to connect with the community and connect with the public and really tell the story.

'Don't tell me the dairy story unless you are going to admit to the bobby calf bins, and tell me you are going to do something about [them], because that's what you're going to get caught on every single time.'

Bobby calves are the by-product of the milk industry. They are mostly male calves not required for milk production, which are sold on quickly or raised for beef. While there are strict industry guidelines on how the calves are treated, there have been examples of poor treatment on certain farms and the issue remains contentious.[3]

Death is as much a part of animal-rearing as life. If you eat a chop, you must accept that. If you eat a lentil burger, if you're living in a city and buying food – you have an impact on nature. Everything we do, everything we eat, how we live is one big opportunity-cost equation when it comes to nature. You can make value judgements and set your priorities, but you can't discount your own role in the natural world. Germano's concern is that people who have become very prescriptive about, for example, not eating animals, have removed themselves from the food cycle and the ecosystem to become 'omniscient, all-knowing god-like creatures who say, "This is pain, this is not pain; that's how you should live and this is not how you should live."'

The Australian writer Tim Winton wrote in his memoir *Island Home*, 'For someone brought up with a modernist outlook, it's hard to swallow the idea that we belong to nature.' I could not swallow that idea for a long time. Like a lot of modern, relatively wealthy humans, I was confused and unsure of the natural world when I moved to a farm. It is hard to accept we do belong to the earth. The changes we make to landscape result from our needs and wants. Some are urgent, such as the requirement to eat. Some are not urgent, such as the desire to fly at great CO_2 expense to some interesting location. The binary either/or debate that says we either have pristine wilderness or we have slash-and-burn farming is crap. Even a small population will have an impact. We have to balance that impact and create a bridge between the people who manage the broader landscape and the populace who also benefit from their produce.

This is the great melding of eaters, farming and environment. There is a growing alliance at the farming end and the food end, which acknowledges that agriculture and environment can only survive by coming together. The next generation of farmers and eaters increasingly recognise this. When we eat, we digest not only the food but the system that grew the food. Farming systems are influenced by eaters' desires.

Chapter 5

ON FOOD TRIBES

To be a vegan or even a vegetarian in our little town would have been a lonely life a few decades ago. With the popularity of more bespoke diets, it is getting easier. Hell, the local IGA supermarket even sells tofu, though it's tucked away. For any food producer, these new patterns of eating are a growing challenge, conjoined with climate and market supply-chain risk. Eaters are getting more particular about what they eat and how it is grown. But there is not one signal – there are many. Farming today is like taking many calls on a switchboard with an array of different demands.

Take meat, as one example. Australians are big meat eaters by global standards, but consumption is falling.[1] Climate change has been a driver of the trend towards cutting meat out of diets. That might send a farmer down a cropping route: lentils, wheat or barley, perhaps. Equally, there is growing interest in regenerative farming practices that rely heavily on animals and their poo in the landscape, effectively using sheep and cattle to regenerate degraded land by concentrating their stocking rates on land for shorter periods to improve soil health and increase ground cover. I talk about this trend in 'On disruption', but, suffice to say, it will necessarily make you a meat producer.

Whichever system you choose, you need a market of eaters. To extend the switchboard analogy, one caller will demand grass-fed meat and the next will demand lentil burgers – with no chemicals, please – and then ten others will demand cheap meat, don't care how it's grown. To be at the beginning of the food supply chain is to be confused. Understandably, climate change scares people and one of the easiest things to control is what we eat. The latest diet craze can fracture markets, but big food producers have to pay attention to the big trends for eaters.

Our politics have polarised globally and we have also splintered into food tribes. Take the US-based online food store Thrive Market. It boasts products for seventy different food values and allows the customer to filter their products according to those values: locavore, vegetarian, gluten-free, raw, paleo, vegan, low FODMAP, ketogenic. If you want proof the food you're ordering adheres to your dietary desire, you can get a range of certifications, including organic, biodynamic, non-genetically modified, kosher, fair trade, glyphosate-residue-free. You can order alcohol-free, caffeine-free, peanut-free, preservative-free, salt-free, antibiotic-free, yeast-free, soy-free. You can choose boosted foods high in a range of constituents, protein, fibre, omegas, essential oils. Once you set your parameters, you are presented with a range of goods within your value set, including pet foods. So, if you are shopping for your kelpie and you set your filters at 'vegan, BPA-free, no added sugar, "supports charity", antibiotic-free and synthetic-hormone-free', you might be directed to the Healthsome Garden of Vegan peanut and pumpkin dog treats, with 'US sourced proteins'.

For someone who gets most of her food from a small-town supermarket, this stuff just blows my mind. I heard about Thrive Market from Mike Lee, a US food futurist who was in Australia in early 2020 speaking at Evoke, the annual conference of Agri-Futures, the rebadged Rural Industries Research and Development Corporation. Lee helps food companies develop their products and create innovation strategies for the future. He loves working with the industry because he says it's like no other – 'the perfect messy confluence of logic and emotion'. The food industry sounds a lot like politics. In politics, a great deal of analysis goes into the way voters are supposed to think, both before and after elections. It's assumed that large chunks of the public will vote a certain way for a certain reason, yet so much about voting is at the intersection of emotion, recognition, interest and, well, the vibe. Just like the way we eat. Our appetites for both food and politicians are directly connected to the gut.

Lee describes food tribes as similar to political tribes and just as polarised. Augmenting cultural food trends mirrors dealing with political trends: you develop identity and then social media allows you to amplify. Social media allows us to supersize ourselves, to reinforce our values.

'This is food as identity in action,' says Lee. 'Digital media allows you to be that thing more than is excessively healthy, right? So the right gets more right and the left gets more left. It's the same with food tribes. It's easier to go deeper and deeper into the wormhole.'

Unsurprisingly, Lee is frequently asked what the future is – as if it is one thing. He is advocating for a balance because the future is many things. It can't be all plant-based or meat-based or entirely set by one of those filters. It has to be an interconnected system. Lee's hypothesis is that no matter how sustainable a food is when it is first produced, once it gets to a certain scale, it becomes unsustainable. Human nature being what it is, the idea lights up the imagination, so if a little is good, much more is better.

'You have to realise it's okay to eat a little bit of everything and if everybody did that, we wouldn't have these big monocultures.'

He goes back three or four decades to the development of almond milk, when its pitch was about sustainability – which he advises to 'take with a grain of salt for now'.

'Maybe that was true in that moment but now you've gone to the situation that there are so many almonds grown to fuel it, it's not sustainable at all. So that's a really interesting fact because it means you can't pull all of your goals into any one thing. Nor should you, for your health, just eat one thing. We need diversity.'

I have always thought of diversity in cultural terms, but recently the idea of economic diversity has been rolling around my head after years of covering rural political fights, which are basically a power struggle between those with fewer resources and those with more. I think we are losing a lot of the economic diversity of our farmers, which I will cover later in these pages. But I had never thought of diversity in terms of what I eat. Over decades, I have eaten a very consistent diet – healthy, peppered by outbursts of hedonism. I've tried most diets, carnivore, vegetarian, non-dairy, full-fat dairy, high protein, you name it. At my age, though, it seems so much easier to stick to something that works for you. Lee has the best advice of any foodie. Stop thinking about trends. Stop thinking about which diet to follow like a slave. Be a moderate person who eats a little bit of everything. Have full-fat dairy ice cream, just not every day. Have almond milk if you must, just not every day. Moderation is harder when the range is endless, though: it's a lot easier to set yourself to five or ten rules. Humans are not programmed for moderation.

'It's very appealing to dive into a food tribe because it feels like you can have these rigid set of rules and you can go deep in them and don't have to think about anything else. So I get why that's tempting but it's causing a lot of issues.'

Lee describes how we got to such a confusing place. The global food story of the post-war era starts with Olympian-scale yield leaps. Norman Borlaug's Green Revolution of the 1950s and '60s consolidated industrial food production and it was wildly successful. The progress staved off a lot of hunger. It was so successful partly because of its focus on a few foods. So the yield increases but the diversity shrinks. Lee says 75 per cent of our food now comes from twelve plants and five animal species. That is mind-blowing to me.

'We exchanged the natural biodiversity of all the different flora and fauna we have for a highly concentrated system supported by heavy inputs.'

The output expands, the basic ingredients shrink and the supermarket explodes. There is an illusion of choice because there are many more products than were in my grandmother's supermarket all those years ago.

'Ask the consumer about diversity and they will say, "Of course, I have so much choice." The average supermarket has 80,000 different products. But if you walk down a cereal aisle and you see all these different brands, a lot of these foods are made out of the same four or five different things. We traded ecological biodiversity in exchange for brand diversity.'

This is where the cultural food story changes in the western world. I loved to shop for clothes as a teenager and a young adult. Clothes were an important cultural marker, an essential part of identity. But my twenty-something son buys most of his clothes from second-hand stores. He couldn't care less about brands. Many of his generation signal their values through food. He is vegetarian and so were a lot of his friends at college, most of them choosing that tribe in the first years of university. US surveys of youth attitudes have found that teenagers spend more money on food than clothes.[2]

'Food has also become that kind of expression,' says Lee. 'It's not just about the calories that are going into your body and how they make you feel, it's about the identity and how you want to express to the world. And this idea that food is identity is massively disruptive to the big food system, to a consolidated food system, because however many identities there are in here, there's that many ways to look at how we want to eat food. The problem is our consolidated industry has not been able to service each one of you as individuals, so we look at you as one giant lump. Or two giant lumps of people.'

That's where the disruption comes into the equation. In politics, the disruption of the usual voting patterns has been the big story of the last decade. Disruption has hollowed out the media industry, leaving many journalists unemployed. I did not realise this disruption had hit the food industry. The fact that it has hit food means it is necessarily shaping farming (I will cover this in 'On disruption').

This is another story of power. These niche brands are like the guerrilla force of the food industry, or the independents of politics, starting up, innovating, expanding or selling, moving on to the next trend. They are nimble and turn on a sixpence. They drive new food tribes to establish new markets, with a view to selling new products. Lee says pretty much all of the innovation is coming from small food brands (who knew someone would buy BPA-free, vegan dog treats? At Thrive, they figured it out). A company like Coca-Cola could not establish a 'mega brand' from scratch now. 'A company like [Coke] thinks of all of us as a mega segment and we are all going to love it. Those days are over, we are just too fragmented and too digitally connected and powerful.' You don't get into that many loungerooms at the same time now. Like my own industry, no one reads one news source anymore.

Startups are stealing a great deal of market share from big entrenched food companies, creating an explosion of brands, many to service those smaller food tribes that have unique ways of looking at food.

Lee gets paid to help retailers, so he spends his time thinking about three main values: health, sustainability and experience. They are the three values that most 'discerning' consumers want now. When eaters want 'health' as a value, they want the food to improve their health. This is 'functional food' as medicine. The rise of the term 'superfoods' is an example of the health value. We have all seen the lists which usually include things like avocados, nuts, berries, leafy greens, turmeric and seaweed. The 'functional food' industry was worth $247 billion in 2018.

'Sustainability' is more complex. More than half of eaters value sustainability. According to Lee, 66 per cent say they want to support sustainability globally, and that rises to 73 per cent for millennials.

Then there is the 'experience' factor: the taste of the food, the place that it comes from and the story attached to it. The provenance.

The problem is that when you cross those values with the harried single parent rushing into the supermarket after work to fill the fridge, are they thinking health, sustainability and experience, or are they thinking price, flavour and ease of preparation? The other thing is that no one knows what sustainability tastes like. When you eat your favourite meal, do you sit back in your chair, sigh with satisfaction and say to yourself, 'That was so sustainable'? Lee says probably not, though I am particularly satisfied when dinner is produced from our own place.

'There's a lot of logic and science that goes behind the farming and the manufacturing of food, but all of that can be completely upended because someone doesn't like tomatoes. Food is emotion and I implore you that as long as we need to think of logical solutions, you also have to think emotionally. You have to accept the fact that the consumer will be completely irrational. And we can't resist that, we have to embrace that and work with that.'

So much of the appeal of food is literally the gut and the heart, informed by the past but also very much in the moment. So food is a personal, selfish thing. It concerns the I – how does it make me feel? Does this taste good? Can I afford this? Lee says there is a selfish end of food and there's an altruistic end. The goal is to join those two. For that concept, he looks to the Danish architect Bjarke Ingels and his concept of hedonistic sustainability. 'Hedonistic sustainability is the idea that you can actually be sustainable but increase the quality of life while doing so.'

Lee's example is the difference between two electric/hybrid cars, the Toyota Prius and the Tesla. The Prius is worthy and functional. The Tesla, for those who are into cars, is definitely the more attractive car. The Prius says 'If you want to save the planet, buy this car'. The Tesla says 'This car is fast and sexy. By the way, it's also sustainable'. Lee's mission is to fuse those two ideas for food. To go from 'this is delicious and it's sustainable' to 'this is delicious because it's sustainable'.

The really fascinating thing, I think, is that those small producers and food startups remind me of the niche operators, including some of the best regenerative farmers, who are really committed to 'a cause'. It is the cause that connects them to their eaters. You can argue about whether the cause is legitimate or not, but the common thread is the full view into the system. Those farmers invite people into their landscapes and their businesses, and in the process they are buying not only the food but also the story of the food and often the story of the family who grew the food. That builds trust, and for a lot of people that is more delicious.

For me, this explains why Big Food is taking up the small brands. The startups have built the connections to their eaters. They have an authenticity, which in a very noisy world is worth a lot. If you are a mid-sized farmer looking at these trends, you might be saying, it's okay for them because they have the time to fart around with a few cows. Don't mistake the trend, though. The trend is not necessarily the return to an old-fashioned farming system, or a small-scale operation, or particular model. The trend is to transparency, to see into the food grower's business and her life. Many eaters want to choose.

Transparency means the food process has become the product. Seventy per cent of consumers want more transparency in their food, according to Lee, and in China it is slightly higher. In China. The demand means the process will be harder to hide. This is the unparalleled opportunity for food producers. It is also a threat for those who cannot stand behind the virtue of their process. This is a big point for farming so let me repeat it. If farmers can't stand by the virtues of their food production processes, they will fall behind.

Lee has identified the 'primal scream' from a portion of eaters who want to be closer to their food. For urbanites, that might mean concepts like urban farms and community gardens. It also means eaters in cities and regional areas tracing back their food to their source farmers.

Fancy restaurants used to manipulate food so they could hide the fact that it came from a farm and turn it into something that was uniquely made by their chef. In the last twenty or thirty years the best chefs are saying they are only as good as the food that the farmer grew for them. They cannot turn bad stuff into good stuff.

This trend in human eating in both the west and the east is the most exciting thing to happen since the return to unsliced sourdough. I cannot imagine a greater opportunity for farmers to speak directly to the eater of their produce, whether that be wheat or beef or lamb or vegetables or fruit or lentils. Farmers have power if they wish to use it. More than that, if you combine this trend with Lee's message on the disruption of smaller brands, there is an opportunity for the calculated, risk-taking farmer to grow a niche product *and* set the terms. In Australia, I think of the growers in Western Australia of chia seeds and lupins for flour for gluten-free and paleo eaters. Likewise, the banana growers up north who began making banana flour from previously wasted bananas. It is a popular product, traditionally used in Africa as a cheaper alternative to wheat flour, but now loved by grain-free eaters. Literally anything is possible in this disrupted market. This makes food production a very exciting space if we can get over the economics of the middle and the culture of the commodity – I will come to these wicked problems later on. Suffice to say, it turns out that people do care about farming.

But back to our eaters.

The first restaurant where I noticed a kitchen garden out the back, in the 1990s, was Canberra's Ottoman, run by Serif Kaya. Kaya and I had a mutual fondness for fresh figs. I only discovered the fresh version when I moved to the farm. Three enormous black Genoa fig trees bear fruit nearly every Easter, apart from in drought. Most of the time The Farmer just lets them drop. He is a man of moderation. I have a penchant for gluttony and have spent many Easters sitting under the canopy, eating too many figs with the old Labrador.

Of course, chefs have long cared passionately about food. Matt Moran is another high-profile Australian chef with a kitchen garden outside one of his high-end Sydney restaurants, Chiswick.

American chef Alice Waters has been a key figure in the farm-to-table movement in the US for the past three decades, famously serving a single peach on a plate for dessert, listed on the menu as '[farmer] Mas Masumoto's peach'. The American chef who supercharged restaurant connections with the farm is Dan Barber, whose book *The Third Plate: Field Notes on the Future of Food*, first published in 2014, is now a classic of the global paddock-to-plate movement. He concentrates on farm-to-table cooking at his New York Blue Hill restaurant, and Blue Hill at Stone Barns Center for Food and Agriculture – a working farm and education centre.

Barber has flipped around the seed-breeding tradition of concentrating on yield and robustness, in order to concentrate on flavour. How would a *chef* design seeds? A chef would design seeds to do the job of flavour in order to keep the cheffing bit as simple and as flexible as possible. Revolutionary, huh? Yields have long driven seed-breeding because the seed company that can breed the best-yielding, most robust and resistant variety is automatically seductive for farmers whose only way to increase financial return is, usually, to increase yield.

Wheat is the obvious example. When The Farmer was young, wheat plants were tall and spindly. Often the plant would fall over, making it a pain to harvest and leaving The Farmer with a whole lot of stalk that was consuming plant energy that could go into the seed – the bit that makes money. Over decades, varieties were bred shorter and with more yield.

So Dan Barber's subversive idea to breed for flavour might prompt farmers to ask, 'Will it pay?' The job of people like Mike Lee is to find a way to make it pay. For his part, Barber has established Row 7 Seeds, a US company that sells vegetable seeds whose crops are particularly flavoursome. Lee gushes over Barber's Koginut squash variety. When Lee tried the roasted squash, he thought someone had covered it in half a kilo of brown sugar. Barber's potatoes – the Upstate Abundance Potato – taste like they have a slab of butter in them, even when they're baked simply with a bit of salt.

'Barber's approach is to start at the root of the issue and say, "If we want more people on a plant-based diet, how about we make the plants taste better? Let's not support all the other industries that try to make the plants taste better. Let's just make the plants taste better."

'This is about how you tell the story of sustainability in plant-based diets – on the back of experience, on the back of flavour, and how you can connect that flavour back to what happened in the land, instead of coming right at you with a bunch of climate stats. Climate change is real and it's important, but people don't eat stats, they eat food, and we have to marry the two very strongly.'

Lee has been highly influenced by the Japanese concept of *omakase*. This concept is based on trust between the chef and the eater. The good chef knows not only the best thing on the menu but the best food in season in their market. So by ordering *omakase*, you are saying to the chef, 'I leave it in your hands.'

'That chef will not take your order. That chef knows what's happening in the ocean, what's being over-fished or under-fished. The chef is one and the same as the fisherman. What you are saying is, "I leave it to the supply chain to tell me what I should eat. Not because I want to save the ocean" – yes, you will do that if it's done well – "but because I want you to show me the best flavour out there." It's a hedonistic thing.

'This is what it is to explore and eat and have fun. It's the double-edged sword that allows us to scale sustainable causes into the mainstream. Then the guy sits next to me and orders twelve pieces of tuna. This is what the big food system is set up to do – find the handful of things we love and just go deep on them. It doesn't have to be this way.'

Here we return to the problem of scale and yield being the only variabilities for the food grower or producer. So, the beef producer scales up everything to make a living wage and it is in their interests for the eaters to eat as much beef as possible. Steaks for breakfast, lunch and dinner. Lee acknowledges that big food is predicated on finding the one food, growing that crop year on year, and doing it at scale. The economic model has demanded it. Big supermarkets have demanded it, whether it's fruit or lamb or vegetables. Big supermarkets do not want your beautifully tended fifty flavourful cauliflowers; they want five thousand, and every year, please.

Lee was working with grain farmers for a food company in Washington state. He asked them what they wanted to grow. That was confusing enough, because farmers usually grow what the market will take. But Lee asked, 'If you could grow anything to take care of your land, what would it be?'

They came up with a mix of wheat, barley, millet, flax and canola, crops that have been around for a long time. 'They know millet is very good for microbial action in their soil. I asked, "Why don't you grow it?" They said it was only grown for bird seed in the US. There was no incentive to grow it.'

Lee wanted to work out how to change the usual cycle of wheat on wheat. He believes that every decent farmer knows what it takes to look after their soil, they are just not incentivised to do it by the marketplace. That's the problem he was trying to solve while improving diversity in the food chain and the environment. (Though it should be said here that most Australian farmers do not grow the same crops year on year – they have a rotation of crops and fallow or resting paddocks with pasture.)

So Lee's job was to think of a product that could help farmers grow crops that regenerated their land and still paid a decent income.

He came up with crackers. In the US it is a $4.5 billion market. It hadn't changed in a long time and it's an easy product to understand. Now he had demand and he had the capacity to scale it up if it worked. He describes crackers as 'the meatball of the baked goods industry'. It is a forgiving product that can change as the crop rotation changes; there is a connection between the cracker and its eater, and via a better process for the land and the people who farm it.

'Varietal Crop Crackers. You don't start with that mix in Australia. You could ask what Australian farmers want to grow and then incentivise that. That's the mind-shift I want to employ with people. We can look at consumer trends, what's out there – and it's important to do that – but we as producers of food don't have to take any of that as gospel. If we don't like the future we can change it.'

This stuff turns food on its head. Sceptical me says it's marketing. But it also shows leverage and getting ahead of the market by acknowledging some practices need to change, and offering a solution to bring about better environmental outcomes. The impetus has to come from the food industry thinking outside the square to work out what eaters want and reach back into the farming process to satisfy these eaters' demands according to their values. A, I am doing the right thing by the farmer. B, I am doing the right thing by the planet. C – and most important – don't come at me with it if it tastes crappy.

Political me says this is power for farmers. It requires the connective tissue between the farmer and the eater. Sometimes that is the farmers reaching out. Sometimes that is the eater. Most times it is someone in the middle. And the person in the middle usually makes the money.

You might say all this is referencing the high end of food only, the people who have a choice and a budget to care about what they eat. But the point is that it sets trends. And, as happens in fashion with couture, these trends tumble down the chain. They are to be harnessed and ridden because they almost always signal the track forward. And before you know it there are kale chips at the corner store.

The problem is that a large portion of commodity growers feel trapped by the economic model, riding the rollercoaster of price and the seasons without the energy to innovate. They are exhausted by dealing with uncertainty, leading a portion of farmers to adopt the brace position. It is very hard to think clearly when your head is between your legs, kissing your arse goodbye. Part of the reason for this uncertainty is the current economic state of play in farming. Economics, wrote the economist Kate Raworth, is the mother tongue of public policy. It demands attention. So the history of Australian agricultural economics is the story of how we got to where we are today. To ignore the role of public policy in agriculture's operating system, as if farmers just came up with this whole show themselves, is to deny our history.

Chapter 6

ON ECONOMICS

The deregulation agenda of the 1980s is seared into my memory, not just because my journalistic consciousness began in that era. The international appetite for privatisation and removing regulation was gathering pace under leaders like Margaret Thatcher and Ronald Reagan, who were committing to an 'economically rational' agenda. In Australia, from the 1960s onwards governments had gradually begun the work of stripping farm protections, with the Hawke–Keating and the Howard governments really accelerating change.

John Kerin was Labor's minister for Primary Industry and Energy through the 1980s, when he played a key role in the gradual abolition of tariff protections on agricultural imports. He puts the capacity for change among farmers down to a growing understanding in parts of the industry that high protections levels were adding to production costs. The mindset, he says, was of 'us still being a colony with imperial preference well into the 1980s'. Remember that

Britain had joined the European Union a decade before, primarily to consolidate its own economy. The idea that Australia would continue to gain preference was so last century.

Kerin surveyed the industry landscape and recalls there were at least seventy-two agricultural marketing boards, including three for eggs in Queensland; and one for brown onions and one for white onions. 'I never learnt whether the supply of purple onions was regulated.'

Minister Kerin gave Australian farming an enema. Many of the least efficient businesses fell by the wayside. A portion got better at what they did and a fair swag got bigger to cope with greater competition. The unerring message was to get big or get out. Farmers largely responded, but not without some loud wailing.

Thirty years later, farming as a whole has mostly done what governments have asked it to do. Farmers acted with the self-interest that supposedly drives the market. They opened their businesses, many of which were welded to historical, cultural agronomic traditions. They took on more research-based solutions to gain the revered market edge, even while that research was also being privatised as funding was ripped out of government departments to be taken over by agribusiness.

Kerin was not without some sympathy for farmers. After all, he was not only an economist but the son of a poultry farmer. He still thinks deeply about the issues he grappled with in government. Blessed with a desert dry sense of humour, he recommends his 726-page memoir for insomnia. It does include much of his policy thinking, and he regularly speaks to the University of the Third Age about his experiences.

While he remains of the belief such reforms were needed, Kerin also had a nagging feeling that there might be some hairs on British economist David Ricardo's theory of comparative advantage. That is the idea that a country should only concentrate on producing goods when it can do so at the most efficient and cheapest price. For example, if you grow beef and wheat well, but can't produce cheese as cheaply nor as well as the French, embrace a good *fromager d'affinois* and let your Australian dairy farmers and cheese-makers embrace a career change.

'As a practising politician grappling with the actual world of the 1970s to '90s, I had intellectual and practical problems with Ricardo's theory, but was intimidated by my better educated, economically driven peers. Even if I questioned the relevance of the theory to the times we were in, I remain chastised and woefully disregarded.'

Kerin was trying to walk the line between some measure of economic efficiency and an equal measure of national sovereignty. That is, being competitive enough to earn export dollars without being too reliant on other countries for basic goods and services in times of say, a pandemic. As we have seen, this remains a critical question for food production, even in countries like Australia.

'I think we have a need for a few basic heavy industries,' he says. He mentions steel, chemicals, electronics, cement, glass, paper and packaging, oil refining and an efficient energy supply to ensure Australia is not excluded from new industries and thus can service existing light industries, like food manufacturing, advanced manufacturing and construction. 'In other words, I don't think we can only have a services-based cum "barista economy" that's other than mining, energy and agriculture to the exclusion of manufacturing.'

When he was minister, he asked questions regarding the disproportionate power of larger nations, which still subsidised or had competitive advantage through sheer weight of working population, money or political heft. His inquiries were met with 'choked incredulity or shocked squawks' from public service and advisors. So the minister rolled on with his duties.

He had setpiece meetings in magnificent castles and palaces in Brussels to beg other countries to wind back their agricultural subsidies. The trouble for Australia remains that other countries have starved and are thus quite protective of their food producers. Those countries, in Europe and Asia, steadfastly ignored his requests, and pretty much have refused subsequent Australian trade ministers ever since, notwithstanding a number of free trade agreements. In public, Kerin sang from the song sheet on free trade, though its reality to him was like the curate's egg. Good in parts.

'We then-purists held the line and I wandered the world with my lines learnt off pat, with answers to every dopey line of argument put to me . . . I remained in Coventry, severely chastised, crushed and doubted by my peers as not being "sound enough" as an economist. Perhaps a rebel with a cause,' Kerin said.

In other words, he believed in free trade with conditions. Since the reforms of the Hawke, Keating and Howard governments, there has been a great consolidation in agriculture into larger and larger lumps of land, combined with the loss of national manufacturing industries. The top owners by value in Australian agriculture in 2021 are global superannuation funds, large banks and asset management groups. Large corporations have traditionally dominated the stuff going into farming, like chemicals and equipment, as well as transforming the stuff coming out of farming, such as baking the loaf of bread or pasteurising the milk. The actual growing of food, for the last century at least, was mostly done by the family farmer. Now the large corporations are moving into the business of growing food. They are attracted by the capacity for annual returns, growing demand and longer-term capital gains, and their interest is driving up Australian rural land prices. This has farmers both cock-a-hoop at their increased equity but also slightly nervous about whether they will be outrun.

The structural changes I see, brought on by global economics, are squeezing the life out of mid-sized multigenerational food producers. They are caught between the agribusiness companies that set the prices of the products they need, and the commodity traders that set food prices at the other end. They are also caught between environmentalists and farm advocates who want to place farm landscapes wholly in the realms of either economic production or ecological wilderness.

Sometimes it takes an outsider to provide perspective. In the grand deregulation plan, Australian and New Zealand farmers are considered the winners. We have scale, we are relatively innovative and we export. Farmers from other parts of the world are blown away by our natural advantages, notwithstanding our climate of extremes.

Every time James Rebanks comes to Australia, he is in awe of our farming scale. The man who rose to prominence via Twitter sharing pictures of his Herdwick sheep mob turned out to be a writer of note. His first book, *The Shepherd's Life*, was a bestseller both in the UK and Australia, and his most recent one, *English Pastoral*, tells the story of how farming has changed since his grandfather's time.

From his little farm in the Lake District in England, the man known as the Herdy Shepherd first came out here for a gap year. Our vast paddocks blew him away, literally. The young Rebanks got homesick and returned to his wonky fields in the fells. But not before he absorbed the scale of the operation.

'I think there's something profoundly different between a new-world landscape, which is set out rationally, or on a bigger scale, or from the get-go was more overtly capitalist, than there is from the old-world crooked-field landscapes. That's not to say there aren't lots of good things in an Australian context that can be wonderful farming. But I'm not sure those two should be competing with each other. I think we need to make our farming work for wherever we are at in the native ecosystems.'

Like many young farmers, Rebanks grew up wanting to embrace changes being wrought in agriculture. It was the 1980s and economic rationalism was upon us. Rebanks was seduced by all the books that were informing that view. 'I knew even when I liked it, it was hard.' Aged twenty-five, he received a Friedrich Hayek scholarship through the Mont Pelerin Society. The man whom the world loves for his traditional farming ways was also well versed in the economics of Hayek and Milton Friedman – espousers of free-market capitalism, free trade and small government.

'It was a cold-blooded view of how the world works, based on supply and demand, but I was briefly seduced by it. I thought, this explains why we are struggling. We just don't think about this ruthlessly enough. I think later on, when I came back to the farm, that's when I had to face up to the limitations of that way of thinking. I suddenly was faced with all these choices. You think, no, this destroys land. This destroys community. It destroys all sorts of things you can no longer ignore.'

James and Helen Rebanks' farm is small by Australian standards, a couple of hundred acres. He runs a very old breed of sheep called Herdwicks, a hardy type that can survive the bitter cold winters and they are run on permanent pastures. He is positive that sustainable farming is not profitable in his part of the world because the only way he can make the farming pay is to 'turn tricks and hustle'. He could wrap it up in a bow or create a community-supported agriculture venture and ask people to pay a third more than the shops because they might like his books or his values. He could create a good brand and he might be able to charge 10 per cent more, but he can't charge 30–40 per cent more, which is what he reckons he'd need to look after the place sustainably. 'I think it is that black and white, sadly.'

He didn't always think the current economic model of farming was unsustainable. While he was at Oxford University, he read lots of economics and watched other young farmers. He thought perhaps they could modernise. His dad was struggling under farm debt and Rebanks was looking at the changes in farming and wondering why they did not apply to his family's place. He worried his father didn't cost anything properly like the modern farmers.

'[My father] said to me, "Don't you dare cost anything, because if you cost anything on this farm you will discover nothing is worth doing." At the time, when I heard that, I thought my dad was insane. He is in charge of my life and my business and he doesn't believe in economics. And now I look back and think there is something in that. It's not insane. He did it because he thought it was the right thing to do and the right way to look after a piece of land, and he was almost confused by why anybody would think about it in any other way.'

So the Rebanks family didn't buy into many of the wholesale changes in the 1980s and '90s, but James saw plenty of farmers who did. The two best farms in the county were owned by someone who went for scale. They bought the best equipment. They were 'the rich farmers', with 120,000 pigs. They had everything going for them – scale, cash flow and, it turned out, debt. They went bankrupt twenty years later. For Rebanks, it was a wake-up call. He thought that those two farms had been the winners of modern farming, but they'd failed and their owner owed £16 million.

Years later, on a book tour in the US, Rebanks landed in an event called 'the Practical Farmers of Iowa', a gathering of 400 families whose style of farming was regenerative. He asked them why they were interested in this kind of farming – they were supposed to be the winners of the modern world that remains sceptical of regenerative farming in favour of the power of scale and high productivity.

They did not feel like winners. 'They said, "There is only one way to do business in that landscape now. There's only one grain company in town that buys what you produce. There's no local market." They basically realised it was a road to nowhere. A handful of corporations are going to farm the whole thing. There are no jobs in town. No future for any of them. Ninety per cent of the farmers we met hated it. They could see right through it. They could see it was a disaster.'

So why is that bigger-farm-cheaper-food model failing for all but the top? I think the simple truth is the food price does not account for what economists call the externalities, which include environmental costs and sometimes labour costs. Rebanks points to the scientific statistics that show a species decline of 13 per cent in 'average abundance' across the UK since 1970 and 15 per cent of species threatened with extinction.[1] 'As we intensify farming, nature is pushed out.' Often the landscape, the farm worker or the farmer – or all three – are left to pay part of the costs of food so someone else down the line doesn't have to pay. And perhaps those eaters can't afford to pay. But someone has to pay.

I ask Rebanks if the price of food is fair.

'We are getting food with prices that are a hidden subsidy, and the hidden subsidy is the destruction of soil, the destruction of ecosystems, it's the trashing of old farming systems, it's the use of unregulated immigrant labour across the American Midwest, in working conditions that are making people ill. The externalities are massive. [So, no], you're absolutely right, [the price of food] isn't fair.'

Whenever we question the costs of production of food compared to the price of food in the modern farming system, we always come back to the eater. A section of eaters cannot afford the price of food as it is. Rebanks says he has had the same questions as I do about the farming system, but always considers that 20 per cent of British or American people can't afford to pay more than they do now. People can't afford to pay more for their food because they are on low or no wages, and wages have to be low, we are told, so that we can produce cheap goods, so people can consume more. Aren't we chasing our tails?

Rebanks no longer believes that farmers growing cheap food is working for poor people. Look at America, he says. It has the cheapest food in the world – Americans spend 7 per cent of their household budget on food. Does it mean there's less poverty in North America? No, it doesn't mean that at all. The devaluing of food is linked to the devaluing of labour. It's linked to the disappearance of the middle class in small and even big towns and cities. It's about badly paid work. There are basically two ways to earn a living in Rebanks' little town in the UK. One is to work in a supermarket, where there is very little career progression and quite low wages. Or it's logistics – moving stuff in and moving stuff out.

'Your options have shrunk from thirty years ago, when there were a whole bunch of other ways – owning a small business, having a small farm . . . which have disappeared.'

He has described many little towns in a nutshell, though I would add nursing, teaching, aged care as some careers available in smaller places in Australia. But supermarket jobs and truck driving are the nub of it. Farming technology has gone ahead in leaps and bounds, so farmers grow more with less need for manual labour.

Here again, pull a thread on a farm and it takes you to the big questions. 'I think if you or I talk about making food more expensive and we haven't got an answer for the poorest people in our society, then we are on really tricky ground, aren't we?'

He is absolutely right. We can rant and rave about the economic system grabbing farmers by the short and curlies, but unless wider economic structural changes are going to take place, we will never change things.

The best study of the shortcomings of modern market economics emerged from an argument in favour of modern market economics. It came from a Princeton professor of economics and former vice-chairman of the board of governors of the US Federal Reserve System. In 2018 Alan Blinder was prosecuting an argument for free trade and lamenting why the public did not see its benefits. He concluded, 'The single biggest reason why economists can't sell free trade may be philosophical; the world view that underpins the discipline of economics differs dramatically from the world view of most people.'[2]

For economists, he wrote, the central goal of the economic system is producing goods and services at the lowest possible cost and then distributing them to people who want them. Economists concentrate on the wellbeing of the consumers – for our purposes, the eaters. In Blinder's telling, we work to earn an income in order to consume. To eat. To buy stuff. '[Work] is not an end in itself, nor a direct source of satisfaction or self-worth. The interests of producers, including the value people get from their jobs, count for little or nothing in standard economic calculus. In fact, work is scored as a negative – something people dislike and do only to support their consumption.

'But what if economists have this wrong? What if people care as much (or more) about their role as producers – about their jobs – as they do about the goods and services they consume. That would mean economists have been barking up the wrong tree for more than two centuries. Maybe the public sees the central goal of an economic system as providing well-paid jobs, not producing cheap goods. If so, the standard case for free trade evaporates.'[3]

Blinder describes one of the key contradictions in modern farming. His argument identifies that producers of all forms have taken second place in the drive to increase the supply of cheap goods and services for consumers. Farm policy pushes to favour the value for the consumer over the value that the producer takes from her work. (The irony is that any producer is a consumer too.)

Blinder argues that while the ordinary punter can intuitively understand the idea of supply and demand, comparative advantage is counterintuitive. Comparative advantage, according to Blinder, 'holds that two countries can both benefit from trade even when one can produce everything more cheaply than the other'.

'If Countries A and B trade with each other, Country A can specialize in producing what it is best at, Country B can specialize in producing what it is least bad at, and then the two countries can trade to their mutual advantage.'

Blinder is obviously frustrated by what he sees as a knowledge gap between econocrats and the 'economically ignorant' who question the tenets of economic wisdom. Leaving aside who is right, the gap becomes a political opportunity. And hey presto, like a rat up a drainpipe, populist politicians see the opportunity: 'Defenders of free trade also have to contend with populist politicians and well-financed opponents who find foreign workers and firms easy scapegoats for domestic economic woes.'

Blinder was writing of the Trump era, but Australia has its own politicians who have demonised foreign workers. The reason populist politicians are able to do this is because, as Blinder accepts, 'every move toward freer trade creates both winners and losers'.

Australia knows that. Think car workers, think garment manufacturers. I think of the Electrolux factory, just two hours from our place in Orange, which closed in 2016 after a seventy-four-year history, leaving 300 people out of work, to take its manufacturing plant to Thailand, where the labour rate was $2.50 an hour.

Blinder offers alternatives. The winners could 'in principle compensate the losers and still have something left over for themselves' and then everyone could see a benefit for trade. Economists should do a better job at communicating with the public, 'but at the end of the day, they may simply have to accept the inevitable: convincing most people of the value of free trade is a losing fight'.

The food growers who can produce at the lowest cost in the world win the prize of the highest returns. That might be Australia and New Zealand, due to our size and scale. That win is important to the economy as a whole, because it makes the country wealthier by increasing export income. Yet when I've asked farmers who aren't in the top echelon if they are winning in the constant race to improve productivity, with the demands of the changing climate, many will say no. That is why some of those farmers are voting for those populist politicians.

The reforms in agriculture since the 1980s have meant decoupling the idea of food from farming, to put food on par with the plastic spoon or lip gloss. Is food production different to any other business? The economists say no. In direct contradiction, governments and agribusiness have urged farmers to ramp up their scale to feed the world. There will be 9 billion people on the planet by 2050! Hurry! We have to feed them! These are contradictions. Either food is essential or it's no different to any other commodity.

Think of the challenges of farming like this. You are working at a standing desk while walking on a treadmill, which is split in two. One side of the treadmill goes slowly, consistently. That side is nature's cycle. So many days' gestation for livestock. So many months from the sowing to the harvest. The other side of the treadmill is accelerating. That side is technology, geopolitical disruptions, scientific knowledge, financialisation, changing tastes. Some farmers stay wholly in the slow lane. Some farmers stay wholly in the fast lane. Some have a foot on both sides.

That is how Mike Stephens characterises farming. He is an advisor who founded consulting firm Meridian Agriculture in Victoria. He completed a diploma of farm management in his twenties, a Churchill Fellowship in his forties, a masters in his sixties and a PhD at Melbourne University in farm succession in his seventies. His experience in consultancy, farm management and now as an agricultural academic makes for an interesting combination, which utilises ground truthing and the rigour of data and research. For his PhD research, he drew on 6000 Australian broadacre businesses and analysed 116 of them. His conclusion was that only thirty of the 116 businesses will continue beyond the third generation. That took Stephens to a bracing conclusion. Only a quarter of the current 50,000 or so broadacre farms have the scale and income to survive being passed on to the next generation of farmers. So, in coming decades we could see the landscape of farming and our rural areas change a lot.

'If around 15,000 is all that's left in broadacre agriculture, there won't be a primary school between Harden and Wagga,' Stephens says.

He discovered about half of the 50,000 Australian broadacre farm businesses can't meet the living and education needs of their owners unless significant off-farm income is generated. Without that income, those businesses simply cannot withstand the vagaries of changing climate and the market.

Of the rest, a further quarter lacks scale, but with some off-farm income, leasing or share farming they have the potential to achieve the scale required.

The final quarter has the scale required both to withstand the vagaries of climate and market, and to achieve the three main aims of family farming, which Stephens names as handing on a viable business, retaining enough money to fund retirement and enabling sufficient resources to pay out non-farming family members.

'The majority of farm businesses make insufficient profit, too irregularly, to have a long-term future,' he says.

After entering the industry at fifteen, Stephens has watched as ag moves from being a protected industry to a less subsidised industry, or from 'feather bedding' to standing on its own two feet; though, he says, there are still a fair few indirect subsidies or industry supports for agriculture that farmers 'don't like to admit to'.

The stripping of protections over the past three decades has thinned out farming businesses. As we begin the 2020s, Stephens contends that others are being pushed into corners by rising rural land prices. Unless farmers have scale and strong management, they cannot afford to keep so much capital tied up in the land prices with so little return.

'Because of the land prices, you can't afford to grow, but you need to grow to stay still because of inflation. Even if there was a direct relationship between production and profit, you need to double your output every thirty years in round figures to stay still.'

Stephens says there are a lot of farmers 'mucking about' with smaller operations who treat their business like a full-time job when it does not and possibly cannot pay them a full-time wage. Perhaps they have a partner working off-farm, a factor which makes their family situation viable. 'Money is not important to everybody, as long as they have got enough to do what they want to do.'

Which sounds a lot like Blinder's meditations about the value people place on their jobs. Profit is important, but for some it's not the only priority. Or Claire Booth's findings in her Nuffield Scholarship – that some farming cultures care more about their capacity to grow stuff than they do about their finances. As Stephens reminds me, some people work from 1 July trying to make as much money as possible until 1 April, and then minimising tax, try to bury as much profit as possible until 30 June.

Here, we touch on a very tricky element of measuring what is actually going on in farm businesses. No one loathes tax as much as a farmer, even while many advocacy groups are eager to ask for tax dollars. Tax minimisation is a given in business culture. Farm accountants and lawyers specialise in complicated tax structures. That means it's even harder to get a handle on farm businesses across the nation. We are often told that the top 20 per cent of farmers are doing very nicely, thank you very much, and the rest just need to pull their socks up. But as far as I can tell, ABARES doesn't survey every farmer every year, or even the same farmers every year. So farmers move in and out of this top 20 per cent. Some might have a cracker season then make no money for the next five years. Some might be always in the top 20 per cent. The narrative from industry is all about positive stories but we simply don't know the details. I am happy for someone to prove me wrong.

There is definitely serious money being made by parts of the industry. Farm management deposits are the tax-free savings squirrelled away by farmers in good times in order to cope with hard times. Deposits held in January 2021 were worth $5.2 billion – a hell of a lot of collective savings. But they were held by only 10,823 accounts, and the same farm entities can hold multiple accounts.[4] Even if all the accounts were held by different individuals, that would only represent 12 per cent of the industry. So as far as getting a clear picture of the health of the industry, Stephens says, 'We don't know that stuff and we won't know that stuff.

'What we do know is some farms are getting bigger and they appear to be successful. The only way you really know if a business is successful is to get a good look at the people, the farm and the books. And without seeing all three, you just don't know. I've had people quoted to me as being fantastic farmers and I know what their financial situation is and I know it is far from fantastic.'

The figure most used in financial analysis is gross farm income. Stephens suggests that a $500,000 gross farm income is a healthy-sized business if the family has done up the bathroom and kitchen, had the overseas trip, [privately] educated the kids and bought the new car. He adds, if they have adult children to take over and not too much crop expense, 'That's probably okay.'

'But 70 per cent of farmers are below that number.'

There are some unpalatable truths around performance. Stephens says farmers in that 70 per cent bracket may be perfectly happy to continue what they are doing. 'Just, as a taxpayer, don't ask me to fund their habit.' If individuals with a minimum net worth of several hundred thousand dollars, or more likely several million, cannot make enough to live on, that's their problem, not the taxpayers'. He says towns will continue to decline as they have always done as farm businesses fall by the wayside. Does that matter? People can still get to schools and workplaces; they just have to go further. Stephens doesn't think there is a role for government in making too much policy around the structural changes in farming. That is, government policy shouldn't be designed to support structural changes that might help farms that are failing. People need a social safety net but businesses, including farm businesses, cannot expect never-ending support.

But if we keep following the same path, where does it lead?

Stephens sees two scenarios in the near future. In the first, global interest rates move to more like a historical norm and foreign investment money flows out of agricultural businesses as it has done in the past. In this future, Stephens sees wonderful opportunities for family farmers who are ready to buy them. This would entrench some of the mid-sized and bigger farms firmly into the landscape.

In the second possible future, interest rates remain low. Even with low interest rates, there would be a slowdown in land prices. Stephens cannot see how farms can continue to live on rising land prices when the yearly return from the business of farming is not bringing in good cash returns. 'At some stage, someone needs to call in some of that money.' Maybe banks start to pull money in; that would halt the increase in the price of land.

As for corporate farming, most now is driven by investors looking for a safe investment in managed funds rather than specific agriculture shareholder companies. And much of the managed funds comes from superannuation money. That is because when you are taking care of a portion of so many pay packets every week, you need somewhere to park that dosh. Most of the corporate money is in cotton, grain or, increasingly, horticulture. Stephens sees fund management continuing to invest in agriculture until these companies can make better money elsewhere.

Either way, he sees no reason for the community to give a toss about farming over any other industry. The reality is that 70 per cent of the population is too busy getting to work on time, putting food on the table and stopping the kids from fighting, to worry about this stuff. And he's right about that. Most don't have the bandwidth to care and fewer assets than the average farmer.

But what about food?

Food growing, he says, is no different to any other business and as a nation we have not starved or come close to starving since the early colonial days in 1782. 'In Europe, where the whole population understands what it's like to go hungry, or in Ireland, where they have had famine, they will value agriculture because its importance is handed down between generations. We don't have that attitude in Australia.

'It's a modern, globalised world and we can buy food anywhere. We're not talking about farmers being yeoman now and getting up in the dark, saddling up the horses or walking behind a plough.

'If we expect the community to really care about Australian farming then we need to ensure that farmers are quick to stamp on any unacceptable, inappropriate actions in relation to the people they employ, the animals they hold and the land they farm. [In 2019 and 2020] some farmers have in noticeable circumstances failed on all counts.'

Stephens represents a progressive strand of farmers who have taken on big agricultural reforms and run with them. These farmers are on board with the economic realities of the globalised world; they are realistic as to where the industry is at; and, notwithstanding a lifetime working in farming, they are dispassionate about its virtues. And of course we *can* buy food from anywhere now. The product may have been through a number of processes in different countries so, anyway, which is the producer? Are noodles made from Australian wheat but milled and processed in Indonesia into mee an Australian product or an Indonesian product? But, if Stephens is also right about the broadscale change in who farms – only a quarter of broadacre farmers being sufficiently viable to hand on – does any of that matter? 'Nobody is walking off penniless, we don't see abandoned broadacre farms.'

Yet I have a nagging feeling. If the current 80,000 or so farm businesses become 800 mega farms, it will have implications for how our food is supplied and how up to 60 per cent of our landscape is managed. The larger a farm becomes, the more remote it becomes from oversight and, in a sense, from democracy. The roots of that word are from the Greek *demos*, 'the common people', and *kratos*, meaning 'in strength' or 'rule'. In other words, you could say, we are removing the country from the majority of its people.

Farming is so damn complex that we can't talk about the last four decades of market reforms without talking about the rise of a 'market first' philosophy. Many terms are thrown about and increasingly neoliberalism is the label most ascribed to this market philosophy.

Neoliberalism is a loaded term. I don't like it as a term because it brings on a culture war. By neoliberalism, I mean obeying the market at all costs. Perhaps rampant individualism is a better description, because it correctly reflects the chaotic and less organised nature of how the market-first philosophy developed. In any case, market-first philosophy is generally associated with privatising and outsourcing government services, and removing constraints or regulation around business. A neoliberal would argue that any constraints on competition are a threat to economic freedom. Neoliberalism was associated in the UK with Thatcherism. In the US, it was Reaganomics. In Australia, this market philosophy began in many ways with competition policy towards the end of the Labor Hawke and Keating governments, and doubled down under John Howard.

The lack of constraints on competition has led to oligopolies in agribusiness and supermarkets, confuseopolies in water markets – where fragmented marketing prevents buyers from making informed decisions – and monopsonies in food-processing markets. This is an inherent contradiction in competition policy.

I wrote earlier about Michael Symons' wonderful food history of Australia, *One Continuous Picnic*, written nearly forty years ago.

Symons considers himself a left-leaning liberal but argues that neoliberalism has 'systematically corrupted liberalism' by granting liberty to corporations at the expense of democracy. He says that money has overtaken all other considerations in farming. 'Capitalism wipes out food as a prime consideration all over, not just in peasant society and not just for Indigenous Australian considerations of food. The [corporate] farms . . . are all about money, they are not about food. That's a broad case I'm making, but I'm only more convinced, the further I have gone, that our whole way of thinking and language is shaped so much by money that people don't even notice.'

Symons is a man who takes his food seriously. In the 1980s he and his partner, Jennifer Hillier, set up a little restaurant in South Australia called the Uraidla Aristologist. *The Aristologist*, meaning a student of dining, was Australia's first known cookery book, published in 1864. The restaurant was established in a time of money, big hair and shoulder pads. Later in the decade, Michael Douglas would play a banker in Wall Street declaring greed is good. Symons was spending his time picking zucchini flowers.

In 2021, he says Australian food has come a long way. Tomatoes have improved and the committed eater can acquire decent ingredients, though often from around the world. Symons is reassured that in some quarters people are much more serious about the central importance of a good meal to health and happiness, made with fresh, seasonal and local produce. But there remain the politics and the economics of food, still as stuffed as a fancy zucchini flower.

Symons' thesis about money overtaking all else had only hardened when I interviewed him in 2020 about the existing food model and the structural changes in farming. He had just published *Meals Matter: A Radical Economics Through Gastronomy*. My spark of interest was lit from the paddock; his came from the plate – and we meet in the middle to agree there are some fundamental problems in our food chain. To be clear, farms have to make money to be viable. But the profit imperative pushes everything, the food as the product, landscape as capital, and communities, as workers bow to the price of the food. It must be cheap and it must be plentiful and it must be all year around. The people and the environment must take a back seat to the market.

I'm convinced that thinking about food and farming helps define your politics. The process of considering food and its origins, how it's grown, who controls its supply into the market – whether it's the local market or the supermarket – makes you think on fundamental questions about the role of the state. Should the state step into society and to what end? I'd say that the thesis of this book is driven by concerns about the black hole in the food and farming policy space. My internal argument centres on the regulation of the space and whether it is even possible for governments to get it as right as is humanly possible. The last decade of politics has not convinced me that more government regulation would be done well, but without change I have grave concerns that Australia's food producing landscapes will be increasingly owned by fewer and fewer people.

Symons is convinced government is presently so under the sway of business that interventions are bound to worsen the situation. He wants financial thinking to again be subservient to the gastronomic. Just as the family is organised around meals, so too political society should again adopt a banquet structure. Liberalism allows for representation (government is the head table in Symons' world), but only citizens get a seat at the banquet. Corporations are not, he points out, mentioned in constitutions around the world and should not be given the same rights as individuals. They have no seat at the table. If corporations get into the banquet hall at all, they are there as a guest and will only be tolerated if they display perfect manners.

So, again, the dinner table brings us to the foundational questions of how we want to organise our world. Symons' philosophy might sound anti-liberal because so often liberalism is lumped in with the market model. Yet his argument is that liberalism, for the early thinkers, was a flatter structure, a more collaborative effort. Original liberal thinkers like Thomas Hobbes and John Locke understood that self-interested individuals would follow their appetites and thereby get together with others to sustain themselves.

Politics and economics arose around how to make sure everyone was fed. And that makes the food system vital in determining the organising of our very societies. Symons argues that the capitalist imperative twisted liberal thinking to suit the profit motive. Consider Adam Smith's famous quote: 'It is not from the benevolence of the butcher, the brewer, or the baker that we expect our dinner, but from their regard to their own self-interest. We address ourselves not to their humanity but to their self-love, and never talk to them of our own necessities, but of their advantages.' Symons argues that in context, Smith is talking about 'self-interest' in eating well, rather than financial gain. Smith clearly values the mutual benefits of sharing food and an understanding that economics – stemming from the ancient Greek *oikos* (ecos) – grew out of the study of the household, around the kitchen table. Liberalism, argues Symons, is clearly food-based.

'It's not a big theory. People are just trying to do the best and eat properly and grow something for it. If you really believe the change has to come from the ground up, well, the ground is a lot lower than the trade union, say.

'It's more likely around the dinner table or in the garden – that's where people are doing the everyday material things. That has to determine the politics. It has to emerge out of that. You can't say, "Oh well, we all believe in equality so a corporation is equal to a person." We are all equal because we are at the table together and no corporation ever comes [to eat] at the breakfast table. I'm fairly convinced that the true liberal is working with everyone.'

That concept requires a localisation of sorts, which I wrote about in my last book, *Rusted Off*. I had noticed the reclaiming of politics by local communities and the resolving of local issues by local people because Big Politics was not delivering. Big Politics has delivered big parties and big donors. Little Politics saw local communities creating models from the ground up, such as the Voices for Indi movement that sent Cathy McGowan to the federal parliament in 2013 and kept that power in local hands when Helen Haines won the seat in 2019. The concept for the Voices for Indi movement literally came from 'kitchen table conversations'. In the process, Voices for Indi created a community-focused model and policy priorities arose from distilling their conversations into a plan to take to parliament. As the movement has spread, the 'kitchen table conversation' is the organising method, in little towns and in big ones. Sit down, have a meal, talk about the heart of your community and what would make it better.

But if Little Politics ever turns to food, it might mean a reclaiming of local produce, or at least a much shorter food chain within towns, regions, even nations, to complement the long global supply chains that are also required. Though some reclamation had already been happening with the rise of micro farmers and coffee culture, and the return to local bakers and millers, we witnessed its amplification in the first few months of the COVID pandemic. When the supply chains of large supermarkets stumbled, local supply chains were forced to take up the slack.

The weird thing is, in the same decades as the government removed protection barriers for domestic food production, a portion of Australian eaters began thinking seriously about the pleasure of food, good ingredients and cooking. These two trends grew from the same political and economic climate. Symons puts it down to marketing, as big companies moved from production and distribution processes into the consumption end of the economic food chain. 'That meant selling people the idea of the pleasure of food and drawing attention to different recipes, and so on. Since the 1960s the whole marketing of food has changed and that included sensory evaluation of food,' Symons said.

In the 1980s Symons was called an idealist and naïve for wanting fresh seasonal produce, cooked simply and well. People will never go back to wanting that simple fresh local food, he was told. In 1984, he gathered with a small band of gastronomy freaks and, he laughs now, there were forty-five people interested in the entire continent. They were all about fresh, local and seasonal.

Everyone is a fresh food person now, though – even the biggest player in the Australian food retailing industry. Woolworths announced an investment worth $110 million in Sydney for a 'fresh food distribution' centre on an 8.2-hectare site in Western Sydney in February 2021.[5] The company's coffers were significantly boosted after eaters were forced to stay home and cook more in the 2020 lockdown. Eaters also shifted to buying groceries online.

The distribution centre will be split into a fresh-food facility with a fully automated dark warehouse for pantry goods. Dark, because it doesn't need lights without humans. The restructure of facilities will reportedly cause significant job losses – some 1350 redundancies.[6] Those workers will be able to return home and order fresh food and pantry items, but they will have no jobs to pay the bill. Which takes me back to Professor Blinder. What if people care as much (or more) about their jobs as they do about the goods and services they consume? 'That would mean economists have been barking up the wrong tree for more than two centuries.' Woof.

Chapter 7
ON POLITICS

I hope you are starting to see that everything in this farming caper is intricately connected to a thousand other things, including those existential challenges humanity faces in this century; to recap: climate change, water shortages, soil loss, natural disasters, zoonotic diseases, population displacement and geopolitical trade wars. We are hitched to this planetary engine and we can see parts of it seizing up. Politics is the grease in the machine. If politicians do their job and set the rules to look after the planet and its communities, the wheels turn faster and the world progresses. If they don't, it grinds to a halt. In Australia, I would argue that political parties are no longer serving land managers very well.

Political representation in such a complex policy space as agriculture requires finesse and sophistication. Yet it is hampered by old ways of thinking. Farming is a wholly owned subsidiary of conservative politics and conservative advocacy groups. Conservative is not the problem here, it is lack of competition in the ideas department. I reckon that lack of contest is the reason we don't have an integrated sustainable land, food and farming policy that anticipates the challenges of climate change.

The federal agriculture minister is always a National MP in a Coalition government. But the Liberal Party's rural representatives are more widely distributed and hold more seats. In recent times, the Liberals have taken the trade portfolio from the Nationals. Farmers have, historically, voted for the Liberals and Nationals, and currently these are the parties that continue to represent most farming electorates in Australia. The Nationals tend to throw their weight around when you consider their fairly low level of representation in the federal parliament (some 5 per cent), and the visibility this engenders would be handy if it were used for hard policy work rather than boneheaded games, morality tales or personal ambitions. Usually it is used for the latter.

Labor's 2018 national platform contained markers for holistic approaches to agriculture, such as point 133, encouraging 'more sustainable and efficient land and water management practices through a whole of government approach'.[1] (It also is heartening to recognise in point 60 that 'land and water are the basis of First Nations spirituality, law, culture, economy and wellbeing'. If only the non-Indigenous would take up a similar approach.) But Labor is not visible on agriculture, with many in the party privately admitting that rural seats are a lost cause. Thus the party's policies remain a series of motherhood statements. Meanwhile, decisions like the blanket suspension of live cattle export in 2011 following a *Four Corners* report leave a stain on Labor's reputation in the beef industry, particularly in electorally vital states like Queensland. The subsequent Federal Court decision that minister Joe Ludwig 'committed misfeasance' in public office when he ordered the ban proved that policy on the run doesn't work.

Politics touches so many parts of agriculture. You will find political points woven right through the book, but in this chapter I want to land specifically on Australian politics for three strategic reasons that have been amplified in recent times: trade with China, agricultural labour supply and technology. There are some plain truths developing in all these areas that mean business as usual into the twenty-first century will not work.

In April 2020 the then foreign minister Marise Payne and prime minister Scott Morrison pirouetted onto the world stage to call for an investigation into the COVID-19 outbreak in Wuhan, China. Beijing followed up with a swift retribution. Its government whacked an 80 per cent tariff on Australian barley in April 2020, just as The Farmer had sown the crop.[2] Barley is Australia's second-largest crop and is a particularly important part of Western Australia's cropping mix. China is our biggest barley market by far and Australia is China's biggest supplier. That barley decision had roots longer than COVID but the timing of the decision was unmistakeable to even the dullest of political strategists.

Days after the barley tariff, Beijing banned beef imports from four big Australian abattoirs. Wine was next, following accusations that Australian winemakers were 'dumping' product into the Chinese market, by selling it for less than its cost of production.[3] By October 2020 Chinese mills were discouraged from buying Australian cotton. The individual Australian industries refuted all of Beijing's claims against them. A month later, the Chinese embassy gave a 'dossier' of fourteen disputes to Nine's *Sydney Morning Herald* and *The Age* to outline Beijing's anger.[4] The grievances included Australia's call for the COVID investigation; the Morrison government's tearing up of the Victorian government's Belt and Road Initiative; banning Huawei from the 5G network; foreign interference legislation believed to be targeting China; and foreign investment decisions that cited ambiguous 'national security concerns', including those related to agriculture and animal husbandry.

The trade spat exemplified how the edifice of modern farming is a tower of blocks, and removing the lower storey can leave it teetering. Individual decisions can ricochet for years – see the live cattle export ban. These are not arguments against parliaments changing rules, if that is what elected governments decide. It is simply to say regulations have far-reaching consequences and must be deeply thought out.

My Chinese heritage does not qualify me to speak with authority on China. Hell, I don't even have language skills. I would simply make a few observations from both a farming perspective and a Chinese-Australian perspective. The first point to make about trade is on market diversity. China is our number one trading partner, but the percentage of individual agricultural products varies. For example, China takes 10 per cent of our wheat compared with nearly 80 per cent of our wool, as at December 2020.[5] Not many other countries supply wool. There appears to be a good reason China didn't come for our fleece.

Dr Scott Waldron, a senior research fellow in the school of Agriculture and Food Sciences at the University of Queensland, argues that tariffs were designed to maximise economic coercion while serving domestic purposes as well. The tariffs imposed by China were levied on produce to 'reduce costs for China, or indeed bring long-term strategic benefits including the protection of local industry and import diversification'.[6]

In other words, all the Australian goods that attracted trade barriers could be sourced elsewhere. Beef, barley and wine can be sourced from domestic supplies or other markets.

'A substantive barrier would cripple the Australian [wool] industry,' Dr Waldron writes. 'Such barriers, however, would also cripple Chinese worsted mills that depend on Australian fine wool to make higher-value apparel like suits. Unlike barley, there are no alternative suppliers of fine wool, and China has finally come to terms with limits to domestic fine wool production.'[7]

So Beijing's tariffs had the dual effect of attempting to change policy in Australia while strengthening China's domestic industries and diversifying its trade markets. It pays to remember that sometimes it is not all about us.

The second point is on tone. Farmers are used to dealing with the global export market. The sharper end of the industry is aware that bad politics make for bad trading conditions, both domestically and internationally. Indeed, the president of the NFF, Fiona Simson, suggested after the barley tariff announcement that the 'megaphone diplomacy' by some in the public debate was not helpful.

Yet the political parties that claim to stand up for farmers are the clumsiest in dealing with our biggest trading partner. Witness the shouting by the likes of Nationals MP George Christensen: 'We can keep giving in to China's threats, and selling off our country, or we can make a stand for our sovereignty.'[8] Or China critics such as Liberal MPs Andrew Hastie and James Paterson, as well as Labor senator Kimberley Kitching, who refer to themselves as the Wolverines, like some undergrad Dungeons and Dragons club. Or the Liberal senator Eric Abetz demanding during a parliamentary inquiry into issues faced by diaspora communities that Australian-born research fellow Osmond Chiu and two other Chinese-Australian expert witnesses pledge their loyalty to Australia.

'Instead of being asked about complex issues facing multicultural communities or how Australia could benefit from a more diverse Parliament, I was asked by Senator Eric Abetz to "unequivocally condemn" the Chinese Communist Party,' Chiu wrote in the *Sydney Morning Herald*. 'Presumably, the association trying to be made was that, by virtue of my ethnicity, there was some likelihood of divided allegiances.'[9]

Chinese rhetoric has also escalated. Beijing must have been aware that introducing the tariffs would hurt Australian farmers, who are an important political constituency for the Coalition government.

Farmers were not the only target of Beijing's ire. The defence forces are also a solid political constituency for the Coalition parties. The release of the Brereton Report into alleged unlawful killings by Australian soldiers in Afghanistan was to provide an unofficial opportunity for Beijing's scorn.[10] Zhao Lijian was China's deputy director of the department of information in the foreign ministry when he tweeted a digitally created image that purported to show an Australian soldier holding a bloodied knife to the throat of an Afghan child.[11] When Scott Morrison demanded an apology, Hua Chunying, director of the ministry's department of information, doubled down on Zhao's tweet, saying 'Afghan lives matter'.

The tenor of the debate is critical, not only for our agricultural producers who rely on export markets, but also for Australians of Chinese heritage, who are caught in the rhetorical crossfire by dint of our ethnicity. The Chinese-Australian community is the relationship bridge into Asia. People with common interests build deep ties. Unfortunately, the pivot to Asia is always about getting rich. We can make money! There's such a big market! Asia is getting richer so now we must pay attention! So much of economic diplomacy is transactional. I've heard it in the China rhetoric for decades. Positive trading requires deep relationships. As the geopolitics slide into greater uncertainty, Australia needs to cohere.

When it comes to trade, 2020 was a big year for farmers, resetting their perspective on the relationship with Australia's biggest trading partner. Beijing's trade action was a warning. It sent farmers and global traders looking for new buyers, not to replace the China market but to diversify. If China is paying a premium, any farmer will happily oblige, but the big lesson from 2020 is to have options B, C and D.

As we head into a new planting season preceded by rain, farmers are surveying the global trading landscape more realistically and hedging their bets. As for Australian barley, it found new buyers in the Middle East. With the price of canola rising in 2021, country drivers may see more of the pretty yellow crop replacing stands of barley, as farmers take the economic and political signals into account.

A cropping program is designed to ensure a mix of risk and supply needs, balanced by prices and outlook. It is a delicate juggling act that must take account of the crops or grazing preceding it, soil needs, markets and the global conditions. The China trade spat added yet another consideration into the mix.

The pandemic exposed plenty of holes in our global food systems and farm labour was one. Australian farmers have long found it difficult to source labour. Depending on who you talk to, it is either because Australians don't want to work in sometimes difficult conditions for low wages, or because Australian farmers provide terrible work conditions and unfairly low pay. We have to acknowledge it is both at different times. As a result, holidaymakers and foreign backpackers have filled the void in exchange for working holiday visas. Pacific workers have also provided their labour for wages to return to their families. When our borders shut, neither option was available. The industry had no underpants.

Supermarkets have tight specifications for fresh produce and if the seasonal labour force is not available to harvest it at the right time, the crop rots. The want of pickers saw crops worth hundreds of thousands of dollars ploughed into the ground all around the country. Lindenow organic vegetable grower Kane Busch told the ABC he chopped up 50,000 celery plants – worth $150,000.[12] The average wage, $27 an hour, was not enough to entice locals to work on the farms that needed labour. Milk was dumped, livestock euthanised and crops were mulched.[13]

Mid-2020, the horticultural industry warned it was facing a shortfall of 26,000 workers. A $1 million federal government trial in the 2020 budget, to encourage young Australians to fill harvest roles, offered up to $6000 in payments. By March 2021 it had attracted only around 600 Australian workers. The federal agriculture minister David Littleproud blamed the states for failing to come up with large-scale quarantine arrangements, saying he was ready to stamp visas and allow workers in. His National Party colleague and New South Wales agriculture minister Adam Marshall blamed the federal government for not authorising the necessary travel arrangements.

Temporary migrant workers are estimated to fill half the jobs on vegetable farms and a third on fruit and nut farms in Australia. Overall, around half the total casual and contract workforce used on farms were from overseas in 2018–19. That does not include those from New Zealand but it encompasses backpackers and the seasonal worker program. Meanwhile, total agricultural jobs are declining. In the two decades from 1996 to 2016, jobs in ag fell by nearly 20 per cent, according to ABARES.[14]

We are not alone. The UK relies on 75,000 temporary farm workers from the European Union, while farms in France, Spain, Germany and Italy tend to rely on workers outside the EU. The UN Food and Agriculture Organization estimated a shortfall of a million farm labourers across Europe during the pandemic. China and India also rely on a migrant workforce for farms.[15] This is a worldwide problem.

Labour contractors supply many harvest workers in Australia and there have been terrible cases of exploitation. I also know farmers who attract the same domestic pickers (for stone fruit) every year because they are treated and paid well. But it is insecure, hard yakka, only suitable for those who can work flexibly. It is not well paid. To be frank, we have set up a globalised food system that leaves both the workers, the farmers and the eaters vulnerable. We outsource our farm labour to temporary and migrant workers as we outsource our food service jobs and our food delivery jobs, our cleaning, our aged care and assorted menial tasks to temporary workers.

No country has solved this problem yet. Here, the NFF is advocating for a dedicated 'ag visa', which would come with an industrial cop to oversee the farmers and workers and to provide accreditation to the workplaces. It would cap places and provide pathways to multiple entry visas and in some cases long-term migration. The United Workers Union wants to see an end to piece rates and a minimum wage, a royal commission into systemic exploitation in the horticulture sector and an end to the reliance on overseas temporary visa workers.

In a funny way, the unions are aligning with the sentiments at least of Australia's longstanding Liberal treasurer Peter Costello. In 2006, he argued against a guest-worker economy, on the grounds it would create a two-tiered citizenship system. He said the secondary status held by guest workers meant they were not expected to assimilate and were vulnerable to exploitation.

'Our culture and history is [*sic*] not compatible with the introduction of guest workers or different tiers of citizenship. Our concept of an immigrant society is that all arrivals are offered the opportunity to become full, first-class citizens.'

Emma Germano, who actively raised the issue of labour exploitation prior to becoming Victorian Farmers Federation president, says labour shortage is a complex issue. She agrees some farmers do the wrong thing and says every report of exploitation should be followed up by the Fair Work Ombudsman, with the offending farmer fined and forced to repay wages. But globalisation has played a part as well, which is why so many countries rely on guest workers from other countries and regions. Then there's urbanisation: as potential workers move to cities and larger regional towns, the pool of labour dries up. Finally, we have to recognise there is a cultural piece. Farm labour is seen by some as lowly work. It is associated with peasantry in some cultures. Who wants to do that work?

Perhaps robots will pick your tomatoes. Certainly agricultural technology is touted as the magic solution to labour shortages, not only for picking your fruit and vegies. Swarm drones will selectively spray weeds and your farm will give you digital feedback, essentially telling you what is going on in its engineered and natural systems. Climate change is amplifying the need for smart solutions to agriculture's problems and agricultural technology – which I will refer to as agtech – is held up as the holy grail.

Sarah Nolet and Matthew Pryor are the founders of the AgThentic Group, an advisory and investment group that works with state and federal governments, companies and individual farmers. In their investment arm, Tenacious Ventures, Nolet and Pryor fund and support startups in agtech. Nolet is a computer scientist and systems engineer from the US. She has worked with the defence industry but switched over to agriculture after a gap year living on South American farms. I wanted to talk to her because I inhabit the political spaces of agriculture so what I see on the horizon is the fractious, defensive and politically reactive. Nolet is at the other end, where people are looking closely at their systems and feeling empowered to try new things. And these people are probably looking at markets rather than governments to change their worlds.

Nolet argues that the NFF's goal of getting agriculture to almost double in value to $100 billion by 2030 misses this whole other market opportunity for agtech, which sits alongside farming but is not exactly farming. The farm products and service sector is worth $500 billion globally, heading toward $700 billion.[16] But policy makers are stuck in the same groove they have been in for decades, with their simplistic mantra that farmers must increase productivity by growing more with less.

Agtech falls through the cracks of government because it is multidisciplinary: it requires agriculture, energy and innovation to talk to each other. Here we hit a big theme of this book. The interconnectivity of farming and food to everything else means too often that no one thinks strategically about their place.

Yet there is no shortage of examples of Australian farm innovation by private companies, including those supported by Tenacious Ventures. Their first investment was Goterra, a system to dispose of food waste by putting fly larvae or maggots in shipping containers to convert waste into animal feed. Because the containers are small, the system allows for a decentralised food waste system that can be transported wherever the food waste and the people reside.

Another example is SwarmFarm's weed-seeking robots, developed by a young farming couple, Andrew and Jocie Bate, in Emerald, Queensland. The couple flipped the idea of acquiring ever-larger machinery to develop lightweight robots with names like Oscar, Juliet and Kilo, which, among other things, identify weeds and micro-spray them. These little bots have a capacity to run around the clock without the need to break. And the really clever and generous bit is that the Bates have created a system to allow others to keep improving the agtech. SwarmBot is the autonomous vehicle teamed up with SwarmConnect, a platform allowing third parties to build other applications to use the robots so it is not limited by their own company's innovation. SwarmBot is the equipment (as the equivalent of, say, the iPhone) and SwarmConnect is the platform for others to join (think the app store). The targeted nature of such robotics avoids blanket-spraying a whole paddock, meaning reduced use of chemicals and inputs. SwarmFarm has also been backed by Tenacious Ventures.

But there are two factors that make agtech both an exciting and also a frustrating industry to work in. The first is that state and federal governments have a narrow idea of who should benefit from any funding; that is, farmers from a particular state or from the nation, when the reality is that innovations bleed across borders and into other sectors. The beneficiaries of innovation may be people or industries remote from the initial concept. Ultrasound technology was developed for humans but is now also used in animal embryonic transfer. Vehicle technology for the car industry brings great benefits for agriculture robots.

'Our view would be that by developing the technology here, and making sure it works here, that means our farmers have access to it first. It's tailored to solutions here. Otherwise the technology is coming and we just have to buy it from others and get second access to it,' says Nolet.

The second consideration is that if agtech can make it here, it can make it anywhere. Australia is the ideal test pad as global warming bites in our dry continent, myriad climatic zones and variable ancient soils. We are already export-oriented and Australian farmers grow lots of different things.

While the politics of climate remains conflicted in Australia, industries are dealing with the reality of global heating. Nolet has been thinking about how farming might look in the 2030s. One of her subjects is the fishing industry. Fishers report that stocks are moving into different waters due to the impact of climate change. International fishing quotas determine who can fish where, but if the fish have moved from the area a nation 'owns', who actually owns the fish? What happens to the stranded processing assets of fishing companies primed to bring in fish from longstanding grounds that might soon be empty or far less full? Meanwhile, environmentally aware eaters want a diesel replacement on the fishing vessels so they don't have to think about the carbon emissions per kilogram, not to mention a solution to the plastic wastage and pollution of nets and assorted equipment.

So the fishing companies are looking at technology such as electric boats, and energy infrastructure, which enables them to run decentralised processing plants to get their costs down. That means issues such as the changing or depletion of fishing grounds, carbon neutral fishing practice and processing infrastructure must be solved by, or for, the fisher. This is even before his nation fights over trade and environmental policies to determine who owns the fish he wants to catch, where they have gone and how much of the stock should be left for sustainable fish populations. That is so different to how the fishing industry has had to operate in the past. To navigate these changes, says Nolet, the tactics and strategies you need to keep a sustainable and viable fishing business will be very different than in the past.

She says that the challenges for farmers on land are changing rainfall patterns and higher temperatures. They require a rethink of farming, which might include transitions to new crops or regions, or growing niche products that suit the changing climate. Early movers are already thinking ahead. More than a decade ago, the family winery Brown Brothers, for example, invested in new vineyards in Tasmania, and has been working with CSIRO since then to develop new grape varieties that will withstand tougher conditions.[17] Other growers might consider a switch to niche products: rather than a standard crop like wheat or canola, perhaps they switch to a premium food product which sees customers pay more for their food. Crops like chia seeds, quinoa and coriander seeds are some of the niche crops that have gained traction in the past decade. Farmers might need greater storage capacity to hold crops longer to give them time to negotiate into different markets. Or they might use future farm-generated renewable energy to add value to their crops to get better prices, such as by further processing the produce.

Renewable energy will also provide extra income for farmers who can sell into local power grids – as Claire and Brendan Booth are planning – while some farmers will also be able to sell carbon credits gained from sequestration from planting trees, improving soil or changing cropping practices. And perhaps future farmers will be able to manage all this remotely because they don't want to live on the land that is their livelihood.

'That's a legitimate possibility and it is not how we have thought about farming in the past,' Nolet says. 'I do believe we'll see changes in the jobs in ag, but most of the jobs agtech does are jobs that people cannot or don't want to do right now. Certainly we'll see reductions [in jobs] in some cases, though due as much (or more) to consolidation than agtech.'

And right there is the elephant in the room, which circles back to farm labour. Replacing farm workers with robots and corresponding artificial intelligence cures some of the farmer's headaches, but what about the communities who need work? The future will come with better, more automated technology, and that has significant implications for rural places. Technology may attract more people to farm while replacing a portion of farmers in the process. There are big changes coming down the road into farming communities and we don't know what the future looks like.

Food is politics. Politics resides in the food systems we have created. It is inescapable and there is a pretty good reason for that. It has been accredited to many people but I wish I had said this first: we are only nine meals away from anarchy at any one time.

We often think of big government as an interventionist government. Anyone who suggests the new 'deregulated' economy is free of politics or intervention is simply not watching. At all. Likewise, anyone who suggests that free trade agreements allow free trade across borders is living in fantasy land. Every government has no-go areas. Even before the COVID spat, the China free trade agreement ruled out tariff reductions on sugar, rice and wheat, among others. In negotiating a post-Brexit trade deal with Australia, the UK government was sensitive about beef, lamb and sugar. Australia is touchy when it comes to foreign land sales and migrant workers even though we have discovered agriculture relies heavily on backpackers and temporary workers. The point is that every country has its line in the sand and that means there is no such thing as even playing fields.

Being hungry is something that everyone fears. More than five minutes' thought could tell the average policy maker who's concerned about the nation's future that it makes sense to have a strategic food policy. Are we producing what we want? I find it incredibly frustrating to know that much of the work has been done. Our politicians, our advocates, simply refuse or are incapable of joining the dots.

A strategic food plan would determine the missing bits in the food system. It would look at how diverse we want our food system to be, both in what it produces and the people who grow it. It would even make sense to go for a share of that $500-billion-dollar agtech opportunity that Nolet has identified. A plan would identify the opportunities and give people and their businesses something to aim for.

Yet in recent years, governments have looked a bit like a reverse duck – thrashing about on the surface while nothing is happening underneath. To be fair, that does undersell some pretty interesting work that has been done over the years in odds and sods. For example, Australia has a world-beating Landcare network, which is spruiked by the government as a key part of its commitment to protect, support and conserve our ecosystems. It is (mostly) connected with land managers on the ground who have intimate knowledge of the capabilities of their landscape and waterways. Likewise, Australia has a cracking Indigenous ranger program to connect people to country, in ways that grow leadership, confidence and land management skills. It's been so successful, Canadian First Nations people have sought the advice of Australian traditional owners in looking after country.[18]

Australia already has a fledgling natural capital account program, which measures the state of our landscape, vegetation, water quality and air quality among other things. This is essentially our natural balance sheet, taking account of our natural resources and whether they are moving up or down. It could be expanded and regionalised to reward managers who improve the condition of their land by increasing biodiversity and lowering emissions. Regional assessments would supercharge it and its overall findings could be embedded in a monthly accounting system, giving the country as good a view on the state of our natural assets as we have on our economic assets from the national accounts. Farmers and environmental stewards can help reduce emissions, improve these natural assets for future generations, and ensure the nation isn't penalised for not acting. I will flesh out these ideas of natural capital in 'On natural value'.

We have world-leading scientists and economists who have already contributed to the design of global systems in this area, which could form the basis of ecosystem service payments to land managers, both Indigenous and non. We have had programs like the Australian Rural Leadership Foundation and the Rural Women's Award, which have trained a number of generations of smart young leaders, ready to take on the challenges of growing food in a warming climate.

What we lack is government leadership. At least twelve departments are involved in national food-related programs, covering responsibilities in agriculture, fisheries and forestry, industry, education and employment, finance, foreign affairs and trade, families and housing, Indigenous affairs, health and ageing, infrastructure, prime minister and cabinet, regional Australia, environment and treasury.[19]

This dissolution of responsibilities was pointed out by the National Climate Change Adaptation Research Facility (NCCARF), a cross-disciplinary organisation designed to support decision makers to manage climate change risks. It sought to address the fact that the old cost-benefit way of assessing food policy was no longer adequate, given there were now broader 'health, social and environmental drivers'.[20] The report was all about the relationships between food policies, food security and climate change. It focused on six areas where food security could be significantly impacted by climate change: agricultural production; biodiversity and ecosystems; land use; resilience to natural disasters; water scarcity; and biosecurity.

NCCARF recommended chucking out the government's siloed mindset on food security because – to paraphrase – it is not a very smart way to look at the subject. It found that Australia's fragmented approach leaves room for inconsistencies, overlap and gaps. In short, the report urged a simplification of the bureaucratic systems to combine food strategy with climate change mitigation and to streamline Australia's approach so that it's consistent, both within governments in relation to their own departments and between different levels of government, federal, state and local.

It also recommended creating a more diverse food system that delivered food security across the spectrum, including at a regional and local scale. It's often assumed that because Australia exports a lot of food, we must be a food-rich nation. In my region of food growers, the best food often goes to export. Food deserts are real. The NCCARF report urged the creation of food-security policies that are more diverse and complete, rather than an 'agrifood export/import binary approach that focuses heavily on economic benefits of exporting'.[21] Hallelujah to that.

NCCARF was a useful, science-based organisation, established by the Howard government. It was gradually starved of funding, first under the Abbott government in the 2014 budget and subsequently in the 2017 budget of the Turnbull government and its then treasurer Scott Morrison. It was finally declared deceased in 2019.

In 2021, the different departments remain in slightly different guises, with another twenty-four federal agencies, which have responsibilities in food and food-production-related programs. And that is before you get to the state governments, which actually have the responsibility to enforce food regulations.

For all those bodies, for all that brain power, we have no overarching thinking to pull it all together; no one who sees the missing links, the contradictions or the pitfalls. No one who thinks about the risks, or how the system could better deliver for people and their local communities. The federal government has been warned many times about the holes, if only they would dust off the reports. It's all there. It just needs to be connected.

Chapter 8
ON THE MIDDLE

Ernst Engel was the head of the statistics department in Saxony in the mid-nineteenth century when he completed a budget study of 153 Belgian families and concluded: 'The poorer a family, the greater the proportion of its total expenditure that must be devoted to the provision of food.' Later economists extended the theory to whole countries by arguing the richer a country, the smaller the share of income spent on food. Engel's law remains pretty much entrenched among economists.[1]

As it happens, Australians, Americans and the British spend the least of their income on food.[2] This country grows a lot of food and it is relatively cheap. It has made us blasé about where food comes from and who grows it. Boggabilla farmer and sometime independent candidate Pete Mailler often quotes Engel's law when he is thinking about the conditions for Australian farmers. He believes that as a result of Engel's law, the middle family farmers are hollowing out. This is why he thinks that matters: 'The reason the middle is important is that typically they have an emotional connection and an emotional aspiration to pass the land on better. They are the best stewards because they care about it. They don't look at it as just a business, or think in terms of what they can get out of it.

'I'm not saying the middle is always right or that they are always well directed, but they are the ones that care about the land the most. They are the ones who generally want to leave it to the next generation for a genuine opportunity. Corporate farmers typically don't care two hoots about the next generation. They make dispassionate investment decisions, they invest, if it doesn't work they divest.'

Mailler is a grain and cattle farmer. He has been both an advocate and a critic of the industry for years. That makes him unusual because there are very few farming advocates who are also openly critical of the weaknesses in farming. As a speaker at conferences, he can be bracing. He's a bit of a Jiminy Cricket of Australian agriculture. His message for politicians and industry is to wake the hell up on the climate, on finance and on structural changes in our food production. He wants more honest and courageous leadership in government and in industry, and he has tried to have a go himself. He worries about the lack of connection between the average eater and food producers. He argues that Engel's law necessarily means that as society's wealth increases, the mid-sized family farmers disappear to the point where farming is not sustainable because the rewards for being a farmer diminish over time.

This means the challenges to farmers, such as climate change volatility and the need to be the lowest-cost producers in the world, will see many go out the back door – as predicted by Mike Stephens' research – just when other countries are ensuring their own food security. The population's right to food often comes without understanding the obligations; the demand for cheap food is essentially asking farmers and/or farm workers, as well as the landscape, to forgo their own rights. That is, the right to a fair price for growing and tending to that food. It also means these workers are bearing the burden of environmental stewardship and land management without any reward except a fuzzy feeling for the next generation or land manager.

'If the opportunity for affluence is greater elsewhere, then the ability to attract the best minds – the human capital – to agriculture is significantly hindered, as is the opportunity to attract the right kind and quantum of investment – the financial capital – to underpin the essential natural capital. If you want the best minds and patient capital then you need to value the enterprise in line with its fundamental importance. Engel's law highlights that it doesn't and won't happen by itself. There must be some form of intervention to ensure at least an equal opportunity for the sector, reflecting its fundamental importance. Historically, agriculture may have been over-rewarded, but it is now under-rewarded,' says Mailler.

He points to the stunning rise in land prices, evidenced in the 2021 Australian Farmland Values report from Rural Bank. The median price per hectare of Australian farmland increased by 12.9 per cent in 2020 to $5907 per hectare. It is the seventh consecutive year of growth and marks a twenty-year compound annual growth rate to 7.6 per cent.[3] Land prices are going gangbusters.

Mailler describes the price rise as 'a symptom of the disconnect between the agricultural real estate business and agricultural production business. There is an ag investment bubble occurring that is simply unsustainable in the real world without intervention and/or protection'.

I have a distinct memory of being in a cab in Sydney as a young journalist when a story came on the radio about assistance for farmers. It was the hangover of the 1980s drought. The cab driver started talking about farmers 'privatising the profits and socialising the losses'. It was the first time I had heard it and the conversation stuck with me because I have heard many similar comments since that time. Farmers have to acknowledge there has been a culture of handouts in farming, and they are often poorly targeted, too. Governments give scant regard to long-term strategy when it comes to doling out money. If there is a strategy, it's about reelection.

The memory of the longstanding protection of agriculture tends to muddy the water when we think about food production now. Politicians, industry and the public seem to think there are only two options. Either there is protection, or there is the free market . . . except it's not a free market. Farmers, in Australia and New Zealand at least, have got much more efficient at what they do. The question for the next three decades is how to survive the structural and environmental changes coming fast down the pipeline. They are the continued contraction of farming businesses and the continued consolidation of land into larger and larger parcels.

I think these trends are amplified by the water-trading system in the eastern states. Climate change, water shortages and global economic instability make the whole dynamic more complex. Those three elements, an unholy trinity, are problems that crimp agriculture like no other industry because it has maximum exposure to all of them. 'Our problems are the world's problems. They are the manifestation of everyone else's problems, so talking about agriculture in isolation is part of the problem. People want to blame farmers for things without even understanding why it's like it is,' says Mailler.

Let's talk about the physical realities of Australian farming. Australians outside farming probably think of it as broadscale cropping and grazing; of waving fields of wheat, or, increasingly, the yellow fields of canola that are plastered all over social media in spring; of green paddocks with gambolling lambs and placid sheep and cattle. These images are the result of advocacy bodies that are largely run by broadacre farmers and the companies that deal with them. The media, and the history of farming after colonisation, amplify the picture in the Australian imagination of the sheep, wheat or cattle farmer as the quintessential food grower. So it's probably good to take a reality check of what Australia produces for us and other countries. And this involves a close look at land use.

Our cities are a mere pinprick on our national map. They take up a sliver (0.2 per cent) of our land mass. Our cropland and horticulture are larger, but still only a smidgeon (4 per cent). And for all the fights over water usage in the Murray-Darling Basin, irrigated agriculture in cropping and livestock accounts for less than 1 per cent of land. You understand the battle, though, when you realise that irrigation accounts for about a third of agriculture's economic value. Forestry for wood production is just 2 per cent; mining, manufacturing, housing and waste take up less than half of 1 per cent of land. Just less than a quarter of the land (23 per cent) is dedicated to conservation, which might include managed areas like defence fields and stock routes. The majority of land is taken up by grazing on native vegetation (45 per cent) and when you add it to grazing on modified pastures (9 per cent), you have just over half of Australia covered. So, farmers are managing nearly 58 per cent of the land mass or thereabouts.

There were about 86,000 farms in 2020, accounting for about 2.6 per cent of jobs and 2.2 per cent of GDP.[4] Farmers manage the Australian landscape through a combination of leasehold, freehold and native title. Native title covers 40 per cent of Australia, either exclusively or in conjunction with other rights. Pastoral leasehold covers about half the country, with crossover between the two. Indigenous farmers are an important part of the industry and the land management system. For example, since 1996, the Indigenous Land and Sea Corporation has invested $1.2 billion and returned 6.1 million hectares to the Indigenous estate, through a range of business partnerships ranging from cattle production to aquaculture and bush foods.

The land most intensively used for agriculture is along the east and southern coasts of the continent. That intensive management makes up about one-sixth (13 per cent) of the country, but it accounts for nearly all the farm production, due to its climate, soil and access to markets. A third of that intensive land is given to cropping. Wheat and barley take up most of the cropping land while a sliver (2 per cent) is used for fruit, vegetables and nuts, and an equal slice (2 per cent) for sugar and cotton. Two-thirds of the intensive land is given to livestock grazing.[5]

Far from riding on the sheep's back anymore, Australian agriculture is riding on beef cattle, which cover nearly a half of all grazing, and of that national mob, half is exported. Beef is our number one agricultural export.

I think of Australia as a huge land mass that has grazing animals on more than half of the continent, with a sweep of more intensive cropping that supplies the bulk commodity markets with things like wheat for your bread and barley for your schooner, with pinpricks of incredibly intensive food production, mostly fed by the river systems – the nuts, fruit, vegetables and seeds. These food producers are commercial growers. From there, the food system splinters into smaller and smaller producers, micro farmers, community gardens, community-supported agriculture and your average backyard vegetable grower. So in the breadth of the variety of people who grow food, these varied food systems are separate but interconnected.

We should also talk about some other realities when we're thinking about the middle. To understand what farming is now, you have to understand how rapidly deregulation hit food producers from the 1980s to the turn of this century. There was a clean-out of food growers, a swing in the drafting gate for the farmer. It came with a measure of adjustment funding, to be sure, but it was brutal and ripped through the social fabric of some agricultural places. It was a fundamental pivot from the years when director-general of postwar reconstruction H. C. 'Nugget' Coombs was advocating a decentralised nation of farming communities, growing food and contributing both in an economic and a social sense, but underwritten by government support.

The other value of unpicking the history of deregulation is to understand how minutely federal and state governments have directed what, where and how farmers should grow their products. Since colonisation, individual policies broke up large blocks to more closely settle inland areas. Governments kept farm-gate prices high to encourage greater production for export. Governments subsidised superphosphate fertiliser so farmers would apply more and push land harder. Governments actively wanted settlement in inland areas and said the development of a yeomanry would do the job. Farmers were not acting in a vacuum. Historically, there has been strong encouragement for certain business behaviours in this very oldest of industries. The current state of food production is the sum of its history, multiplied by global circumstances.

There wasn't ever one moment that the market forces switch was flicked. It was a series of decisions, mustered by an influential policy community and a change in economic fashions going back to the 1980s. The values of that decade were forged in 1970 when Milton Friedman wrote his much-cited essay in the *New York Times*, 'A Friedman Doctrine: The Social Responsibility of Business Is to Increase Its Profits'.[6]

Friedman was from the Chicago school of economics, a school that had no patience for any market failure or any social responsibility beyond profit.

The influence of the Chicago school on our nation's agricultural economics has been teased out by Sydney University academic Bill Pritchard, who examined speeches of the Australian Agricultural Economics Society presidents in the late 1960s and early '70s.[7] They were actively pushing for an 'industrial' agricultural landscape and they weren't having much truck with farm advocacy groups. The 1970 address celebrated the success of agricultural economics as a discipline while lamenting the failure of the uneducated farmers who ran advocacy.

From the 1970 president's address: 'Many of the farm leaders are highly intelligent and dedicated men, who lack the educational background, supporting staff and time to brief themselves properly on complex economic issues. Most of them have the practical man's scorn for a rigorous analytical approach, particularly when it comes up with unpalatable answers.'[8]

The following year, the president acknowledged that the structural adjustment might need 'the skills of sociologists or demographers in collaboration with economists' for the resulting painful changes.[9] By 1972, as Gough Whitlam was bringing Labor back into government, the president outlined a vision that has been realised in today's farming landscape: 'Over the middle term from 1978 to 1990, my hope is that we will see two developments. The first is that there will be a strong development of industrial or large-scale agriculture. This may or may not involve corporate farming but it does imply a sizeable swing away from family farming in the traditional sense . . .

'What I mean by an industrialised agriculture is one where farms are typically much larger than they are today in terms of capital, volume of production, turnover and managerial competence; where the approach to management and production is far more "industrial" and profit oriented than it is today; and where the traditional values of rural living and ownership count for far less than they do among today's producers.'[10]

The priority was for industrial agriculture to override a type of agriculture more connected to 'rural living' and, thus, local communities. Change was happening globally. President Richard Nixon's agriculture secretary Earl Butz was urging farmers to 'get big or get out' by planting fence row to fence row in 1973. But the phrase has historic precedence in the Australian parliament at least before Butz said it publicly. A little-remembered Western Australian Labor MP, Fred Collard, was accusing the then National Party's primary industries minister Doug Anthony in 1970 of the same mantra: 'It is obvious that under the existing situation, the great cry of the government of "get big or get out" will only be a temporary thing. While this scheme might solve a problem in one area, it will create many problems in others. If the government continues with its policy the country towns will lose their populations or have them seriously depleted.'[11]

Given what was going on in the influencing profession, it is no surprise that Whitlam began agricultural reforms in earnest. In 1973, Australia and New Zealand lost their status as privileged suppliers of agricultural products when Britain joined the European Economic Community (EEC), as it was then – now the European Union. Ties were being cut with the colonies; physically closer neighbours were being favoured over cultural cousins. This forced the child to get out of the house and look for other havens. Emerging markets for food became not only desirable but a necessity.

Whitlam's 25 per cent cut to tariffs across the board, in line with the recommendation of the Industries Assistance Commission, was the first major crack in the protectionist armour – a move a Coalition that included a Country Party could never have done at that time. In fact, the push had been a long time coming but had been resisted by Country Party firebrand and leader John 'Black Jack' McEwen until he retired in 1971.

While howls of opposition to the moves came from the Coalition benches, Malcolm Fraser's government did not change any of Whitlam's reforms. Then the Hawke and Keating governments doubled down, tearing down the ramparts for global competition. Agriculture minister John Kerin initiated further changes. Kerin and his successor, Labor minister Simon Crean, set about forcing industries to compete globally, which put a lot of pressure on any organisations that formed farmer collectives. The Howard government followed, dismantling most of the remaining protective agricultural infrastructure.

A prime example of the practical effect of competition policy is the Australian Wheat Board (AWB). The AWB took all Australian farmers' wheat for export to sell into global markets. It had particularly provided small to medium-sized farmers some measure of leverage against larger multinational corporations. After the 1994 Council of Australian Governments (COAG) agreed to a National Competition Policy, the switch was finally flicked for full deregulation. Any policy that stood in the way of free markets was to be thrown on the bonfire. It forced the deregulation of the dairy industry and the removal of any price supports.

The wheat export monopoly was surprisingly durable, notwithstanding recommendations from the Industry Assistance commissions in the 1970s and '80s. After it was privatised under the Howard government, a very public scandal involving one of the AWB's largest customers – Iraq – began the demise of the single desk.[12] The Rudd government deregulated the AWB, before it was sold to the Canadian agribusiness Agrium, which then merged with Nutrien, the largest agricultural input supplier in the world, and the world's largest seller of farming inputs like potash, nitrogen and phosphate. AWB's marketing arm was finally sold to Cargill, the largest agricultural processor and trader, and the largest privately owned company in the US.

This is a pretty typical outcome of competition policy in the agribusiness sector. It was the last big piece of the deregulation puzzle and global traders were cock-a-hoop. There are four grain trading firms today that dominate around 70 per cent of the grain and oilseed market, mostly corn, soy and wheat. They are known as ABCD: Archer Daniels Midland; Bunge; Cargill; and Louis Dreyfus.

Any political reform for a significant constituency comes with many adjustments. Before 2000, milk prices for dairy farmers were prescribed by state governments. In July 2000, the Howard government forced dairy farmers to a more commercial footing. Milk prices fell 19 cents a litre and the 'adjustment' package was funded by a levy of 11 cents a litre of milk.[13] It was the largest adjustment package in Australian history at the time, costing $1.92 billion. In the last two decades, the number of dairy farmers has fallen by 55 per cent across the country.[14]

Longstanding conventions and a certain status for food producers were removed at a mind-boggling speed. It was twenty years of the most intense changes, not only in business operations but in the place of food production in the economy and the identity of farmers within the Australian imagination.

I am not arguing that some of this did not need to be done. There were plenty of boondoggles in the old structures. Nonetheless, there are important points to make. The architects of the series of policies knew this path would hollow out rural communities. The reforms were designed to create leaner, meaner, bigger businesses. As agricultural economists said back in the 1970s, they wanted to industrialise the basis of agriculture. The reforms were not designed for the rural communities. These two competing aims remain at odds as Australia heads into the 2020s. No government has addressed the contradiction.

The other point to make is that competition policy has created less competition; that is, fewer farm businesses competing or negotiating with much larger corporations such as agribusinesses, food processors and supermarkets. This fact, combined with leaps in technology, has had the impact of denuding rural communities, including jobs in the agricultural sector. Competition policy means everyone competes to grow your food at the cheapest (in the short term) possible price and the eater is the winner. It's a nice enough theory. So this means shaving your costs on the inputs like labour. It also means that because the natural resources are not valued as an asset, the farmer needs to push the landscape. The biggest crop at the cheapest production price means not only the greatest income to the farmer but also the greatest capacity to buy out the neighbour and pay off the debt. That is the current market incentive. Fewer food producers, fewer diverse products produced, fewer diverse economic models. Think of farming travelling down the same path the supermarkets have. Will there be a Woolies, Coles and Aldi of food production? I don't know but I reckon it's worth asking the question. The rest of the food chain has gone that way, from the farm input companies to food processing to food retailing. These are some of the most concentrated markets in the world. For example, the 2020 merger of two of the three largest agribusiness suppliers in Australia – Landmark and Ruralco – means almost half of rural merchandise stores are now owned by Landmark's Canadian parent company, the gigantic Nutrien.[15]

Governments used to help all farmers with price support and tariff protections. As a result, there was a greater proportion of small to medium-sized farmers, and the larger farms had much less of a share of land, income and output. Now governments have chosen to make it easier for larger, well-resourced farms to operate. That is a government choice: their policies favour these operators. Such operators are not necessarily more efficient, but they certainly have more access to capital.

According to the statistics, the average Australian farmer is fifty-eight, male with thirty-seven years' experience.[16] Over the life of his career, large farms have grown from 3 per cent to 15 per cent of the farm *population*. You might say that is a modest jump, given the push for economies of scale over those decades. But those large farms also hold *two-thirds* of the land, and produce *two-thirds* of the output and income.[17]

ABARES makes no bones about who the government thinks is best capable of running a farm, writing this in 2020: 'The structure of Australian farms reflects market conditions, which tend to see the best managers operating the largest farms . . . Increased farm size has supported improved productivity through several channels; providing access to better technology; allowing better and more flexible labour management (supporting higher labour productivity); better knowledge management; diffusion of better farm management practices; and access to positive economies of scale.'[18]

This is a common view, but some academic papers are starting to challenge it. A paper on productivity and farm size by well-respected authors in the *Australian Journal of Agricultural and Resource Economics* found 'that constant or mildly decreasing returns to scale is the more typical scenario'. 'Specifically, regardless of size, farmers' ability to adopt suitable production technology is essential to maintain productivity performance and to be resilient in the face of challenges.'[19] Access to information and technology are key and often that means the need for more resources, but there are plenty of examples out there of well-run small to medium farms.

Still, it is true that Australia is losing its small to medium-sized broadacre farm producers. The government preference is clearly for farms pumping out more yields and thus doing the heavy lifting for balance of trade. The executive director of the Australian Farm Institute (AFI), Richard Heath, has spent a lot of time thinking about the often-conflicting goals of farm policy. He is torn on the question of pursuing policies that hollow out farming to the very large and the niche. He acknowledges the productivity agenda is gutting mid-sized farming.

Heath describes the conundrums facing Australians when it comes to thinking about food. Australia has not decided on what it wants when it comes to production. Australia's government has not thought much about the relationship between food production and regional communities. It has failed to articulate how it will maintain its landscape and its communities.

'There is not a right answer. I would like to have a middle group, and I would like to have vibrant regional economies where there are still people living in towns and lots of businesses. But it's a "like". I think most Australians would like that, and, again, they would probably expect that [the middle] would be there. They would expect the landscape would be there with towns, so that when they go for holidays in the country there's actually services and things to do and people to see.

'But the reality is there is an expectation of food to continue to be delivered at the price it is and the share of income that it is. The expectation is that the price continues to be driven lower and that's actually not compatible with that expectation.'

Competition policy and competition measures drive so much of this environment: 'They rely on very fundamental or pure market theory that everything has a value. But so much of what people are expecting and would like to be delivered in terms of vibrant regional communities, [they] expect that to happen for free. They are not putting a value on it. And when something is expected to be delivered for free, it doesn't happen and it certainly doesn't fit into competition measures.'

So cheap food and productivity advantage large operations, and large operations are considered more efficient, according to the government, which means they employ fewer people and have access to money to spend on technology. As Sarah Nolet described in 'On politics', farmers will not necessarily have to live in the rural communities closest to their land. That might mean fewer people in rural communities in the absence of other industries. (And before anyone shouts 'mining', that industry employs fewer people than agriculture.)[20]

Is there any edge for the smaller operation over a large one? Heath says the medium farm can have advantages when it comes to livestock grazing, particularly with rotational grazing (a common element of regenerative farming but with a longstanding history that predates the recent 'regen' label). 'You can get to a point where scale does diminish your capacity to do things at a granular level . . . But I'm not sure that's enough of a difference. The good big operators are still performing pretty well.'

When farmers really get into the fine management of livestock with rotational grazing or GPS tracking on livestock, or precision pasture management which maps soil, biomass, nutrients and yields, they can do better than a large-scale operation. Heath says the sweet spot is being big enough to make the tech pay, but small enough to keep a close eye over the entire operation. 'There's a point there where I'm confident you are going to get the best growth and returns you can. That's per animal per hectare per unit, but go to 200,000 cattle and the scale just beats it anyway. So it's comparative. There's a management advantage but I'm not sure how you make that pay.'

There is, then, a fork in the policy road around whether governments should design food and farming policy for the top 10 per cent or the other 90 per cent of farmers. When I put that to Heath, he could only reply, 'Welcome to my world.' Does government supercharge policy for the top operators? Or does Australia broaden the objective for food and farming policy from producing a lot of export to producing a diversity of food, and maintaining the economic diversity of food growers with some measure of resilience?

Heath is conflicted. He believes removing all supports promotes innovation but it requires an uncomfortable walk through the valley of death. Australia must decide whether to start paying for environmental and landscape outcomes, in the ways the rest of the world is beginning to do, or to continue to remove supports, as New Zealand has done, and hope market innovation drives change.

'I know in practice that's what you need to drive the change to get that innovation happening, but it will be hard for a lot of people ... and you have to have confidence to get to the other side. New Zealand went from being the most subsidised agricultural nation on Earth to literally overnight saying "No more." There was massive pain. As a result, what came out the other end is what I think is one of the most innovative ag nations on Earth.'

Right through our interview, I could hear Heath arguing with himself. For a man who considers food and farming policy every day, it's comforting that he has no answer for the questions I have been grappling with; the dilemmas that stretch across many different ministries and many different jurisdictions; and the choices that are laden with value judgements about our priorities. After three decades of market-focused reforms and a range of spectacular market deficiencies playing out before us during the pandemic, perhaps people are starting to reassess the shibboleths of conventional economic wisdom.

It's fair to say that organised farming advocacy has from the 1990s mostly grabbed deregulation with both hands. Since its inception, the NFF has focused on the capacity of farming as an export industry. It has bought into the idea that Australia should feed the world; leverage off comparative advantage and long global supply chains; accept big capital injections and the rationalisation of farm businesses into lean, mean fighting machines. Competition ruled the day. Farmers were exhorted to buy out the neighbour to build a business that could surf the volatility of globalisation. So it was a surprise that the AFI's annual essay competition topic in 2020 asked entrants to write on the question: 'Are competition measures delivering a fair go for farmers?'

This is something I have pondered since I stepped onto farm soil. Why would farmers willingly accept a competition policy that not only removes their own rights to collectively bargain but also allows oligopolies like supermarket retailers to dictate the price?

Here's an example. A dairy farmer from Kyogle in New South Wales, Shane, posted a fiery video to Facebook in 2018. He stood outside his farmhouse, visibly seething and speaking directly to his smartphone, having just received his milk cheque. 'I'm a proud dairy farmer . . . I work very hard. But I'd like to say that I worked this month [July] and we just got paid in August for a whole month. I worked for $2.46 an hour. Something has got to change. You can't keep this shit up. People can't expect farmers to continually work for nothing. That's basically slavery.'

The rational economist would say Shane's business is his own choice, the market is paying a price, and if he doesn't like the price, he should go and do something else. Notwithstanding Claire Booth's Nuffield realisation that some farmers prioritise their identity as a food grower more than money, a family does need to feed themselves.

Economics would say that if enough people get out, the supply falls to a point where prices rise again. Except do they? Heath agrees that the food market does not behave exactly like the textbooks predict it will.

'What is delivered at the farm gate through market mechanisms is based on the premise of pure markets, and markets aren't pure. There's not perfect information . . . The [Australian Competition Consumer Commission] report said milk processors are still able to get enough milk. The reason they are able to get enough milk is because of productivity gains and the efficiency driver. The middle has been hollowed out, being driven by more efficiency measures.

'A market economist would say [that is fair]. I think for a lot of people, though, if the objective is keeping vibrant communities, then, no, it's not fair. It hasn't worked in that respect. If you ask a low-income earner in Western Sydney who can still buy a litre of milk, she would say, "Yes, it is fair because I can still afford milk."'

My problem, though, is that if Shane is working for $2.46, it's a wage we do not accept through the industrial relations system. Heath says, and he's right, that if the milk is supplied to the processor and the supermarket, someone is accepting that price. But let's not pretend this is an equal playing field.

As the Australian Competition and Consumer Commission (ACCC) found: 'There is a significant bargaining power imbalance between farmers and processors. Farmers also have limited access to price and market information compared to processors. Farmers rarely have the opportunity to negotiate prices or contracts with processors. This has resulted in contracts that allow processors to transfer risks onto farmers through terms that: allow processors to reduce farmgate prices mid-season, (and) reduce farmers' ability to switch between processors. There are also ineffective dispute resolution processes. The ACCC's view is that these issues are harmful to the efficiency of the industry. It found farmers had limited access to price and market information compared to processors.'[21]

The federal government has since taken up the ACCC's main recommendation for a mandatory code of conduct for large dairy processors. A review of the code is expected by the end of 2021.

But consider this. In 2016, when processors retrospectively cut their prices to dairy farmers, as Australian consumers we were briefly forced to consider our buying choices. The surge of publicity around this meant more people understood a smidgeon of the complicated system that allowed processors to 'step down' or force farmers to return some of the money they'd been paid for milk already supplied. (Imagine any other business accepting a situation where you pay back some of the price you received!) Consumers blamed the big retailers and their $1 milk, which was designed as a marketing ploy to drag people into stores. We rallied, some of us moving our money from $1 milk to branded milk, in the hope the dairy farmer would see more of the money. It lasted for about eight months, before sales returned to cheap milk. We went back to supporting the status quo, and thus the trends to the largest and the cheapest continue.

I have watched government policy and markets encourage bigger farms and devalue economic and ecological diversity in favour of a more simplified approach to land, concentrating on growing one or two products. Markets favour the outsourcing of all functions. A farmer can contract out all the jobs she needs done in order to do them with fewer employees. But if farming becomes only about the scale and the economic bottom line, our social and environmental diversity will be as smashed as the avocado on your toast this morning.

Why should we keep the mid-sized farmers? Because my grandmother told me I should never place all my eggs in one basket, long before I had chooks. I have watched for decades many middle growers remain intimately connected with their land. So here's to the middle, growing a diversity of goods for the supermarket trolley, the kid in Asia or the local farmers market. Here's to the people responding to their landscape, checking their soil, noticing the seasons and hedging their bets for the long run. Here's to the people who place as much stock in Landcare's advice as their accountant's. Here's to the people who are connected to their town as well as to their flora and fauna.

If growing food is like any other business, why do we see such an outpouring of support from metropolitan Australia every time there is a drought? I take that support as a seed of hope that citizens care about their food growers. They might even support governments to come up with an interconnected plan that lays out Australia's priorities around how we maintain a diversity within food producers, rural and remote communities and the natural world.

I would rather pay for the farmer who passes up a few points of economic productivity to keep the fallen tree in the paddock for nesting birds. I would rather pay a farming family who is involved in the local community and the netball competition, rather than the corporate titan managing remotely from Switzerland, or the superannuation fund for an obscure professional group. These are value judgements. There is no right or wrong. But, let me repeat, if we eat, we all have a stake in this conversation. We make these choices when we enter the supermarket to buy our food. Eaters are the third party in the relationship between farmers and processors or retailers. Eaters are the watchers, the crucial actors who can shift the balance.

Chapter 9

ON FAMILIES

Australians love an underdog. Perhaps that explains my identification with the small to medium food producers, the ones who are slogging away with one or two employees. But I am in awe of the families who have created larger food production models that don't screw the environment or the people around them. That is the flaw in my bias against the very big. A lot of those at the top of the chain farm well, without losing sight of the importance of place and people. They have taken the productivity messages over the past three decades and mashed them into their value system.

Let me give you some examples. Sue Middleton is a force of nature, a serial enthusiast. She is one of those fellow weirdos who thinks deeply about the integration between agriculture, rural communities and policy. She has done much of this while being part of a family farming business, the Brennan Rural Group, that includes a 5000-hectare broadacre farm, a 755-sow piggery and a citrus orchard near Moora, a wheatbelt town of Western Australia.

Middleton is originally from Queensland, the youngest of three, brought up on a mixed farm. The cultural descriptor that has stuck with me after our many conversations is her growing up with three articles of faith on her family mantlepiece: the National Party, God and the ABC. Since then, she has become a courageous farm advocate and a champion for rural women, willing to call out bad behaviour in politics and farming. She spends a lot of time engaging with animal activists to explain her farming system, and works in the policy weeds in climate change and drought.

For her, modern farming is all about managing risk. Many farmers manage risk by employing very few people and gradually increasing their land size to get some scale. She contrasts her own model with ours, a business with two jobs.

'You own a business that pays you a wage. That's different to ag that creates jobs, and if we are going to get to the $100 billion target by 2030, we need different capital models. Intensification and diversity [of products] created a lot of jobs, it brings in other capital, but you don't own it all yourself.'

Farmers used to feel guilty for working in the office on management and financial planning. That has changed. Deregulation has driven the need to get across the complexity of markets, commodity marketing, retailing, technology, succession planning and climate projections. Like many farmers, Middleton has a week-to-week involvement in the farm business at the financial, marketing and strategic level with her husband, Michael. She's never driven a tractor, and in fact she jokes that tractors are so technical now that she couldn't drive one. She helps organise a workforce that has ten to twelve full-time employees and over 100 in the harvest systems across the various crops. Sue and Michael think of themselves as running a set of family companies because they get their money – the capital – from other family companies rather than investment from big corporates.

'It's a fairly unusual model. We made it up. If you want to go in ag, it's usually a debt-funded capital growth model, or if you want to expand, you buy the next farm. But if you're only debt-funding your future, it's a slow model of growth, though it's still a fundamental model for family farms.'

This was their response to the 'get big or get out' mantra, because Sue and Michael knew the middle farmers were disappearing. The reason they settled on a mix of intensive and broadacre grain-growing was because they were pretty keen on creating jobs in their local area. She speculates they could have borrowed and increased a 5000-hectare farm to a 50,000-hectare farm. She knew from a background in regional development that such expansion into one area, such as growing grain, means you can run a much bigger place on the same one or two jobs in the family plus a few contractors. That was a problem for her. Where other farmers avoid the hassles of extra staff like the plague, Middleton's more intensive model required more time on staff and much more time managing the extra complexity that comes with staff.

The couple was also responding to climate change. It is a big factor for Sue, driving her strategy and volunteer time. Middleton is the chair of the NFF drought policy committee and is a foundational member of the Western Australian AgZero2030 group, an organisation that drives the state's farmers towards preparing for change that has already arrived.

'For me it was climate change predictions. We realised if we didn't have an irrigated ag project, our business might not survive. The family knew about the deep aquifer under the farm since the 1950s, but since the noughties we have lost 20 per cent of our rainfall.'

She recognises that in their expansion of operations, they joined forces with other operators as other families left the industry. The Brennan Rural Group is employing people, and exporting a lot of stuff.

Oranges to Asia and the United Arab Emirates. Fresh snap frozen pigs to Singapore for my relatives to eat their favourite fatty pork. Barley and wheat to world markets. They are pin-up farmers, doing everything that policy makers and economists have exhorted them to do.

So you might think that they are right on board with the current system. And largely you would be right. But Middleton does see the holes in the status quo. She has watched communities change. As someone who cut her teeth in rural development, trying to increase local population, she has concerns about the dominant food production system.

Here we travel back to that fork in the road mentioned by Richard Heath. What is the objective of agriculture in our continent? I've often thought Middleton would do a pretty good job if she were queen of Australia. So I crown her queen and ask her, 'What is your objective for agriculture in this country and this place?'

'If we accept [the idea of] the efficiency of markets, the way you nuance that in policy terms is that food security is really important,' she says. 'It's fine to say we export the majority of our food so we are not food insecure. But we are food insecure in our supply chain. So we have to understand that efficient markets might be the goal, but there's also this other goal – of putting the culture back into agriculture and having local food supply chains that work.'

It is a curse that as a journalist you are trained to see the holes. Many people think that is focusing on the negative. For me, watching farming policy has been like watching an overloaded bus. During the era of protection, it was heavy with lots of suitcases and lots of people. We threw off some excess baggage in the 1980s and '90s. Each time the bus gets lighter, it accelerates. But still we throw off those suitcases. We tell ourselves it's fine because we can't sell the intangible stuff in that luggage to the market. And we keep removing the weight. Next go the spare tyres, the jacks, the just-in-case tools. But we have to get more efficient, so we start to throw off some of the passengers, because, hell, *they* are weighing down the bus. After all, this model only really needs the driver to keep going. Somewhere in the great arc of the thirty-year market-first drive, there was a sweet spot. Have we now gone too far? Are we losing too many people? That is the question that keeps me awake at night.

In 2021, the Brennan Rural Group transitioned. They decided they could be a smaller part of the bigger business rather than owning all the land they were farming. In the process, they are investing in other asset classes and other parts of the food chain. Traditionally, farmers can be uncomfortable about not owning the land beneath their feet (though it is more common in other parts of the world) because it's easy to understand land as an asset class. Middleton told me the transition would create new opportunities and risks, and would free her up to take on more rural leadership roles.

It strikes me that the game of chasing scale never ends. You get bigger, the neighbours get bigger, the corporates get bigger, you are on the treadmill. It is happening nationally and globally, but it's relative. Australia has huge farms with ancient soils, other countries have scrumptious fertile soils and smaller farms. The average size of an English farm in 2020 was 86 hectares; they are having similar conversations about losing their smaller farms. As James Rebanks said, the option of a small family farm is not feasible for most people in his village. Farmers are leaving the land around the globe while larger mobile multinationals are moving into food production, the only part of the food chain that is not dominated already by large companies.

The Brennan orchard at Moora is in an area dominated by corporate agriculture. They have watched the corporate model operate and are fully aware of the advantages of scale. Corporates can capitalise on land-price growth and wear a smaller income in the meantime, she tells me. Which is funny because the corporates say that without having to feed the shareholders a family farm can pull their belts in to cope with a smaller income.

Family farms are often legacy places, to be held on to and passed to the next generation. Family farmers tell me this is a fundamental difference with the corporate sector, which tends to like developing a place then selling (or 'flipping', as it has become known). Obviously some corporates are in it for the long haul, but that capacity to buy and sell properties to get the capital gain is a key advantage of the corporate agricultural developer. Think of it like Sydney or Melbourne real estate. You buy the house, renovate and sell it to reap the capital gain. When the corporate farmer sells a big farm, it usually goes to another corporate rather than dividing it to allow entry to a smaller farm or a new farmer. Sometimes the neighbours get a chance if the larger place is broken up into composite parts and they descend like a seagull on chips. A long-term family farmer, big or small, can't capitalise on the growth in land prices, except to increase their access to more debt, unless they are prepared to cut their roots.

The other key advantage for corporates is their buying power for inputs such as animal products, chemicals, fencing materials – stuff required to get the job done. A big buyer gets a better deal because of scale. So the ambitious farmer, who may be wanting to rule the world, or just stay ahead of the pack, has to bring money in to develop the place somehow. Middleton says their citrus orchard would be a quarter of the size without the equity funder and the bank.

I have an overwhelming sense that the great corporate land-flipping venture can't last without owners getting better returns for the actual growing of food. I put this to Sue.

'Is it a big Ponzi scheme that could crash?' she says. 'Yes, if they are raising capital to finance returns then it's a Ponzi scheme. But . . . you have to find a model if you want to do the big leap forward. Markets always finds trustworthy models if the returns are genuine, so long as it's not injecting risk into the land market, causing a future collapse that affects family farms.'

Talk to some of the people who advise large family farms and they will say those farmers are doing okay, thanks very much. Andrew Bomm advises Riverina farmer clients in southern New South Wales. He grew up on a farm west of Echuca in Victoria, but the family moved to Wagga after 'mum got the shits', not just with farming but with poverty and the in-laws. The reason Bomm knows about the importance of scale is because lack of scale was ultimately what made his family farm unsustainable.

Bomm and I ran into each other in 2019 at a renewable energy conference for farmers in the federal seat of Riverina – our mutual federal electorate. It was shortly after local MP and the then leader of the National Party Michael McCormack had said that only 'inner-city raving lunatics' were concerned with climate change. There were a whole lot of farmers in that room, some driven by concern over climate adaption and others just looking for new ways to diversify their incomes. Bomm was there to understand the opportunities for his clients in renewables and energy production.

He calls his business Progressive Agriculture. He provides farm business planning and water market advice. Most of Bomm's clients are large family farmers and a lot of his business revolves around the water trade in the southern end of the Murray-Darling Basin: when to buy, when to sell, how to work within the rules to profit and hedge the uncontrollable risks in farming. In the southern basin, water is strictly metered and that's where development has boomed. The real corporate action is happening below him on the lower Murray, so farmers operating in this part of the world need to be right on top of their game to have a chance of competing with those big players coming into the market.

'Margins on water are so volatile. [In 2019/20] we saw water prices range between $200 and $1000 per megalitre, so whether you get those decisions right or wrong can mean more for your business than anything you do agronomically. It's a very important driver for business and it's a very complicated system.'

Bomm and I have talked over the years about the structural changes in farming and the way the media portrays them. I have been scarred by the raw conversations I have had with the small to mid-sized farmers who feel they are being squeezed out. His clients have their whinges over regulation, but generally they have grabbed the deregulation agenda of food production and water trading and run with it. He is a handy guide to those farmers because he sees such a wide range of families who are thriving. I asked him about definitions. Who are the small to mid-sized food growers, remembering that ABARES says they're those with $200,000 to $1 million in cash receipts?

'You're not really sustainable at $200k a year. Different businesses will have different cost structures. Cash receipts are one thing but profit and loss is another. It's hard for any business under $500,000. It's a hobby farm, isn't it?'

Bomm is not a fan of subsidies. He thinks bad drought policy, for example, limits good farming because government intervention acts as a handbrake on personal responsibility. Drought policy is driven by media coverage and creates the wrong public perceptions.

'With poor drought policy, you do get people who are farming not all that productively or profitably potentially getting supported for social reasons. But it doesn't actually underpin food production. The most profitable and productive businesses require natural attrition in the rural real estate market to be able to scale up their productive and profitable enterprises.'

In other words, these are the businesses that want to buy up the neighbours. Artificially keeping farmers afloat means the less-well-run businesses stay on land for longer.

Bomm thinks the middle is being hollowed out because corporates are buying up farms *and* because families are expanding. Here we are at the fork in the road again. He suggests that governments and bureaucrats probably understand less about agriculture than they do about any other sector of the economy. Historically, corporate agriculture has adopted the tenant-farmer approach, when they buy the asset: they keep the farmer on it. 'So you're charging someone 5 per cent to lease the land back, when average returns across the sector are 2 per cent on asset value.' Bomm thinks that model is reaching the end of its natural life.

Then there is the owner-operator model, where you buy the land and put in a management team to run the place. There is a significant risk with the cost of labour, plus management has no skin in the game. Creating bonuses to manage soil or water or rotations can create perverse incentives.

Ultimately, Bomm sees a key problem as being a mismatch between corporate and family-based agriculture. 'Most of the really clever operators in ag in Australia are on family farms, but they are operating at a scale well below the one they are capable of. So the money coming into agriculture is failing to be paired with those who can best utilise it. I think you need different models, but the problem with the landlord-tenant model is the investor is bearing no risk. They just want return on the asset. [Corporate operators] tend to operate in rigid parameters and they have quite inflexible processes, which don't necessarily work with good [farm manager] operators.'

I know what he means about the mismatch. Historically, big corporates have washed in and out of agriculture. I have seen all the examples Bomm outlines. They poke around districts, buying up land. Sometimes they keep the family farmer on the place, extracting a return – the 'rigid parameter' that Bomm talks about. But it's a model that does not provide the flexibility to ride through droughts and lean years. Or the corporation sells the place and the new owner tips the farmer out, after the previous corporate owner assured the farmer they could stay on until retirement. Some corporates do better, employing and looking after their managers and their families, providing football coaches and willing volunteers for the progress association. I have also seen the corporate move in and bulldoze all the houses and the fences to plant fence to fence. And he's right about family-farm expansion. Corporates tend to gather in particular areas, but in our own district, the big competition for land is from family farmers, keen to expand.

Sue Middleton advised me to talk to other big family farmers to get a better idea of how people were handling the problem of risk. She put me on to Brad and Kate Jones, who live two hours east of Perth.

In late 2020, Brad was mowing oats for hay and had just spent the morning trying to source the parts for the main drive shaft of his hay-cutter. He discovered he had two options. The part could come via Melbourne, and would be held up because of state border closures, or it could come from the US, which would entail a few weeks' wait.

'I will lose some of the quality of the hay but you become immune to these things. It's crisis management 101. You become hardened to it.'

Brad grew up on a cotton farm in Queensland, on which he also developed an aviation business. His family farm was on the Darling Downs but it was sold to Arrow Energy for an oil and gas field. Kate, a former journalist, grew up on the farm where they now live. Her siblings have all chosen other professions. Medicine. Physiotherapy. Investment banking.

Flush with Brad's share of the capital from selling his aviation business, he and Kate bought out four of the neighbours. 'We were in the right place at the right time, so we could expand the boundary by buying . . . Suddenly there were four families gone from the district.'

Middleton is the only farmer I have ever heard express such a wistfulness at buying out other farmers. I asked Brad why so wistful. Does he feel guilty?

'Oh no. That rationalisation will continue forever. We have four kids and you can only divide and multiply on a property so many times. We were on the east coast and watching the aggregation by corporates, so there may have to be an exit strategy for ourselves if we choose it. We were very aware that we could offer a corporate the chance to step into a turnkey operation. We always thought that's where value would be. [The scaling-up] was planned, if the opportunity came.'

It is a savvy move in a business sense as they watch what he calls the 'hard and fast' march of the corporates into the southwest of

Western Australia. The cost of land there is cheaper, which means there is less risk to their capital. The state offers big operators scale at cheaper prices than the east coast does. The Joneses manage the farm both as a legacy and as a dynamic high-return operation, offset by the diversity and cashflow of Brad's aviation business at times of year when the farm doesn't bring much in. Brad speculates that the value of the place, which is now 13,500 hectares (it was once 5000), might be $30 million, reminding me that the corporates don't like playing around with farms worth $2 or $3 or even $10 million. He figures it might even be better to pitch the property up to $50 million if he can get its value up there. That's when the corporates really start to prick up their ears.

The Joneses grow wheat, canola, barley, legumes and oats for hay. It was a mixed farm when the couple first took charge of it, but they moved fast, using a radiometric geological survey to better understand the soils and landscape they were dealing with. They ripped out fences and used technology to ensure they were farming in the same soil types as 'the forefathers'. They felt like outliers at the time and Brad openly admits to making mistakes. They harnessed technology to create geographical divisions rather than relying on the old fence lines just because the boundaries were there. If an area shows a higher risk for any particular crop type, they make sure they take lower financial and environmental risks on that land. Better not to throw the kitchen sink at land that resists being pushed.

They recognise the nuance in their land, a reflection of the progressive farming approach I mentioned earlier. They ask, how is it we should farm in *this place?* So often, farmers and governments talk about getting more tonnes per hectare. I would like a dollar for every time I have heard farmers extol the hero of the district who grew a high tonnage crop. To be frank, this stuff easily descends into a dick-swinging competition. Farmers never watch their crops as closely as the next-door neighbour does. Yet this might simply be a reflection of the size of their fertiliser bill rather than profit. That is, most of the profit will end up with the input suppliers rather than in the farmer's bank account.

Brad agrees that the average farmer's measure of the yield in tonnage still amazes him. He thinks of yield as the financial return. He wants an 8–10 per cent return on the crop. For him, the old ways of comparing the yield in the bin are culturally entrenched, including in farm advocacy, which he describes as 'grey, stale males' who just 'aren't very good farmers'.

He hasn't got much time for what he thinks of as 'green-washing' by some farmers and businesses; however, he reckons sustainability should be the number one priority in farming; that it underlies the importance of being closer to the land and closer to the consumer. The Joneses are highly attuned to what the eater wants.

But if he looks past his farm fence to the whole agricultural landscape, he would strip out all advocacy groups and rebuild from the ground up. He would concentrate on educating farmers in finance and marketing. And he would reward growers for good sustainable practices.

'It's about building skills. There's some young people coming home now. Some have been away and gone to uni or done non-ag degrees, but they are seeing farming as a good viable career.'

In a way, Brad and Kate are corporate in their approach – Brad's masters of business administration has driven that. He thinks of himself as the chief executive officer and Kate as the chief financial officer. But he still distinguishes their family operation from a corporate one because 'corporates haven't got the longevity in mindset that we do'. He argues, 'Theirs is working money, ours is working land.'

'We have planted 550,000 trees on this land. We just planted 30,000 over the school holidays, which was fun once the kids settled in and stopped arguing. We have been straightening paddocks in order to join remnant vegetation. A corporate might plant from a [corporate social responsibility perspective but] that's all they're thinking about. We want to link it up so it's going to be beautiful. We are thinking in the future that it's going to be there.'

Yet the Joneses are empire builders and will leave farming if it makes financial sense to do so. Brad's language wavers between that of a hard-nosed businessperson and someone who sees his kids and his grandkids growing up on their farm. I ask him what his children will face if they decide to take on the business in the future.

'Their challenge will be to stay committed. If someone walks in and says, "Hey, we will write a cheque out for" – looking at land appreciation between now and then – "$65 million," that's a pretty hard thing to say no to. That's where the pressure will come. The sheer value because of scale. Someone will fold and go. Corporates will continue to grow.'

'Does it worry you?'

'It's not rape and pillage by any stretch. [Corporates] are sound land managers, but I don't think they would take it to the next level as a family farm would. And so I think that sense of long-horizon-type farming will be gone because the managers will love farming and they will love that particular farm but they will get shuffled around like management does, whereas you don't have that same level with family farms.'

Of course, there are badly managed family farms as well and I'm absolutely prepared to concede that a well-managed corporate farm, in it for the long haul, will easily be a better outcome than a rape-and-pillage family farm. Activists and shareholders have a greater propensity to pressure a corporate farm than a family farm. As one big corporate operator told me, there's a lot of 'family-farm-washing' that goes on, which involves talking up the mythical credentials of such operations no matter what. But, remember, this argument is also about people and communities. A balance must be achieved if there are to be enough humans outside cities to manage land on behalf of the nation.

Brad also raises a potential threat for family farms if corporates suddenly pull out of the market. In safe farming areas, particularly in irrigated land, corporates are pushing land prices up. That increases every farm's capacity to borrow, and essentially makes their existing debt a smaller proportion of the whole. If the corporates were to pull out of the market, it would leave a big hole in the value of all farms.

'[Sue] Middleton's neighbour is Macquarie [Lawson Grains], and if they suddenly exit and pull their profits off the table, is it going to spook the market, which runs on spooks and rumours? I'm not sure they will be in a rush to exit. We have to think about it in the context of the size of their enterprise value. If you're looking at a $100 billion asset [like a bank] and they decide to put 2 per cent of their value to ag, suddenly that's $200 million, which is an enormous ag enterprise and it's only 2 per cent, with which they could kick off their CSR [corporate social responsibility] . . . We are small change. So I think it probably will continue along that way.'

That is, with the clamour for corporate social responsibility, perhaps combined with the imperative to act on climate, they can turn a small portion of their wealth towards landscape amelioration, or as offsets for other projects, depending on government regulations and/or food production. The corporates would be doing something that civil society is asking for. In the process, they can own the landscape and change the landscape at scale. For better or for worse.

And that returns us to that corporate squattocracy. In my local district, one squatter originally took a vast area of land that covers much of our local government area. It was only broken up by the New South Wales Land Acts, which divided the big runs around here at the turn of the twentieth century. Perhaps we are heading back to the past.

Brad's MBA told him unviable industries should not be saved. As an example, I ask him whether it matters if Australia loses, say, the majority of dairy farmers, if we can buy milk cheaper from New Zealand or somewhere else?

'I think that may have changed a little bit due to the pandemic. Now there's probably more of a view that the just-in-time supply chain model is not all it's cracked up to be. I think the shortcomings have been really shown up with this pandemic. It will be a couple of decades before it goes back to that type of model,' says Brad.

'It doesn't really solve the problem for the dairy. Fixing supply chains doesn't fix milk.'

'No, it doesn't, but ... There's a dam near here called Niagara Dam – a beautiful big dam was built but never ever used ...' His voice trails off.

'As in ... that's life?' I ask.

'Yeah.'

We talk about the increasing possibility that very large companies – the big miners, for example – need emission offsets for carbon intensive businesses. 'They could walk out of here and start changing the whole landscape again.' The need for carbon sequestration has the potential to change the land again, as big business searches for carbon amelioration at scale.

'So their proportion will increase because more of them will identify land for that very reason. Which means we are heading to a different landscape?'

'Yes, we are.'

When I check in again with Brad a few months later, Lawson Grains' whole land aggregation is for sale.[1] According to the real estate agent, Lawson is being sold as its backing investment fund is due to expire. That means 105,000 hectares of prime agriculture land is on the market, with an anticipated price tag of around $600 million. Lawson's website says it's a proud corporate farmer and Australia's leading grain farmer. It also says, 'We are long-term custodians of the land, ensuring mutual benefit for the environment and our communities. We are in it for the long haul.'[2] Yeah nah.

Around the same time, in March 2021, Gina Rinehart puts 2 million hectares of northern cattle country up for sale, contained in seven stations with 100,000 head of cattle and a feedlot.[3] Back home, just a year on from the last drought, all anyone can talk about at the dinner parties and the barbecues, at the field days and the Landcare meetings, are land prices. There is excitement about the increased equity, but also nervousness. The question on everyone's lips is how long it can last.

Chapter 10
ON CORPORATISATION

The public face of agriculture has been dominated by men, and a fair portion of men revel in competition. A cohort of these men like to look over the fence to see what the neighbour is doing. They like to compare their . . . er . . . size, their yield, their capacity and their machinery. Deregulation has catered for this particular part of the gene pool in the farming population and amplified it. Occasionally you see other sections of the community pushing back, but after decades of reform you will have no trouble finding gung-ho farmers who are working to be the biggest and the best, with the largest machinery, the biggest crop, the most water and a huge wing of stock.

Since whitefellas arrived in rural populations, big operators have existed in Australian farming. What is changing is that the corporates and big families are expanding their share of land, water and food supply production, and I'd like to consider what that means.

Queensland University emeritus professor of sociology Geoffrey Lawrence has spent a good deal of his career looking at the structural changes in Australian farming. We discussed how the development of European agriculture benefited both the mother country and Australia.

'Britain wanted cheap foods to fuel industrialisation. British capital poured into Australia to build the infrastructure that could facilitate trade. We'd provide the food; they'd provide us with manufactured products. With refrigeration, meat joined wheat and sugar as the staples for the workers' diet (both in Australia and England). Once this pattern of trade became entrenched, it was seen to "work" for both nations, although today we've gone well beyond Britain to feeding an industrial workforce throughout the world. Economists continue to "praise" the arrangement as a great example of comparative advantage – we provide bulk agricultural commodities and buy manufactured goods in return.'

Out of that need emerged a triple burger of much more lucrative businesses to hang off farming. The agribusiness companies supplied the inputs as crop technology took off. The trading houses bought the product to transport it around the world. The supermarkets sold the processed product to the eater. Of those, the trading companies are the oldest as they were developed to take advantage of new opportunities in global economies. That was a big head start. Trading houses such as Louis Dreyfus and Cargill were borne from the opportunity of moving surplus food between countries.

The input companies largely consist of seed and chemical sellers and they began to merge in the 1990s to a concentrated few. Now, four behemoths hold 70 per cent of the global pesticide market: Bayer-Monsanto, ChemChina-Syngenta, BASF and DowDuPont's agricultural division Corteva Agriscience. Bayer-Monsanto, ChemChina-Syngenta, Corteva Agriscience and Limagrain hold 67 per cent of the global seed market.

The synergy of selling the chemicals to work with privately developed seeds was an obvious business opportunity. Genetically modified seeds work in conjunction with herbicides. Roundup Ready canola, for example, means you can spray the crop with herbicides and kill the weeds but not the crop. In 2018, about one-fifth of the Australian crop was grown from genetically modified seed, though the regulations vary in each state.[1]

Genetically modified or not, most of what you need to grow a conventional crop, or take an animal through the average farm lifespan, comes from one of the large input companies. The food-processing and commodity companies buy the product once it's grown and add the value by making it into a retail product. These increasingly concentrated companies are swallowing up other competitors to expand their market share. Cargill began as a family business and is now involved in most parts of the food supply chain, from seeds and fertilisers to livestock rearing to meat processing and shipping. The lines are increasingly blurred between the different parts of the food chain.

The big change coming out of deregulation in the 1980s and '90s was the financialisation of agriculture. Futures markets had been around since the 1800s but their use really ramped up in the era of deregulation as a way for farmers to hedge their bets. Take out a contract and you lock in a price when it's high and – fingers crossed – you get a crop at the end of the season. If you don't, you have to pay out the contract, adding more risk to the business.

The other players are the speculators outside farming who bet on market changes. They are investors who want to bet on food but are not direct producers. So they might invest in a commodity index fund (CIF) that includes food (pigs or corn, for example), along with other commodities like metals and oil. Investors gambled CIFs would rise prior to the 2008 global financial crisis and, as a result, food prices rose.[2] They have long been in the commodity markets, and since Australia turned water into a tradeable commodity, speculators have entered the water market as well.

Then there are the big supermarkets, which reach back into the supply chain to specify the boundaries of the crop – the size of the apple, the protein in the bread, the dimensions of the leg of lamb – and the price they will pay. The local greengrocer described the massive apples available in the fruit markets in mid-2021 after a bumper harvest. The growers couldn't give them away because they were too large for the eater, who wants the perfect apple to put into a lunch box. So again, consumers play a part. Do we want pretty food or good, healthy food? Increasingly, big food retailers will also specify the type of system that grew the food – organic or regenerative or cheapest possible price. All of these systems have customers.

Australia may be dominated by Coles and Woolworths at the moment but competitors like Aldi are catching up. In fact, Aldi, along with Walmart, Schwarz Group and Kroger, is one of the biggest four food retailers in the world. The retail food industry used to have independent supermarkets that grew out of a particular region. In regional and rural centres, a town must get to a certain size to warrant a Woolworths, which in turn means it probably has critical mass to attract other services. Smaller towns like mine are dominated by individually owned stores that operate under the banner of IGA, which is a supermarket chain owned by Metcash.

This acceleration of big players – ones who were traditionally at either end of farming but are increasingly influencing the business of growing food – ramped up at the same time as the old industry bodies were progressively dismantled. Competition reforms neatly removed farmers' capacity for collective bargaining and bulk-buying or selling, while private companies moved into the place of industry trading desks like the AWB. Removing these old industry structures gave farmers only as much leverage as their size, trapped among the large input suppliers, large commodity traders and supermarkets. That has applied a massive amount of pressure to the price received for the wheat or the lamb or the cauliflowers. So scale was what was going to save farming in this restructured globalised world.

Of the old boards, only the Rice Marketing Board for New South Wales remains, to 'obtain the best possible monetary return to rice growers'. No doubt some of the old statutory marketing boards were considered inefficient and clunky, but Geoffrey Lawrence suggests their removal has led to other problems. 'Once the various boards, subsidies and tariff protection, et cetera, were removed, farmers had to sink or swim. Many drowned because they were too small to survive. Farm numbers declined and farm size increased. This is what the free market proponents view as "success" as it means that the market is working its magic – consumers get cheap food from more efficient, larger farms. But many of these remaining farmers are on a technological treadmill, which forces them to purchase more and more costly farm inputs, to reduce farm diversity through specialisation, and to farm in unsustainable ways.'

The industry argues that the changes led farmers to concentrate more on their businesses, educate themselves better on marketing and be more aware of the global trends in agriculture. Either way, as we've seen, the trend is consolidation, encouraged by government and, *sotto voce*, by agricultural advocacy; and a fair portion of consolidation has happened among farming families themselves.

I have no trouble grasping that Big Food and Big Finance – we'll come back to them – are moving into Big Farming: it makes total business sense to own and control the one bit of production that you don't have. The bit I didn't get is how the big players would make their returns. Farming in Australia is marked by drought, flood and higher labour costs than in many comparable countries. But I have since discovered that in a globally uncertain time, there is all this investment money 'sloshing around the world', to quote finance journalist Alan Kohler, and it is looking for a safe haven. Because of its size and its deregulated food-growing regime, Australia has large parcels of land where the government really doesn't butt into your life as much as it might in more subsidised markets.

Sometimes globalisation, particularly in the food industry, feels like a second wave of colonialism. There are large corporate and state players wandering around the world, looking to control resources in order to make a profit. The definition of colonialism is around exercising political and economic control over another country. It certainly feels to me like we are losing control of farming to global capital, but Lawrence suggests it is simpler than that.

'It is really just capital doing its thing – looking for investments to make profits,' he says. 'Once, as an investment for corporate capital, agriculture was looked upon dimly. After all, it is highly risky and the returns are often poor. But with dotcom and real-estate bubbles bursting, populations growing and needing more food, and globalisation promoting movement of capital, institutional capital, in particular, began looking towards agriculture. Good farming land gives yearly returns *and* longer-term capital gain. This attracts corporate finance and leads to what sociologists are describing as the "financialisation of food and farming".'

Certainly, the headline returns for the big corporates are heroic. There is such a thing as the Australian Farmland Index. 'Favourable growing conditions, a low Aussie dollar and strong commodity prices helped prime farmland deliver a total return of 14.9 per cent for the year to March 2020,' was the lead on a story in the *Financial*

Review.[3] It was measuring forty-two selected funds 'managed by some of Australia's major agricultural asset managers'. So, off the back of a shocking multi-year drought in the eastern states, the index reported annual returns of 15 per cent.[4]

The important thing to note is that 61 per cent of the businesses assessed are in permanent horticulture, such as almonds, citrus and grapes, as opposed to annual crops – irrigated agriculture. The balance is in grains, oilseeds, pulses and livestock. The index has only been measuring since 2015 and over that time it has averaged 14 per cent, with 7 per cent income and 7 per cent capital gain, even though the capital gain may not be cashed in until the land is sold. It relies on rural land prices continuing to rise. When I read out the 14+ per cent returns to The Farmer, he said, 'Hmmph, they're obviously not working where I'm working.'

Of course, though this index mix reflects some of that global capital sloshing around the world, it does not reflect the broader Australian farming population, so comparing it with all farms' performances is not apples for apples. We could compare it with ABARES figures, which measure all farms above a modest income level. The last figures available from ABARES that pull out the top rung tell us that the average rate of return, including capital appreciation, by the largest 10 per cent of broadacre (as opposed to horticulture-heavy) farms was 8.3 per cent; the average for the smallest 10 per cent was –4.2 per cent.[5] Notably, the equity ratio for small farms is pretty high at 95 per cent, compared with 81 per cent for the largest 10 per cent. Larger farmers are using current low interest rates and more debt to fund expansion. I can't help thinking about when Australian interest rates hit 17 per cent in 1990, and about climate change projections.

Agronomist Kate Burke, whom you met in 'On farming culture', says the corporates provide an entry into agriculture, employment and career paths for people across Australia. As the youngest child and 'the wrong gender', she never got a chance on the family farm. Instead, she worked for Warrakirri Cropping, where she worked with twenty-three staff, none of whom had the chance to work on family farms. Lumping corporates in the same basket, she says, is like comparing one family farmer to Joe Blow down the road. She says you can't generalise between binaries: corporates versus families or big versus small.

'Some employees told me they were treated better, paid better and had a safer work environment in the corporate world. And if the returns on farming are so horrible and no one can make any money out of farming, why would a corporate invest in farming?' says Burke.

Maybe the corporate rush into Australian agriculture is a value proposition. Burke says the idea that corporate ag is throwing cash around is a nonsense. 'Warrakirri was basically using institutional money, they had fiduciary responsibilities and the decisions involve twenty times more thinking and analysis than the farm next door would do. We couldn't pay over the odds.'

Richard Heath of the Australian Farm Institute reckons Australian farming land is still underpriced by global standards. I would add that many of the top 100 agriculture companies that have made a big splash into the market are pension and other investment funds with patient capital, which can sit and wait out a drought. Never mind food production at scale. That is income working at scale.

'When you get big enough to geographically diversify in Australia, as severe as the droughts have been, if you've got farms all around the country then you spread your risk and look at those performance indexes: it's a really good return. It's counter-cyclical to other investment classes. It's just a good strategic, diversified investment for funds managing billions and billions of dollars and the need to spread their risk. It makes a lot of sense.'

Still, there are red lights going off all over the shop for me. Many of those large funds' portfolios have exposure to permanent plantings, particularly in the southern basin. In July 2019, the Victorian government released a report by the water consultancy firm Aither. It observed: 'During periods of future extreme dry water availability [*sic*], existing permanent horticulture may demand essentially all surface and groundwater available in the connected Murray region.'[6]

The Victorian water minister, Lisa Neville, said she would personally review all licence applications for 2019–20 to ensure the risks to the environment were minimised, and that Victorian entitlement holders did not increase due to more extractions.[7]

Neville was backed by the Almond Board of Australia, the industry body that called for a moratorium on state governments issuing new water-use licences in the Murray Valley that 'threatened the future capacity to deliver water to existing irrigators thereby maintaining a diversity of farm production'.[8]

So how can all this money, from big investors who are presumably well advised, be thrown into growing things that look increasingly uncertain within the constraints of the system? It makes no sense to me. And I am not alone. Many farmers, financial types, environmentalists and academics are questioning it. One overseas fund manager asked me if it's a 'pump or dump scenario', in which properties are developed and then on-sold – the last one being left holding the can.

Looking for answers, I stumbled across evidence given to a federal parliamentary committee by Ed Peter, who runs the global fund Duxton Asset Management, known as Duxton Capital in Australia. For him, agriculture is the 'gift that keeps giving'.

'We're probably the biggest farmers you've never heard of,' he told the House of Representatives Standing Committee on Agriculture and Water Resources in 2018. The committee was set up by the then treasurer Scott Morrison to examine the hurdles for large-scale superannuation investment in agriculture. Peter rattled off a list of Duxton's holdings: 30 dairies; 130,000–150,000 cows or 2 per cent of beef production; about 5 per cent of the wine industry around Mildura; and 5 per cent of the Australian apple crop. That doesn't include 17 per cent of Darjeeling tea, or 30–35 per cent of Jamaica's sugar. Nor does it take into account Duxton Water. The company earnt a reported $90 million from the sale of temporary water alone in 2019.[9]

Peter's investment logic for agriculture is based on his capacity to wait while the price of food remains at all-time lows. That is interesting to me because of the much-talked-about advantage that family farms have had over big corporates. (That is, the corporate needs to feed the shareholder whereas the family farm can ride out the troughs on little or no income as long as they are not up to their eyeballs in debt.)

Peter argues that when interest rates go up, the four big asset classes – bonds, residential real estate, equities or shares, and commercial real estate – will tank. Yet the three asset classes that do well with inflation are metals/mining, energy and agriculture. Peter's strategy has been to buy at the bottom of the cycle because if an agricultural business can make money when the commodity prices are really low, the land prices are usually low. And if you get to hold a safe asset, plus have the potential for more cashflow when the prices rise, then that's where he wants to be.

Peter takes the opposite view of farming to many fund managers, who shy away from it because the rates of returns have been low. That's because of the low prices for soft commodities – wheat, livestock, coffee, cocoa, sugar, corn, wheat, soybean, fruit. If he can buy into agriculture at the bottom of a cycle and still make a single-digit cash return on a farm asset, it makes sense to him because if inflation hits, he's sitting pretty. 'Ag is a gift that keeps on giving. As long as I husband my land, I will get a return every year. So from my side, that's why we do what we do.'

Peter argued that fund managers usually don't understand agriculture, so traditionally they have been reluctant to go near it. He estimates that of the $110 trillion of institutional investor money across all investment classes globally, only $28 billion goes to agriculture. So if global capital does get more interested in farms, where does that leave the smaller farmers? The UN estimates there are about 570 million farms globally, with an average farm size of less than three hectares.

'Australia sits in a very special place in the world. We have the cheapest farmland in the world. There are a bunch of reasons why that is. But also we have some of the largest average farm sizes, which makes us institutional grade already.'

Peter says of the $28 billion invested by institutions, Australia has been one of the largest winners, which shows that large institutional investors are looking here. 'Hancock by themselves in this country has more invested, at least from what I see, than our industry does, as one US fund. Westchester is bigger than Hancock in the country. ABP – the Dutch. Optifarm – heck, we can keep on going through. Any one of these foreign investors is at about the same size as us when I take timber out of our industry investments.'

He is right. Westchester Group Investment Management claims it is the largest manager of farmland assets globally. Look at parent company Nuveen's map of agricultural investments – it spans the globe, spreading risk across Europe, Australia, South and North America. It in turn is owned by New York-based pension fund the Teachers Insurance and Annuity Association of America (TIAA). According to *Fortune* magazine, TIAA has a little less than US$1 trillion in assets under management for its five million teachers and healthcare workers, as well as a steady stream of income from pay cheques every week.[10] Its profits rose 48.7 per cent in 2018 so presumably it is doing something right.

Westchester, as its investment arm, has been in Australian agriculture for a while. According to its investment material, accessed by Geoffrey Lawrence and his colleagues, it saw the flight by Australian family farmers as an opportunity 'to purchase quality properties that haven't been on the market for generations'. Westchester planned to develop a tenant-farmer model for younger farmers who cannot get into agriculture due to the high cost of land.[11]

In a pandemic-restricted world, TIAA-Nuveen is ever more bullish. A company analysis, 'Why Farmland Now', says the short answer is because farmland was a good investment before COVID, and it's an even better investment in the future.[12] The company argues that farming is a 'safe haven investment' through times of economic tumult, and that financial yields are 'inherently tied to food prices', which have not suffered in previous pandemics. Nuveen is expecting 'imminent productivity gains'.

This corporate optimism is a revelation, and in stark contrast to the people I speak to on the ground about the challenges of the 'structural adjustments' being wrought on their lives as these large-scale investments relentlessly roll into the landscapes around them. If Peter is right and this farmland thing takes off permanently, the middle of farming is going to not just hollow out but disappear completely. Because how can the middle ever compete with a company flexing a trillion dollars' worth of muscle?

Peter suggests a simple answer as to why the big fellas haven't entered farming at scale previously. Big investment managers don't understand agriculture. In his eyes, it is no more complicated than that. At the time, he suggested American institutional investors, who are going into agriculture in a big way, were two years ahead of the Australian investors. That was 2018. Which takes us to right about now: 2020–21.

'As people prove that you can make money in ag, you will see people come and invest here,' says Peter. 'At the moment, it's the foreigners. As they have successes, guess what's going to happen? We will catch up. It's sad because any one of the big two Americans is already bigger than our entire industry. It's a shame. They are nice people but we should have it for us.'

'The Americans' are the aforementioned Westchester and Hancock Agricultural Investment groups. Rural and regional newspaper the *Weekly Times* started publishing a 'top of the pops' list for agriculture – the best rough guide to who owns the joint by value rather than land size – in 2016. That edition is the best-selling paper in their publication year. In 2021, topping the investment charts was Public Sector Pension Investment Board (PSP), a Canadian superannuation fund that invests money for Canadian public servants. According to the *Weekly Times*, PSP has land and water investments exceeding nearly $4 billion. To give you an idea of scale, the NFF estimated total Australian agricultural production in 2019–20 at $59 billion.

Australia's Macquarie Bank comes in a close second on the list, with $3 billion in assets. TIAA-CREF is third. In 2021, the *Weekly Times* estimates the top three – PSP, Macquarie Agriculture and TIAA-CREF – own 6.3 million hectares of farmland and have an estimated $8.8 billion worth of local land, water and infrastructure assets under management.

Ownership is not the only way to control land and resources, of course. A 2021 *Guardian Australia* investigation of pastoral-lease data found the person who held the most land is Western Australian mining magnate Gina Rinehart. She controls 9.2 million hectares, or 1.2 per cent, of Australia's land mass, through three different corporate entities.[13]

The biggest corporate landholder of pastoral leases is the old colonial company turned ASX-listed Australian Agricultural Company. AACo's biggest shareholder is the Bahamas-based AA Trust, controlled by the British billionaire Joe Lewis. (He also owns the UK football team Tottenham Hotspur.)

According to the Foreign Investment Review Board, around 14 per cent of agricultural land had some level of foreign ownership as at June 2020. China was the biggest holder, followed by the UK, with the Netherlands, Canada and the US all at third spot. That level has been fairly steady for the past five years.

The board also reported the level of water entitlement: foreign ownership is 10.9 per cent as at 30 June 2020.[14] Canada has overtaken China as the top foreign owner of water. China and the US hold second position with the UK third. About two-thirds of that water is used for agriculture and a quarter in mining.

I tracked down Ed Peter in his Adelaide office, over Zoom. We talked about a lot of things – global agriculture, technology, soil carbon and interest rate cycles. I asked him whether corporate farms, with their advantages, will take over from family farms.

'Let's define corporate. The Kidman family were corporates, but they were family farmers. I've got a farm in the Northern Territory. The family who owned it before used to own 12 per cent of Australia. They are bigger than the Kidmans but they are a family, you see,'

Peter says. 'From my side I'm perplexed because corporate farmers seem to be anyone who is working for a pension fund or a larger institution. But if you are a very large family who has more wealth than many pension funds, you are not a corporate farmer.

'Part of our problem is what we call farm-washing, which is bullshit – there's hundreds of farmers who are absolutely killing it and no one is pointing the finger at them and saying, "Oh god, you're such a fucking evil person because you are making money."'

Peter says corporates have to pay 'full tote' salaries and cross i's and dot t's when it comes to occupational health and safety. 'If your husband hurts his arm, you strap it up and send him back to work.'

He shakes a thick wad of paper at the computer camera. 'If we have an accident, even if it's not our fault, we are talking about it three years later. Every single cut, scrape, injury, what we have done to avoid it and where we sit right now.'

He says the advantages of a corporate-style farm were around purchasing power and analysis, but good families can also access great analysis. The big difference, though, is access to money.

'We can access capital. That's probably the single biggest difference. Our returns on average, even if we are doing world's best practice, tend to be lower, because we have every single person on the planet looking at you for occupational health and safety and your reports.'

So, I ask, it's easier for family farms?

'Point blank yes. Do you have kids? That's called free labour.'

'But you get cheap money!' I said.

'If we get into trouble,' says Peter, 'does the bank even wait two seconds to throw us under the bus?'

'No,' I conceded.

'Yeah! You get in trouble and, god, there will be mediation forever.'

Peter lists a number of challenges for agriculture and they do not include corporatisation. Too many nitrous-based fertilisers acidifying soils; weed tolerance to herbicides; flatlining yields and productivity. These issues are not exclusively Australia's problems and that means raw commodity prices, in his view, are likely to rise. Far more important to the Australian family farmer is the price of iron ore.

'And Australia has the weirdest financial system in the world. No other developed country on the planet has a system like this.'

His explanation goes like this. About 22 cents in every dollar borrowed in Australia is funded from overseas because our savings pool is too small to finance our debt. Europe largely funds that debt. To balance things out we structurally need to run a trade deficit. So we buy finished goods from overseas. We need to have a deficit because every time we get near parity we have to keep on paying the interest rates overseas, and our dollar goes to the moon. Last time this happened in the Global Financial Crisis, world governments said, 'Let's get infrastructure spending going.' As a result, iron ore prices remained stable or rose. We bought less stuff because we were scared. Our balance of trade equalised and our dollar went to $1.18. That did over Australian farmers. That will happen again as world governments say again, 'Hey guys, we need to spend big on infrastructure to revive economies.'

'That is more important than any other piece of the puzzle for the family farm.'

Big companies or big families bring big dollars, which are exactly what governments and farming bodies suggest are needed in Australian agriculture. Remember, the Rural Bank's 2021 Australian

Farmland Values report showed the median price per hectare for agricultural land in Australia increased by 12.9 per cent in 2020, the seventh consecutive year of positive growth. Historically, there is a strong correlation between commodity price and farmland values in Australia, but the report makes the point that trends in land prices and commodity prices started to diverge in 2016, 'widening significantly' from 2018 to 2020, driven by declining interest rates and historically low transaction volume. As 2020 marked the end of drought in many of the eastern states, you would expect land and commodity prices to come back in line. This has not happened. 'Looking ahead to 2021, buying power remains strong, driven by low interest rates and historically high livestock prices, suggesting that the median price per hectare could continue diverging away from commodity prices.' Return on agricultural commodities is not the only game in town.

But there is a contradiction at the heart of government rhetoric, which says that, on the one hand we need a lot of money flowing into farming land, while on the other – in drought, say – we need to keep mum and dad farmers. To marry these two aims and keep the diversity of farms and farm sizes in Australia, and this rural population, a national strategic plan is needed.

When former union boss Paul Howes suggested in 2013 that the days of 'ma and pa farming' needed to end, he was rounded on by the Coalition. The then Labor agriculture shadow minister Joel Fitzgibbon backed Howes' comments, saying there would be more consolidation in the farming sector in future, involving more corporatisation, which would offer more opportunities for high wages, good job security and superannuation.

'We will address the big concern out there about where the next generation of farmers will come from by offering more graduate opportunities with big agricultural companies, equivalent to those companies that we see now mining the nation's oil, gas and coal,' Fitzgibbon said.[15]

The then agricultural minister Barnaby Joyce called Howes' remarks an insult. But Joyce's answer to a plan was encapsulated in the agricultural white paper. More dams. Climate change did not even make the terms of reference.

The tension between food as a financial product and food as an essential for human life is increasingly on display. It's a leap that has been made in the past fifty years as the world economy has developed. We are treating food, and the water that grows it, like any other widget or commodity. Former US president Bill Clinton pointed out that much in 2008 in a speech for World Food Day: 'Food is not a commodity like others . . . it is crazy for us to think we can develop a lot of these countries where I work without increasing their capacity to feed themselves and [by] treating food like it was a colour television set.'[16]

If you talk to people with long memories, there is a sense that corporates get excited every few decades and wash in and out of the system as market conditions change, as Mike Stephens pointed out in 'On economics'. But I think things are changing fast in agriculture. To drive the Murrumbidgee River is to glimpse into the future, and Australians will have to decide whether they want that future. I think the trends towards corporatisation will continue.

Still, like all things, food and farming has its disrupters. A lot of food production doesn't get much attention in mainstream media. And this swathe is worth knowing about as an antidote to the transnational story.

Chapter 11

ON DISRUPTION

Christmas 2019, and, like many others, we were trapped at home in a stifling smoky haze. Temperatures in the high forties were accompanied by winds whipped up by the firestorms around the country. There were blazes to our east, on the New South Wales south coast. The fires travelled up the Clyde Mountain into Braidwood and Canberra. There were fires south of us at Gundagai. On New Year's Eve, my Aunt Libby rang me from a motel room in Eden on the far south coast. She lives at Mallacoota, just below the Victorian border. Fires were approaching the little township and she had fled her house with her partner, the dog and as much as they could fit in the car. She drove out wondering whether she would ever see the house again. It was the house where her kids had grown up. It was full of her artwork, done regularly with passion in the back studio, her meditation.

On 30 December, she sent me a picture of the smoke outside her motel room and we spoke. Then she messaged me: 'May lose contact if mobile towers run out of batteries. Don't be alarmed [terror emoji]'.

On New Year's Eve, the remaining 4000 residents and tourists fled to the beach. Social media was flooded with videos and pictures of the town washed in a deep crimson red. Libby texted: 'Think we lost the house.' She did.

In the days that followed, the smoke seeped into every crevice and crack in our old farmhouse. I woke coughing and thanked the gods that we were not closer than an hour from any fire. Continual blazes burnt from mid-2020 to February 2021. They burnt more than 17 million hectares of land, killed 33 people, destroyed more than 3000 houses and affected more than 80 per cent of the World Heritage-listed Greater Blue Mountains, parts of Gondwanan rainforests and more than a billion mammals, birds and reptiles.[1]

I will admit it has been a deep frustration to me that farmers as a group, people who marinate in the climate, have not spoken out sooner on what they are seeing. A portion still see the climate events of the past twenty or so years as part of a cycle, and thus talking about climate action is to butt up against all of the familiar objections. Or they are reluctant to talk about what they are actually experiencing. Or how it is affecting them. As a conservative force, they hold more power in the political realm than they perhaps realise. Even though most family farmers hold in the back of their heads a desire to leave the farm for future generations, whether they act that way is another matter.

All of which brings me to Tolkien and Tim Beshara. Tim is manager of policy and strategy at the Wilderness Society, where his role is, as he puts it, 'focused on parliamentary engagement,

organisational strategy, public policy and strategic communication'.
He has a long history in environment and agricultural extension, which is the term used for farm training and support. He was the chief executive of Landcare in New South Wales for a time. He occupies the twilight zone between landscape management, agriculture and environment – a zone I have been tracking for the past decade. He is one of those people – and there are a growing number – who has a vision of agriculture that embeds land stewardship at its very heart.

Beshara does not accept the status quo in any one area. He is very good at seeing the threads between siloed subjects and that makes him a valuable person in politics, policy and conversation. Both of us have watched and lived the politics and science of climate change, him much more than me at advocacy level. He has worked for environmental action while I've been thinking about climate change in the context of food, landscape and agriculture, and dreaming of how to create a business model that rewards the good things and discourages the crap things.

Beshara has been considering how you can work on an issue so big and so overwhelming, against such odds, and keep going. In a piece for *Eureka Street* in 2017, he neatly outlined the contradictions – not just those regarding the environment, food and water, but the ones that pervade life, really.[2] Beshara pointed out that no matter how big and hopeless a problem looks, you will never change people's behaviour by telling them it's a threat to their very existence. Because humans aren't very good at facing up to what we cannot control by ourselves. If it's that big, someone else will have to deal with it.

He used the themes of *The Lord of the Rings* to deal with the personal angst of a seemingly impossible job description – saving the natural world and motivating others to join the cause. Those themes are the idea of the long defeat and eucatastrophe. The concept of the long defeat pervades *The Lord of the Rings*. I will let Beshara take up his point.

'This is the idea that so often in the world you find yourself fighting for a cause where there is very little chance of success, but you fight for it anyway because it is the right thing to do and because you can't imagine doing anything else. In *The Lord of the Rings* this sentiment appears time and time again, whether it is the folly of sending two hobbits alone into enemy territory and thinking it will work out well, or the many occasions the heroes of the story rode out into battle against superior numbers.

'In the moments of quiet between battles, the protagonists often mulled over whether there was any hope, or if this even mattered to their mission. Sometimes they would decide there was no hope. Other times they saw glimpses of hope. But most times they resolved that whether there was hope or not, they would push on regardless.'

Change is slow. Imagining a better system, a better world, is hard. You question your sanity. The art of gaslighting – making people question their own judgements – is deeply embedded in politics. When I suggest that the modern farming model in a changing climate could itself be an existential threat to a swag of Australian farmers, most advocates look at me like I am mad.

And that is when I think of Tolkien's second theme. Eucatastrophe, a sudden and unexpected change of fortune for the better. Beshara describes it thus: 'Think about the late arrival of Gandalf *et al.* in the battle at Helm's Deep, or about the arrival of the eagles to rescue Sam and Frodo from the eruption of Mount Doom. To Tolkien, eucatastrophe could only come about if you had faced up to the inevitability of "the long defeat" and soldiered on regardless.'

There are the farmers, the corporations, and the eaters who buy the food, and their rules of engagement. There are the global governments and the trade agreements that determine whether the food enters the country, and the rules around how that happens. There is the land's straining natural capital – the soil, water, critters and trees – already under pressure from the insatiable needs of a food system, for humans, livestock and pets, that does not account for their value. Now the whole show is staggering under the weight of climate change.

Since Tony Abbott took climate change out of the realm of the bipartisan and weaponised it in 2013, the issue has been a problem for a lot of people in conservative country places. For a long time, 'climate change' were trigger words for the rural conservative voter.

That is slowly changing. To continue the Tolkien analogy, watching farmers awaken is a bit like the March of the Ents. The hobbits tried to rouse the trees to help but Treebeard told them they were not troubled by the Great Wars. 'I do not like worrying about the future. I am not altogether on anybody's *side*, because nobody is altogether on my *side*, if you understand me . . .'

But Treebeard is spurred into action when the hobbits take him past the razed forest. 'Many of these trees were my friends. They are trees I have known from nut and acorn. They have voices of their own.'

I have come to accept that farmers won't rise up like Treebeard and his woody friends, though a group called Farmers for Climate Action have been working quietly behind the scenes. In 2020, as my aunt was still waiting for her new house to be built, the NFF managed to land a policy on climate change. Getting farmers to agree is a lot like mustering chooks because it requires buy-in from all the largely conservative state farming organisations, plus the NFF's own executive. In this case, the Farmers for Climate Action group and some committed individuals, including NFF president Fiona Simson and CEO Tony Mahar, were the kelpies to help muster the NFF towards a policy that accepts climate change and supports an 'economy-wide aspiration of net zero emissions by 2050'. While the language is qualified, the NFF position places agriculture where it can take advantage of the 'social, environmental and economic opportunities' of a low-emissions future. It is a laggard in the sense that the Meat and Livestock Association committed to carbon neutrality by 2030 way back in 2017. The Western Australian farmer group AgZero2030 has a similar goal. But by nailing its colours to the mast, the NFF left the political party most associated with farmers, the National Party, looking useless as tits on a bull, given it had historically resisted any action on climate change.

In the spirit of the eucatastrophe, I can see ways that our farmers can have a key role in climate change solutions in 2021 and beyond. Those optimistic shoots have bloomed since the summer fires and the early pandemic run on food. I know I could talk to a different farmer every day who is looking for new ways to work, such is the energy in parts of the sector, particularly in the younger generation. The bottom line is there are a lot of good people doing good things to grow food in a changing climate. A number of them are also spurred on by an urge to break the vice-like grip of an economic model based on a competition policy that is creating less competition, fewer farmers and fewer farm businesses.

The rising interest in alternative models is happening for a number of reasons. First, notwithstanding the demand for cheap food, a portion of the market also wants farmers to treat their environments with respect and care.

Second, there are obvious social, environmental, and even legal challenges to the current chemical-based conventional food-growing model. Eaters are increasingly concerned about the blanket use of glyphosate, for example, and many weeds have developed resistance to glyphosate anyway. Australian farmers must prepare their farming systems for life beyond the ubiquitous herbicide, among other practices.[3]

Third, scientists have illuminated the path we face as the climate changes. Whether politicians, advocates or individuals recognise it or not, farmers will be forced to adapt to blunt measures like carbon tariffs on international borders.

The changes in food markets, social licence for chemical usage and trade markets such as carbon tariffs are beyond the farmer's control, but they all increase pressure on any farming system from the outside. This is not new. Already, of the non-tariff measures affecting agricultural exports, more than half impose biosecurity, health and food safety requirements, such as limits on antibiotics in meat production or pesticide residues in grains.[4]

The fourth factor pushing some farmers to do things differently is from inside the farm. It is the people. It is a growing realisation. *Things cannot go on like this*. As we head into the third decade of the twenty-first century, the obvious human survival instinct requires farmers to grow food in a way that does not harm the planet any more for our children and grandchildren. The argument over what system best does that is subject to furious debate.

Vince Heffernan is a sixth-generation farmer living and working on 1200 hectares known as Moorlands on the Lachlan near Dalton, New South Wales. He is a biodynamic farmer who's long focused on improving the landscape with his former partner and horticulturalist Janet Heffernan.

Vince Heffernan was doing regenerative work to improve his landscape function years before the latest rise in the term 'regenerative agriculture'. He is not urging a 'lock up and leave' approach to wilderness, espoused by some ecologists. He sees a place for land management and food production with a different system. For Heffernan, it is either getting out of the way of nature or putting some things back so the ecosystem can function well. He has planted a range of 60,000 trees and shrubs on his land, fenced off creeks and dams, and developed a fish sanctuary for the southern pygmy perch, ringed by aquatic plants.

'I'm trying to replicate what was there, which was a patchiness, mindful of what Indigenous people were doing.

'We can't turn the clock back. We can't bring the thylacine back or Indigenous people living the way they were, but we can rebuild elements that have gone missing. And we can make these systems work in terms of energy flow and nutrient flow. We can make that happen and still run agriculture. It's not like we can only do one or the other. These issues are sold as a polarity – that you can either be green or a farmer, you can't be both. We can do both.'

Heffernan took himself to university as a mature-aged student to study ecological agriculture at the University of Sydney. He learnt about the trophic chain: if you take snakes, say, out of the ecosystem, the kookaburras either die off or they have to start eating something else. The frog population might explode because there are no snakes. Heffernan has seen this in his creeks and streams. He has also seen the problem with chytrid fungus wiping out frogs, in an ecological pandemic the *National Geographic* has labelled an 'amphibian apocalypse'.[5] He sees tadpoles as the krill of the creek system because they clean the water, but pressure from disease and from the removal of other food sources means everything is eating those tadpoles.

'Take one thing out and you've got muddy water running through the creek. Most people don't even know what a creek looked like. They have no sense that a creek has reeds in the middle of it because [now] the cattle go and eat the reeds every summer. They have no sense of what bird life was there, or what role different things played. We just go in and remove chunks of these chains and create these warps in how these things work. The biggest warp is in the carbon layer.'

Heffernan is a keen bird lover and can name 200 species on his place, but, he emphasises, the diversity of birds is incomparable to the 50,000 species of bacteria that live in the soil. His sense of awe regarding the landscape is palpable as he describes the complexity in thousands of species of fungi, existing in chains that are thousands of organisms long.

Heffernan has found a way to balance the needs of his landscape with his own need to eat, transitioning to biodynamics in the 2000s. He earns income from a Texel lamb flock, using rotational grazing methods that involve very long rest periods for his pastures. He likes Texels for their temperament, their mothering ability and describes the meat as fine textured, lean and sweet. 'Almost nutty.' He uses biodynamic preparations to spray his paddocks to improve soil function and has not used chemical drenches to control worms in his sheep for more than a decade. Worms have been managed by rotational grazing.

His work on his landscape and his healthy flock has been his passion. Increasingly, though, some years ago he was incensed by an economic system that screwed farmers. He was putting in all this time and effort to bring forth the best possible product, only to be done over at the sale yards.

'A lot of what got me into this is being screwed by the supermarkets. Initially, I thought maybe supermarkets are doing it tough. Then I realised they were selling for $100 clean profit. It was a fallacy they couldn't afford to pay an extra $1 or $2 a kilo.'

Heffernan took up his concerns with the stock and station agent, who promptly told him he could find someone else. He was flabbergasted. And he is perplexed as to why farmers and advocacy groups are so vocal about greenies and red tape, yet throw up their hands in defeat when their livestock leaves the farm gate only to be squeezed by processors and retailers.

'[Farmers] have no knowledge of where [their product] goes, how it is handled, what country it ends up in. No other business person I know knows so little about their product. Nowhere else in the world would you put up with this shit. Why are we at this place? Part of it is the supermarkets. They want all product to be the same. They place a barrier in front of the customer. There's no way you can see where the mangos came from. They don't want the differentiation because they want to be able to push that price down. They don't want the farmer to be the brand that they could expect a bit more from. It's all about controlling and not allowing info through, and that's why we have a lot of substandard product.'

Heffernan stepped out of the system. He boxed his lamb, and eaters have to buy the whole animal. You can't say, 'I don't want neck chops, I only want mince and cutlets.' He's not interested in playing wholesaler because he's trying to be a full-time farmer and land carer. People order online and the information is sent to his local butcher, who cuts up the whole animal as per order. He meets customers at a designated farmers market in Canberra or Sydney.

'I turn up at the other end, people give me money and I drive off. It's really simple, and low on convenience for the people buying, but their reward is a better product, a warm feeling and a good price.'

As word spread about his lamb, the restaurants started ringing to ask if they could order twenty legs of lamb or a load of lamb shanks, but Heffernan didn't have enough hours in the day to be a wholesaler. That is where the specialty butcher Feather and Bone stepped in. For the last fourteen years, they have been buying Heffernan's whole animals, supplying the restaurant trade with what they need and selling the rest of the animal through their butchery. That trade has driven the reputation for Moorlands, which has increased Heffernan's business to the home buyer. A *New York Times* review of a local restaurant described the lamb as 'extraordinary'.

'Because my lamb gets into a restaurant, I get a profile, which benefits my business and leaves my customers rusted on, and that's important because they feel good. You don't get [chef] Danielle Alvarez and these others buying if you don't tell your story as well.'

Laura Dalrymple and Grant Hilliard are the retailers of Heffernan's animals: they run Feather and Bone in Sydney's inner-west. They are two of the most passionate advocates I've met for growing healthy food. My realisation on moving to the country was about the importance of the place and the landscape for the local people. It leaves an imprint. Their realisation was the importance of place and landscape to meat. Those elements leave an imprint on the animal as well as the human.

Hilliard had been a sommelier and he wondered why we set so much store by the French concept of *terroir* for wine but not meat. That is, how the animal is raised, where the animal is raised and what the animal eats count for a lot: we are what we eat. This pair take it one step further. We are what the animal eats. They contend that the animal becomes a physical expression of place, time and intent – *terroir* in flesh. An animal raised naturally on a flourishing landscape is healthier for being given genuine freedom to express instinctive behaviour, and it tastes better.

And the customers of Feather and Bone want to know the animal on their plate had a good life and added to the health of the ecosystem rather than detracted from it.

Dalrymple and Hilliard look for regenerative farmers and they only buy meat directly from the farmer. They only buy from farms with no or minimal chemical use. They recognise that occasionally stock will need grain feeding but they say no to continuous grain-fed systems. They won't take stock fed growth promotants and they prioritise low-stress stock handling. They deliberately seek out different breeds of animals to encourage diversity. (This reminds me of Mike Lee asking farmers to nominate the best crop rotation for the landscape rather than food processors telling farmers what they will buy.) Feather and Bone buy the whole animal to break down and use with no waste.

I met Dalrymple at a food writers conference in 2018 and was struck by her energy and enthusiasm for food growers. In a perfect piece of timing, she and Hilliard produced a book called *The Ethical Omnivore* in the middle of the pandemic in 2020. It is part manifesto, part recipe book – a love song to good farmers, land managers and conscious, pleasurable eating. It has cooking instructions for ears, livers, hearts, kidneys and hocks as well as the prime cuts. Bottom line: eat less but better meat.

It lays out their understanding of the interconnectedness of food growing and land management. That the manager, while in control of their own land, has an impact beyond the boundary fences. It is an idea as old as the hills, a conservative idea, espoused by one of the liberal fathers, Edmund Burke. 'One of the first principles on which the commonwealth and the laws are consecrated is lest the temporary possessors and life-renters in it should act as if they were the entire masters, hazarding to leave to those who come after them a ruin instead of an habitation.'

In other words, leave it as you found it. That is sustainability. Or, even better than you found it. That is regenerative. The best farmers try to do this using the prescription for their locality.

In *The Ethical Omnivore* they write, 'The more we learned about soil, plants, animals and farming, the more we've come to understand animals, rare breed or not, are just one component of an extensive natural system, which is only as strong as the health of its component parts. From the complex world of fungi and microbes in the soil through to the insects and animals that live in and above it, every farm is a rich community of diverse interconnected creatures, constantly responding and reacting to each other.'[6]

Far from being too small to make a difference, Feather and Bone's food philosophy recognises that 'each of us is actually an intrinsic part of an interconnected world that shifts and changes according to the actions of each element within it'.[7] The community connections travel far beyond the farm, a fact that is only starting to be recognised in the public debate around climate change. At a farm policy level, that recognition of the interconnectedness of food, farming and the environment is the power (and failing) of land management policy.

Feather and Bone supplies a lot of restaurants and events, often because those businesses prioritise provenance. With the onset of the pandemic, their restaurant and event customers declined by 40 to 50 per cent. It was like those cartoon characters, Dalrymple says, running full pelt and as they sail over the cliff they are still running in mid-air for a short time before the fall.

'We thought, holy fuck! What happens now? But then there was this huge rush – people were buying for the zombie apocalypse and our retail business went through the roof. That helped. It's not the same as the business we had before because there's more work involved in serving retail orders, so we had to employ people, which was wonderful, when everyone else was laid off. We make sure to look after people we employ.'

By spring 2020, the business wasn't quite back up to speed but the increase in retail covered most of the hole left by restaurants and events. And the customer conversations were impacting.

'In one sense, the conversations were the same as the past decade. People had found us because they had done searches of "organic" or "sustainable". There was fear of running out, at first, and they were looking for reassurance. There were a lot of anecdotal stories. It was a fascinating anthropological experiment. People were saying, "Everything has to change now." Of course, they are a self-selecting group and we preach to the choir. They are not the people saying, "God, when will it return to normal?"'

Nonetheless, Dalrymple's sense was that people are looking for answers. When you feel for the first time that the food system is threatened, it might make you genuinely frightened, and people were frightened at the start of the pandemic. Here, we hark back to Stephen Bartos's food security report in 'On risk'. Bartos was directly examining Australia's food system resilience and it came up wanting. The pandemic simply provided another echo of the problems faced during earlier disasters.

But Dalrymple noticed that customers were not just looking for food supply assurance. They were also looking for something healthy that they could trust; they did not want a product 'to cause greater destruction in its production', she says.

Hilliard noticed more attention on food. Where it comes from and how it gets to you. 'Friends of ours involved in the arts world, professionals, lawyers, policy strategists, educators and academics have seen food as slightly frivolous. Now they see food as connected to a series of environmental concerns around water, land clearing, carbon sequestration,' says Hilliard. 'Once you make that sort of leap, food gets repositioned, so I think that's what we've seen with our customer base. That was a consequence of extended drought, fire and pandemic.'

Growing up the child of a diplomat, Dalrymple was the rootless global citizen, educated to appreciate a lot of different places, to be sympathetic to other cultures. It was her brother's wedding in Alice Springs that focused her attention closer to home.

'I borrowed a car and I drove out on the highway out of Alice Springs and it was an incredible afternoon. I was surrounded by all of this red wilderness and I had this most incredible moment. I got out of the car and for the first time in my life I felt connection with land and a sense of belonging. It was very strong but I have no experience of it and haven't grown up in Australia, really.'

Feather and Bone pay over the odds for their meat because they want to sell a particular product that adheres to their principles. In concert with the producer, they set prices based on logistics, market tolerance and what they need to continue farming as they do – the true cost of their food. This also allows both parties to forecast and plan.

They are serving a market made up of people who want food produced in a certain way. As Mike Lee said at the beginning of this book, they are eating according to their values: 'This is food as identity in action,' food as an expression of those values. You can argue with people over their values, I guess, but I'm with the social psychologist Jonathan Haidt on this one. It's pretty hard to change people's moral framework.[8]

Dalrymple admits she is 'evangelical' when it comes to regenerative agriculture because of her experiences connecting with the producers who supply their meat. She cannot understand why other farmers would not immediately change how they work when they see Vince Heffernan's land; also, the price he receives for his lamb. She sees him as not only effecting smart changes on country but also as doing business in a smart way.

But she also understands the defensiveness of some, and admits she doesn't have generations of interactions with land. And, she acknowledges, the good regenerative farmers thrive but not all regenerative farmers are good – 'In fact, there are a lot of shitty ones that do a bad job.'

To many conventional farmers, regenerative farmers are guilty of the worst crime: virtue signalling. To conventional farmers, it looks like the regenerative farmer is saying 'I'm better than the rest', or suggesting that conventional farmers are degenerative. Some might be saying that. But most simply want to explore a different way of doing business. To use the tired old economic slogan that has dogged farmers for decades, they are 'value adding'. They are outlining to the market, praise be, a way of farming that they hope will add value as well as create a better legacy. They are choosing to step outside the economic system that has had farmers by the bottom line for the past three decades. They are connecting directly with customers (another economic goal) in bypassing the big players, the supermarket duopolies, the food processors, the grain handlers, the marketeers, the shiny bums. Surely there is enough room in this very wide landscape for everyone.

And then there are the eaters who, in the face of disruption, are choosing a different way. The eaters who are showing us why we should care about farming. In the May after the 2020 bushfires, I took a drive through the black lunar landscape of parts of southern New South Wales and northern Victoria. Rain had followed the fires and washed away topsoil in many parts of the landscape, a sharp one-two punch to those communities. I was going to Corryong, where I had heard through the bush grapevine of a bloke who was taking part in a community rebuilding project.

Joshua Collings and his partner, Kate Crowley, are creatives. Josh has a video and audio business. Kate is a singer. In 2016 they were living in Kallista in the Dandenong Ranges but wanted to move further away from the city. So they drew a radius on a map and set their search filters at $150,000. They came up with a little cottage in Cudgewa, a beautiful valley just out of Corryong in the Upper Murray. It is a spectacular landscape of green flat land rising up into hills, cradling the little town with a scenic boundary fence.

They started their life there, had a son and renovated the cottage. They dug a vegetable garden and began a community food swap, meeting regularly with locals. Collings and a fellow gardener, Jacqui Beaumont, mulled over the idea of a market garden. That was before the fires came.

Collings is like a force of nature, a natural-born storyteller. He is energised by disruption and became a sort of narrator of the story of summer bushfires in that part of the world. Collings describes the day when the fires got to Cudgewa. He and Crowley had taken the official advice to move to shelter and there they waited. As they emerged, the cottage was gone. Their house, their bus in the frontyard were blackened shells. The only thing unscathed was the vegetable garden, a square of zucchinis. As every home gardener knows, not much eats zucchinis – they are set and forget. It turns out not even that massive firestorm killed the zucchinis. As they toured around town, vegetable gardens were often left beside burnt-out buildings.

After checking life and limb, the town descended on the supermarket to address the next need. Food. The place was still ringed by roadblocks with a squadron of emergency services making sure only residents and authorised vehicles came in and out. This was happening in fire-affected communities up and down the eastern coast of Australia. Staples were the only thing available and prices doubled. EFTPOS lines were down so cash was king. Fire recovery hubs sprang up, funded by government. They were a place to gather, get advice and swap war stories. Problems were being solved. The social interaction was almost as important as the problem solving.

It was a turning point for Collings. 'What was going to be a tiny garden became one-acre gardens in the Upper Murray to create resilience and make sure we always have fresh food. They don't burn because they are so heavy in water and they could produce income for communities who want to be involved.'

Then the pandemic arrived.

Human contact fell away and the food supply dried up again. There was another great retreat. All levels of government had to wind down recovery centres to ensure they did not bring on more devastation to small communities like Corryong, with already skeleton health services.

Josh returned to the idea of a community garden and Acres & Acres Co-Op was born. The stalwarts of the community food swap created a combination of a community and a garden, a venture that could raise money from the sale of the fruit and vegetables while paying workers in the garden. It could address in some part future food-chain shocks, whether due to fires, disease or floods. Here was an answer, also, to the frustration of food deserts in country towns, where residents often buy old, expensive produce.

Acres & Acres became a focus for the community's energy in lockdown. The first garden started behind Josh and Kate's shed on the main street of Corryong. 'With disasters and the speed of the changing climate, food is going to be five times the cost in the next five years. In IGA the prices had doubled and I needed to find a solution.'

More than a year down the track, Acres & Acres is a working food supplier for the people of the Upper Murray. Forty people arrived to the first farm-gate stall and that number continues to grow. Josh and Kate have bought the block next door to expand their operations. Their plan is to use the building as a food hub, with office space, a bottling station, a vegetable washing station and some graphics services for food producers to brand their products. They have employed a bookkeeper and are looking to scale up to a larger processing unit to produce more composting from kitchen waste. They have built a trailer as a mobile food shop and developed a community tool library that other community gardens can use to share resources. As the word grows, more people are coming, so more vegetables need to be planted. As I went to press, Josh and Kate were designing a greenhouse with funding from the local community foundation, the Border Trust. Acres & Acres wants to be able to sell to as many people who will buy.

'It's just like we talked about when you and I first met,' Collings said to me. 'It's working! It's attracting people from all walks of life and abilities from across the shire, and that is what we were aiming for as a group. There's no doubt it's doing that job.'

The garden project is a hub where people working side by side can grow something while talking about their experiences, including of the bushfires. It is part community building, part therapy, part bounty. It has been so rewarding to watch it grow from that crazy idea just after the black summer, in the main street of Corryong. To watch Acres & Acres develop over the past year into something as tangible as carrots and leeks and lettuce is to witness community power in action. Those growers and eaters are nourished by their own produce and their own capacity.

Their reputation is spreading not just among cooks but among community development advocates. The success has come about because it was a locally designed concept, supercharged by seed funding from a range of government and private programs.

At its most basic, that success means the availability of fresh, healthy, locally grown fruit and vegetables. We farm a lot of food in Australia, but by volume much of it is beef and wheat. We are master producers of steak and sausage sandwiches, perhaps reflected in the phenomenon of the democracy sausage at election day. Only 4 per cent of our commercial farms grow vegetables. Only 7 per cent of us – and even fewer of our kids – eat the daily recommended serving of veggies. The number of veggie farmers are declining, with a third lost over the decade to 2018. One-third of those remaining grow veggies on less than five hectares. Josh and the Corryong mob have a goal of gardens throughout the district.

When I think of their model, I think again of the Voices for Indi political model, which came from a community focus to achieve a goal. The Voices mob wanted better political engagement and happened to reinvent political representation. The Corryong mob want to create a better local food supply and happened to reinvent a community food model by instilling community independence from long global supply chains. Taking control of their essentials seemed, well, essential after living through the terrible experiences of the black summer, and then COVID. The Voices model has now spread out from their shock election victory in 2013 in Indi. Two more federal MPs, Zali Steggall (Warringah) and Kerryn Phelps (Wentworth) entered Parliament using community-organised independent campaigns. (Phelps has since lost office.) Voices movements have also spread through the eastern states and across the country, a key component to watch at the next federal election. It is not impossible to imagine communities throughout Australia picking up the Acres & Acres model to recharge their own local food supplies and renew their communities in a similar way.

Josh Collings sourced a lot of his gardening gear from James Hutchinson, a Tasmanian market gardener. James runs his supply business from his Longley Organic farm, south of Hobart. He is what is known as a micro farmer – a model that looms large in food subculture but is ignored in the mainstream farming debates on the national stage. It is as if micro farming doesn't exist. These are not the powerful farmers consulted by governments, or political parties. They are not considered in policy-making because they don't shift export markets or fill major supermarket chains. Yet the micros often have great market connection, via social media or their local communities. Their Instagram accounts are followed closely and intertwine with other growers, eaters and dreamers who think, one day, maybe I can escape the office and don a pair of overalls.

Hutchinson rejects the idea that micro farmers don't make a difference and says the fifty produce boxes he sells to local families will beat the equivalent basket at the duopoly supermarkets on price and nutrition any day of the week.

'Food deserts are very real in city and country,' James says. 'It is about knowing farmers, and people want to know where food comes from. It's a global phenomenon. It's about reconnecting with food we are putting into [our] bodies. I don't think it's a fad, because it was definitely improving well before COVID.'

He puts the uptick in interest down to food security and building resilience. He supplies micro farmers all across the country, to areas about as far from Tasmania as you could get: the Western Australian wheatbelt, Esperance, Albany, Adelaide and Alice Springs.

There are many different models. Community-supported agriculture is common, where the farmer is supported by a subscription model of customers who pay through good season and bad. Some offer customer connections through farm visits, a model that James Rebanks talked about. Some are certified organic growers. Some are larger farmers, already well versed in growing and grazing at scale but who want to play around on smaller plots set aside to diversify their incomes or to provide side hustles for family members. As a way of bypassing the food processors and retailers, this model is the ultimate paddock-to-plate adventure.

The disruption in farming is being driven by the big global and domestic existential threats we have talked about. These elements slice through political agendas that are indifferent, or, worse still, undermining real action. Yet they are tucked into every corner of our lives, from the casual café conversation about the weather to the agendas of setpiece meetings, in the community, in every tier of government, in every boardroom.

I have heard the echoes and warnings right through my conversations with Indigenous people, farmers, scientists, writers, gardeners, citizens of all kinds. Those messages are there in Oral McGuire's words, about the human connection with land, trees and the spirit of fire. They are there in Emma Germano's words about her family's emotional connection to farming. They are there in Pete Mailler's ideas of the rights and obligations of the eaters who demand cheap food, and farmers who demand ultimate control of land without understanding the wider implications of their actions. They are even embedded in the warnings of expert Paul Barnes about the link between our natural resources and our national interests.

They are there in the words of butcher Laura Dalrymple: 'We just don't see ourselves as part of the landscape or nature. That allows us to behave the way we do, with cavalier disrespect and regard for natural assets and also for the people whose lives are spent on the land. It's really interesting because we are not encouraged to think about ourselves in that way. We have a rationalist approach to life and economics and landscape and culture and all of those things.'

It took me ten years of living on this landscape to develop a strong connection to the earth. It was only when I came to this place I understood human interaction with the natural world, with its jagged edges. That a crow could take a sheep's eye without compunction. That nature abhors bare ground. If I think back to life before the farm, nature was a world contained, a play in which I had no part. The writer and scientist Helen Macdonald reminded me that nature is not for locking up behind closed glass. It is for preserving and reflecting our responsibilities back.

Once my brain plugged into the natural world, I could see how you could spend your whole life dedicated to regenerating a small patch of earth. You might even leave a legacy for a time. If you had a tenant on your own block of land, isn't that the kind of land carer you would want?

Disconnecting ourselves as eaters from food growers and land managers is a denial of our own dependence on essential goods: food and all the health it can bring. Equally, disconnecting ourselves as farmers from our impacts beyond the boundary fence is a denial of our dependence on essential natural resources: water, soil and all the natural capital required to grow that food.

Chapter 12
ON WATER

Water is essential to grow food, whether it falls from the sky or comes from a river through a pipe. In nine of the last ten years, the World Economic Forum has identified water crises as among the top five global risks by impact.[1]

We can think of water as one element inside the farming system. And of farming as one element inside the food production system. The food production system is one element of the food chain that produces the meal on your plate. That whole food chain is one element that makes up human health and the nation's strategic interests. And the food chain must operate within the limits of the natural world. This series of links is rarely considered by governments, food companies, a lot of farmers and many eaters. Thinking about all these elements separately is pointless.

Nuts, citrus and olive oil are part of my usual diet but I also rail at water management. Those foods, wholefoods, good healthy foods, are three examples of the produce driving current water markets. It is inescapable, this connection between what's on your plate and how the world's farmers go about the business of growing food. The problem is always to be fixed out there *points inland*, without understanding our own role as eaters. Never is this more evident than with the acrid water debate, both in Australia and globally.

'What do people need to know about water and irrigation?' I asked Andrew Bomm, the agricultural consultant and water policy wonk we met in 'On families'.

'That irrigators are not all robber barons,' he said. And it is true, every time water is written about, a wave of commentary arises around greedy irrigators, and corporate malfeasance and raping and pillaging farmers. At the same time, we wander into cafés and drink our almond lattes and indulge in a little berry friand, made with cheap almond meal. There is a redaction of our part in the morality play. This removes the need to change the way we act because it places the onus on someone else – anybody else – to act. *They* should do something! The government, the robber barons, the little farmer. Someone else.

But we cannot separate ourselves, the goodies, from irrigators, the baddies.

The water debate in Australia is dominated by the Murray-Darling Basin system, which takes in four states and is the oldest system exploited for large-scale food production. The country does have other rivers – not to mention a vast groundwater system, notably the Great Artesian Basin. As the returns roll in for irrigated crops, large and small irrigators, big investors and farmers are looking at other water sources. Remember that Sue Middleton knew she needed an irrigated element to futureproof against climate change. These battles largely escape the daily news cycle but are a portent to the future of large-scale agriculture in a water-challenged environment. Water is the new gold, and the person or entity that controls large-scale irrigation holds the keys to prosperity and production in non-metropolitan Australia.

An example. Fortune Agribusiness applied in 2020 for a licence to eventually extract 40,000 megalitres of groundwater a year to develop one of the country's largest fruit and vegetable farms on Singleton Station, 100 kilometres south of Tennant Creek.[2] In February 2021, the native title holders of this land opposed the plans. The district is 41 per cent Aboriginal land, with a thousand Aboriginal residents in Alekarenge community, outstations and land trusts, according to the Central Land Council.[3] Fortune's head office is in Southbank, Melbourne. In April, the application was conditionally approved by the Northern Territory Water Controller. If it gets through the conditions, eventually the farms will be extracting the full 40,000 megalitres, which would make it the territory's largest water licence to date. The water will be used to grow onions, rock melons, citrus, grapes and other crops.[4]

Another example. The 700-kilometre Fitzroy River in Western Australia was subject to a battle between Indigenous owners and pastoralists, including mining and agricultural billionaire Gina Rinehart, over a proposed expansion of irrigation.[5] Indigenous people wanted to set aside a portion of the river for a national park to protect it from over-development. In 2019, Rinehart began buying up pastoral leases in the Kimberley and then offered to trade tens of thousands of hectares of land to the state for the creation of the national park in order to secure a licence to pump 325 gigalitres out of the river each year.[6] In December 2020, the Western Australian government declared 173,000 hectares along the river as a national park, jointly managed by the Bunuba Dawangarri Aboriginal Corporation and the state's department of biodiversity, conservation and attractions. But that does not discount future irrigation, which will form part of a water allocation management plan for the river's future in 2021 and beyond.

The mother of all examples, though, is the Murray-Darling Basin, a system stretching over one million square kilometres. This is where the longstanding needs of Indigenous culture, more recent farming culture, conservation, law and politics crash headlong. The Murray-Darling Basin Plan determines how much water is kept for the environment and how much is shared between humans and their industries. The grab for water is changing landscapes, towns, food production, fortunes and climate.

Many conservationists, ecologists, water scientists, even lawyers, are angry. (Barrister Richard Beasley, senior counsel for the South Australian royal commission into the Murray-Darling Basin Plan, has written a very angry and funny book called *Dead in the Water*.) Indigenous people are also angry at the state of the river. The Barkandji, literally 'people of the river', were given land rights around their mother, Barka, the Darling, but no water rights. In the basin, Aboriginal people are estimated to hold less than 0.2 per cent of all available water as of 2018. Furthermore, research shows that amount has declined in the prior decade due to the liquidation of Aboriginal organisations – a fact the researchers Dr Lana Hartwig and Professor Sue Jackson characterise as a 'new wave of dispossession'.[7]

The Murray-Darling river system is like the lines on the palm of your hand. It is full of big and little branches that fade into nowhere. It has been irrevocably changed since whitefellas arrived. River infrastructure, weirs and dams have modified the flows and decimated the native fish populations. Human pressure, including human-induced global heating, is squeezing the rivers dry.

In the summer of the big fish kills, Barkandji elder William Brian 'Badger' Bates stood with his cousin beside the Menindee Lakes in southwest New South Wales. Big old Murray cod, golden perch and his totem fish, the bony bream, floated belly-up. Menindee locals filmed the disaster and the videos went viral. Black and white people were angry. The Barka is the heart of Barkandji country. Bates was shattered. Look what they are doing to our Barka, our cod, his cousin cried. Bates cried too.

'I see white people cry. I seen that politician [Jeremy] Buckingham spew his guts up and cry for fish. They laughed at him and all he doing is to help the environment and say this shouldn't happen. We all talk about our families and leaving it for our kids. The government is going to come along and say I'm proud. Look at what I left you, it's just a bitumen road, you know? They got more bends and twists than a boomerang. They can't lay straight in bed.'

Bates is a renowned artist. He was born on the Barka at Wilcannia. The Barkandji's totems are the crow and the wedgetail eagle. Bates learnt his culture from his grandmother, a belief system where the Ngatji (rainbow serpent) resides in the Barka. The Barkandji are responsible for the wellbeing of the Ngatji, so when the Barka runs dry, despair sets in. Bates spent twenty-one years as a national parks officer and knows his country inside out. He spent much of his childhood on the river, swimming and fishing. The white kids would bring lemons and other fruits, plus a bit of flour. Black kids like him would show them how to fish in the weir pools. It still happens, he says. The flow of the Barka has a big impact on crime. When the river is down, the crime rate goes up. The connection is fundamental because Bates's people have been using the Menindee Lakes for 45,000 years, harvesting their catches of fish as well as living on big mussels the size of your hand. It took the river management three years to kill the system, he says.

There was a lot of celebration when Aboriginal people got native title. It gave Bates's people some recognition, but it didn't help their beloved river. The Barkandji as people of the river were given no water rights. Bates says, 'Without the Barka, I'm nothing. I'm not even black. I'm just a refugee without a country because they are not giving me respect for my mother, the river.'

The lakes and the river are still an important protein source for the locals when there is water, particularly for those on low incomes. The state of the lakes and rivers is impacting their food security, already under pressure due to land-based rules.

'They gave us native title and we still got to ask, "Can we go in and get a kangaroo or emu?" Even with national parks, when we say we want an emu or kangaroo they say we can't because it's a national park. You call us native title owners but they don't let us hunt. All we want is some bush tucker to eat. I say the kangaroo and emu are ours. You own the sheep and the bullock and the other stuff, but not the kangaroo or emu.'

The food chain is increasingly disturbed by the extremities of human management and climate change. The Barkandji fish totem, the bony bream, lays a lot of eggs that need water. The river mussel needs water to make it grow. When they drain the lakes, they are killing that food chain. 'We know the mussels – 45,000 years ago, my people sat down and ate the river mussel and the lake mussel . . . If we get too greedy with the river, it will hurt someone. The people we really love the most. It's our job as Barkandji people to protect the river.'

In theory, the Barkandji people's water is included in environmental water – the water allocated to maintain the natural system. That feels like a throwback to pre-census days prior to 1967 when

Indigenous people were lumped in with flora and fauna. Bates describes environmental water for the Barkandji as akin to 'shut-up water'. He would like to see a cultural water allocation to the Barkandji in Lake Pamamaroo at Menindee, managed by the native title holders but for the benefit of everyone in Broken Hill and wider western New South Wales.[8] If that were to happen, the Barkandji Murray-Darling Basin plan would share it but ensure the Barka came first. 'We want that cultural water separate from the environmental water. What they will do, and they do it all the time, they tell you what you want and then as soon as they walk out the door they laugh and say, "This is what we're going to do." They don't want us blackfellas here, we don't know anything.'

Governments have been directing who gets water for a long time; governments have been directing how we farm for a long time. And they pretty much still are because of a framework that rewards money, knowledge and technology.

When the English invaded, they imposed their own system of riparian law. If you had land next to a river, go for it. Yet the colonisers chose a continent whose river systems were far more variable than those they were used to. Alfred Deakin and others acted to ensure water was controlled by the states, via centralised systems. Deakin's objective was 'to encourage the greatest possible utilisation of the water on the largest possible area'.[9] Development, via closer settlement and agricultural production, was the goal and that was supported by public investment in water infrastructure. The key here was that, unlike other countries, the water rights were pretty similar.

This, according to the National Water Commission (NWC), set us up for tradeable entitlements down the track. The states had an eye on economic development, particularly in the regions. This has never changed.

Water infrastructure was planned. The states' aim was to use irrigation water to create 'communities of property-owning independent small farmers as a foundation for a democratic society', writes academic Daniel Connell. Governments deliberately restricted the size of farms to prevent the 'creation of grand estates worked by armies of low-paid workers similar to those developing in southern California'. In New South Wales, our legislators determined farm size would be sufficient for the maintenance of an average family 'through average seasons and circumstances', even though nothing is average in the Australian climate. Water rights were tied to land titles to discourage water market speculation and the development of 'water monopolies and cartels'.[10]

So farmers understood they were there to feed the nation and they were carrying the overt message from government that they were building the foundation of Australian democracy.

The farmers were encouraged by political rhetoric and public infrastructure, and the planning of the policy essentially dictated where they would settle, the size of their farm and what they would grow. Settlement was voluntary, but the place – the home in which they would put down roots – was planned by government through infrastructure. Soldier-settlement schemes and land acts were another version of government direction of policy, jointly funded by states and the Commonwealth to encourage horticulture, mixed crops and grazing on the small blocks. Many of the irrigation valleys were developed directly as a result of government's plans for building the dams, locks and canals. It wasn't a scattered pattern of development so much as a strategic look at where water could be exploited for the development of the interior. Once you add this very direct government planning to the high protection barriers for farmers, you have a multigenerational contract with the state.

Governments were throwing around licences like confetti. Up to the 1970s, licences providing access to water were pretty much supplied on demand by the states.[11] Irrigators could use as much water as they wanted, as long as it was from a defined irrigation area on an annual fixed fee. There was little incentive to conserve water, and while licences were for a set period, the expectation was allowed to grow that they would be automatically renewed. The majority were handed out in the fifty years of a decidedly wet period in the Murray-Darling Basin. Over-allocation has been a major problem. The New South Wales irrigators themselves sounded a warning by opposing the issuing of more licences on the Darling River at a land board hearing in the 1970s.

Australia's water trade started informally, between neighbours. Water bailiffs were an institution along the rivers, and they lived and worked in the communities they served and policed. Informal trade might be a deal between neighbours to swap water allocations in exchange for a price in cash or kind, aided by the bailiff. Instead of sending water to the bloke with the licence, the bailiff sent it to his neighbour. In the 1960s and '70s, temporary transfers of water started, particularly in drought or drier periods, though each state applied the rules in a slightly different way. By the 1980s and '90s, water allocation was just one of a range of economic reforms under the microscope.

The effect of these changes was to discard the notion of closer settlement policy in practice. You hear the rhetoric to this day, pretty much every time you see a politician in an Akubra. But economists and governments began to let go of the idea that small farms were a foundation for anything, let alone democracy, from the 1960s.

These trends, combined with growing global environmental awareness, led to the push to change longstanding agreements around water management. By the 1990s, there were economic pressures and environmental pressures for smaller government to address over-allocation. And no wonder. Demand for water was still increasing and total water usage, according to the NWC, increased by 65 per cent in just over a decade between the 1980s and '90s.

The push for a water market gathered a head of steam with support from agricultural economists and the irrigation lobby. Land and water were split asunder and water was created as a property right in and of itself, able to be traded to the highest bidder. The change represented a massive cultural leap from the foundations of Australian rural policy development. This is how the NWC put it: 'There were concerns that breaking the nexus between water and land would privatise a community resource, and that rapid trading of water out of irrigation areas would lead to stranded assets and adverse regional economic impacts. The development of markets was the clearest sign of the change in policy objectives away from regional development and towards overall economic efficiency.'[12]

The government sales pitch was that it was for the greater good. Water would flow to the best use product; in other words, the crops that get the best prices.

The big water reforms of the last few decades emerged from the 2004 National Water Initiative agreed by state and federal governments to collectively get their shit together. We'll come back to that initiative shortly, but first let me lay out water architecture.

States are responsible for water management under Australia's constitution, but the really momentous reform was the Water Act 2007, authored by the then water minister Malcolm Turnbull, which allowed the Commonwealth to bust into national water policy on the grounds of adhering to our international treaties. These are environmental agreements Australia has signed to act on things like climate change, biodiversity, significant wetlands and migratory birds.

The Water Act 2007 changed the rules of engagement by acknowledging past overuse of water. It sought to tip the balance back in favour of the environment. The act says the Murray-Darling Basin Authority and the water minister must 'take into account the principles of ecologically sustainable development; and act on the basis of the best available scientific knowledge and socioeconomic analysis'. The Howard government committed $10 billion towards a Murray-Darling Basin plan. At its most simple, the plan is about how much water can be taken out of the environment and used for humans. Then the humans' water is used or traded: water having been untied from land titles to become a commodity in its own right. Once you have a water licence (the bucket) and an annual allocation (the water in the bucket), you can grow whatever crop you like. Government does not direct what is grown in Australia, with the exception of the brief, abandoned, half-arsed 2020 Water for Fodder program.[13]

By 2012, when the Murray-Darling Basin Plan was implemented under the Gillard government and its water minister, Tony Burke, the share of water returned to the environment was 2750 gigalitres per year. This was in stark contrast to the 3000 to 7600 or so gigalitres per year suggested by the Murray-Darling Basin Authority's own guide, published the previous year and modelled by scientists.[14] The downgraded figure was the political fix to keep the states on board but it is at odds with the Water Act.

And now there are five main players in national water governance. The states and territories cover water allocation, water trading procedures, monitor water use and determine water sharing plans. As always, the states all go about things slightly differently. They are the housekeepers of water.

The Murray-Darling Basin Authority oversees water trading across the system and ensures the states comply with those rules. This means the authority has to keep the states in line, check their homework and manage the politics. This is a no-win situation and as a result states can obfuscate and bluster while not fulfilling their obligations. (For example, in May 2021 New South Wales was told to revise almost all of its detailed water sharing plans because of policy inconsistencies, technicalities and failing to consult with First Nations representatives.[15]) New South Wales Nationals leader John Barilaro specialises in the performance art of threatening to walk away from the plan because it wins him brownie points in some parts of the regions.[16]

The ACCC also checks water-market and water-charge rules, which are set by the federal water minister. These rules are meant to reduce barriers to trade and be transparent. They are as clear as mud. The ACCC is supposed to ensure water infrastructure operators can't discriminate against individual water users. This does not always happen.

There are the water infrastructure operators, the old public irrigator boards, now privatised. In my neck of the woods, that is Murrumbidgee Irrigation. They create the rules for operation and trade within their network (allegedly checked by the Murray-Darling Basin Authority). They run the infrastructure and deliver the water to irrigation customers and allegedly deal with compliance. They can also privately trade. I would argue there are deep conflicts in one body doing three things: delivering water and running infrastructure, policing, and privately trading.

Finally, there is the federal government water minister, who oversees the Murray-Darling Basin Authority and the ACCC. Under Coalition governments, mostly that is a National Party minister.

In his conception, Turnbull wanted registers of water entitlements and trades to be compatible across the nation. That hasn't happened. And he wanted nationally consistent water accounting to ensure that water accounting methods and the measurement of water across Australia meet common standards. That hasn't happened. Disorder and distrust have ensued. These five players intertwine like a bunch of university students playing Twister.

The water scientist Professor Peter Cullen was central to brokering a plan for the water reforms of 2007, and in that year, in a speech to New Zealand scientists, he outlined the goals of the 2004 reforms, the National Water Initiative.[17] The goals were to:

- understand how much water we have and how we use it
- determine how much water we can take and still have healthy rivers and secure groundwater
- restore over-allocated systems
- give users clear entitlements to water
- allow users to trade their entitlements
- enable effective water planning to protect key ecological assets
- use best-practice pricing to encourage efficiency in water use.

The only point missing from Cullen's list was engagement with local communities. The complaints box is full.

Of his listed goals, it's clear we do recognise an entitlement and allow users to trade their water. Of the other goals, there is no transparent way to understand how much water is in the system.

Though Cullen died in 2008, before he could see water reform and community trust break down, his speech shines a light on how those who devised the reforms saw them playing out. It is worth unpicking Cullen's speech to take the temperature of the water reforms now.

Cullen predicted climate change was going to make water less reliable. He was correct. Numerous reports, including that of the interim inspector-general of the Murray-Darling Basin water resource, 'Impact of lower inflows on state shares under the Murray-Darling Basin Agreement', published in 2020, have found climate change is a big driver of less water in the system.[18]

Cullen predicted perennial plantings like nut and fruit trees would become fewer because annual crops provide more flexibility, especially when there are unpredictable water supplies. He was incorrect. Thirsty perennial plantings have expanded exponentially in the southern Murray system. Australia is now the second-biggest exporter of nuts after California.

Cullen predicted irrigation properties would become larger but less land would be irrigated. He was correct that properties would become larger but the overall area under irrigation has expanded.[19]

Cullen predicted prices for water would rise. The price of water has certainly risen.

Cullen predicted dairy farms would leave irrigation districts. He was correct. In 2019, there were fewer than 6000 dairy farmers in Australia, compared with 22,000 dairy farmers in 1980.[20] Water reforms have accelerated the decline in dairy diversity that began with the deregulation of the industry. Australia is now a net importer of dairy products.

No one could say government didn't know about the structural adjustment playing out now for those communities.

So Australia has not really hit its goals when it comes to water management. And water trading is a dog's breakfast. Its hallmarks are a lack of transparency and the crossover of too many responsibilities in the different governing bodies and agencies.

The legacy of bad market design means the rules are ripe for arbitrage, which means the buying and selling of the same asset in different markets. The ACCC water market inquiry report in 2021 outlined a failure of governance, though it did not support a re-hitching of water rights to land.[21]

The ACCC found: brokers operating in a mostly unregulated environment, allowing conflicts of interest; improper reporting of transactions; scant rules on manipulating prices; no overarching body to monitor the market participants; and lack of transparency in trading processes. Furthermore, trading doesn't equate with the physical river systems because the transaction does not count the loss of water (conveyance) when moving it around a massive river system that encompasses four states. Nor does it account for the environmental impacts of trading water in different places. Changing river conditions and reduced capacity are challenging the assumptions that underpin the current trading rules. Add to that a lack of trust in the market and its institutions and you have a dog's breakfast.

This tangle of conflicting regulations has practical consequences. 'The complex nature of the Basin's market settings means the market's trading systems and opportunities are best understood and leveraged by professional traders and large agribusinesses with the time and knowledge to analyse and navigate them,' the report found.[22]

Red flag, people.

Those on the ground closely relate to all these findings. But that last quote stood out for me as a reflection of economic reforms in the last three decades. Those reforms have not *deregulated* the market into the fantasy natural economic state as espoused by market champions. Rather, natural resources, including our most important one – water – have been *re-regulated* to favour a different group. Protective trade policies may have favoured the smaller to medium operators. The market reforms favour the wealthier operators. This is not a free market. This is not a fair market.

People are like water. They find the cracks in the rules and flow through them. Notwithstanding high-profile water-theft convictions, most of the egregious behaviour on river systems has been allowed to take place *under the rules*. This has created economic, social and environmental perversities. It is the classic case of rule beating, going to greater and greater lengths to get around the rules. This has created skewed outcomes and the natural system has been changed beyond measure because of it.

We do have to recognise river systems will never return to a completely natural state.[23] The binary choice often presented in the media – farming versus environment – is pointless. If we want to eat, we need to come to an agreement as a nation about the amount of water to take, and the amount to save, from the natural world.

Our most precious resource can now be traded like shares or real estate, but without the transparency of those markets. This has amplified the value and access to our water for speculator, behemoth or small farmer alike, but favours those with access to the best information and analysis. That is not the average family farmer. This imbalance is causing division. Water trading has created a Hunger Games in communities along the rivers, which I would argue has not benefited the country, nor in a lot of cases the small to medium irrigators. The structural change is hollowing out some towns. It is creating a two-speed economy in country Australia.

Chris Olszak spent more than a decade from 2000, during the millennium drought, working as an advisor to governments. The drought broke but he realised the complex policy issues around water, its allocation and its scarcity were not going away. He was one of the co-founders of Aither, a consultancy focused on water policy, working with state and federal governments.

'People were on board with the journey of sustainability and economic efficiency through that period, when the National Water Initiative was being championed by Peter Cullen. But we have lost the punters. Good decision-making around natural resource management requires tough compromises. There's no right or wrong answer and people need to be brought along.'

Olszak says the polarisation that water policy engenders is not helped by the lack of shared understanding of how the system works, let alone the complex policy. This point has been echoed by Mick Keelty's review of water. Keelty's key recommendation called for a 'single point of truth'. There is no longer an independent forum such as the NWC because it was abolished in 2014 by the Abbott government. The environmental movement, Indigenous people and the irrigators have largely lost faith in the system, making consensus harder to achieve.

For all the criticism from stakeholders of the Murray-Darling Basin Plan, Olszak still thinks Australia is well-off compared to countries that have yet to set the basic machinery in place to measure water extraction and understand what is sustainable for their river systems. 'Point me to an example where an environmental program has returned 20 per cent of the resource to the environment like in the southern Murray-Darling Basin. Imagine if we could do that with carbon.'

In his mind, things really changed again when the Californian nut growers discovered Mildura. As the largest nut exporter in the world, California was ripping through its water resources like nobody's business. And why? Because nut demand was going through the roof and their water was not subject to the same caps on extraction that are in place in Australia, especially for groundwater.

Nuts have been grown commercially in Australia since the 1830s. The industry moved to the Murray in the 1960s and '70s and there they ticked over with other horticultural food crops. But in 2015, the Californian drought pushed the almond industry to look globally to diversify its climate risk, given its dwindling water supply. That state was producing 80 per cent of global export almonds. They found Mildura. It had an existing horticulture industry, perfect climate, perfect soil and plentiful and comparatively cheap water.

'They came quickly and at scale and have utilised the water market to invest in some pretty substantial orchards,' says Olszak.

That demand, plus the Asian free trade agreements signed by the Coalition government, supercharged horticulture, not just for nuts but for grapes and citrus. By this time, 20–30 per cent of water entitlements had been purchased or acquired by the Commonwealth for the environment. The reduction in water entitlements available for irrigators and the increase in demand created a price boom.

Reformers are fond of saying the water markets were designed to deliver the best and highest-return products. The opportunity cost has been to some crops that are struggling to compete for water, particularly if they are reliant on water markets. The dairy farmer cannot use water to grow fodder for her cows in dry years because what she makes from her milk won't pay for the water. The rice farmer cannot grow his crop until water is so plentiful that the price drops to a level where he can receive a return.

In the rational world of economic textbooks, free markets have perfect information with full transparency. The people in the equation behave in the way they are supposed to behave. Business people do what business people need to do – that is, maximise their returns, cut their costs and carry on into the sunset. What if we don't always act like rational economic players? What if we value priorities other than return? What if we think of balance sheets in terms of the whole landscape? In terms of the communities we live in or the people we employ?

That's where things get messy and the real world sets the textbooks on fire. Exhibit A: Aither's 2020 report into the water market.[24] Olszak and his colleagues found there will not be enough surface water in the lower Murray to meet demand in extremely dry years, given the current boom in permanent plantings of nuts and other crops in the southern Murray-Darling Basin. The report spelled out that new investors should be mindful of their water supply before planting. At the time of writing, there were still new trees going in.

Aither's findings had a few conditions. It assumed there was no carryover – the water that irrigators hold from previous years and are legally entitled to use the following year. It also assumed no inter-valley trade. Both these factors can help horticulturalists get by. The report warned 'previous estimates of existing permanent horticulture water demand are likely to be underestimates'.[25]

'Existing and projected permanent horticulture demand is expected to push the limits of water supply in very dry periods', it said.

Demand will exceed supply. Prices will rise in drought.

Aither also made this point: 'Based on what is known about how the market operates and has behaved in the past, we can assume that the market will not act perfectly rationally in the future. This means that estimates of water availability in this report are likely to overestimate supply for horticulture.'

Olszak resists the idea that the market isn't rational in terms of supply and demand. It is more about the combination of thousands of individual farm businesses who make different long- and short-term decisions. In other words, this may mean that outcomes in a model might not eventuate in practice. For example, if a rice farmer is willing to pay for water at $150 a megalitre, while the dairy farmer next door might pay $300 a meg, you would assume if the price goes over $300 a meg, everyone in dairy and rice will sell their water to the almond growers.

'It doesn't always happen like that,' says Olszak. 'People have a longer-term view on these things. So you might have a dairy farmer who needs to maintain their herd. They want to keep up their mix of pastures they grow on their property. Or they might just love farming and they are willing to go around and farm. To me it doesn't make them irrational to not sell water when the price is high, they just have different objectives and a longer-term view.

'I think the point is there was a bit of a wake-up call that the water is not going to definitely appear and be there. You've got to buy it off someone and they've got to be willing to sell.'

While irrigators get a lot of attention, we seem more able to accept towns running out of water in times of drought and shortage.[26] In January 2020, an ABC investigation found fifty-five towns across New South Wales, Queensland and in parts of Western Australia and the Northern Territory – a fair swag of them Indigenous – were either out of water or at risk of running out.[27] Though the drought has mostly eased in 2021, it means only that the issue is off the front pages until the next time.

Human and animal communities cannot exist without water. Droughts have been occurring every decade. The fact that we regularly accept that people are at risk of running out of water in a developed country makes me want to shout, or at the very least write in capital letters: THESE ARE ESSENTIAL ISSUES OF NATIONAL STRATEGY REGARDING OUR BASIC RESOURCES IN A CHANGING CLIMATE.

The irony is that since the pandemic, regional living has never looked so good. Let's not cut off regional centres at the knees just as metropolitan people are starting to see the benefits of moving out of cities, and many employers are starting to realise that workers can deliver from a variety of bases. A town with a secure water supply is way more attractive than a town that needs to truck in bottled water mid-drought. Many tiny towns rise or fall with economic circumstances. In future, their water supply may be the determining factor, with bureaucrats suggesting that bottled water may become the *only* way they can survive. This might be okay for a town of a few hundred, but it obviously won't work for larger centres, hence the roll-out of emergency water infrastructure funding in New South Wales at the height of the last drought.

Australia's water supply and its managers need to inspire more trust in the system at a time when trust in governments is at a premium. So governments – state and federal in the case of water – need to get the basics right. For example, there is not a lot of detailed data about water use by industry because governments don't ask irrigators how they use their water. Geospatial satellite imagery can already determine which crops are grown. If governments used the masses of satellite data at their disposal, there would be more intelligence about what crops are going in, including new permanent plantings like almonds. This would tell governments what the demand is going to be like. As should be very clear by now, new technology is going to be crucial for policy makers grappling with climate change.

'Creative destruction' is a term coined by the Austrian economist Joseph Schumpeter in 1942, as 'the essential fact about capitalism'. Bret Walker SC, who led the South Australian royal commission into the Murray-Darling Basin, used it in his final report when he described the many submissions from river communities regarding the social change that had resulted from changes in water management. Having heard complaints about water buybacks, the loss of annual cropping (in favour of permanent plantings) and overall reductions of 'irrigated water', he wrote, 'Whatever the merits of these complaints, the fact is clear that market forces work through "creative destruction" in Basin irrigation communities as much as in urban rust belts.

'There can be no doubt, for example, that the constant progress in mechanization and chemical assistance to agriculture continues to reduce the opportunities for many (especially less skilled) willing workers, whether employed or contracted, permanent or seasonal. Yet no-one complained about these forces, which explain deserted villages better than the Basin Plan.'[28]

It is true to say that farming communities have undergone many technological changes that have reduced employment on farms and helped farm owners improve their productivity. But which came first? Did people move away because jobs were not available, due to mechanisation? Or did other job opportunities come up elsewhere and attract labour away – potentially making greater mechanisation necessary? These are things land owners would not yell about because they have benefited from them. Workers who've lost their jobs as a result of productivity gains have less political leverage, which also explains that silence.

More expensive water hits irrigators in their pockets; I have, however, spoken to irrigators who are happy with water going to the environment, as was the plan in the Water Act. Though Walker was not inquiring into the water trading regime, I believe he misdiagnoses the community angst over the water market. He is describing the common view that trading is simply a case of better farmers taking out the dross, or, as he puts it, 'The farmer with the most profitable business plan, or the plan which generates most revenue, will tend to bid higher prices.'

'It is thus in the nature of things that smaller, less ambitious farmers will either suffer large cost increases, or give up irrigated crops. It is to be stressed that this is not an undesirable side-effect of the market — it is the overt intention of those of us who devised and supported it.'[29]

The nuance he misses is that this is not 'best in show irrigator' against laggards. This is three things. This is highest-return food against lower-valued food. Almonds over milk, pistachios over rice, table grapes over oats. This is a fundamental restructure of the food we grow and the people who grow it. I ask again: do we want to become a nation who only grows beef, wheat – and almonds? No government has ever asked that question.

This is also highest resourced irrigators, who can spend time and money playing the markets with all the technology, time and advice that it requires. So while governments talk the talk of family farming, are they talking top twenty farming families by value, or the average family farmer? This is also a geographical lottery, where whole regions become the winners because a particular food suits their climate. The winners in 2021 are places like the lower Murray, Griffith and Shepparton. That outcome is proportionately detrimental to those regions that produce lower-return food, like Deniliquin, Blighty and Jerilderie. As a political reporter, I can pick where the swing booths are as a result of those economic equations.

Schumpeter's 'creative destruction' was also used by irrigator, agricultural researcher and SunRice board member Dr Leigh Vial, who with Andrew Bomm wrote a paper called 'Creative Destruction in the Australian Water Markets'.[30] Its subtitle is 'Broadacre irrigation in the southern MDB is set to change dramatically: Is this the creative destruction we want?'

Vial and Bomm take creative destruction a step further. That is, every irrigated business seeks a reward for not only water but also the land, labour and capital applied to irrigation. Schumpeter pointed out that an economic system will only function in some sort of equilibrium if all factors of production – land, capital and in this case water get some reward. I believe we are heading to the point where water (via its value on the temporary market) commands the bulk of the return from almost any broadacre enterprise, leaving little for the labour, capital and land used. Another red flag. And an indicator of more social adjustment (and therefore political disruption) to come.

Vial and Bomm describe big changes in the market, the communities and the environment that I have also witnessed. Some irrigators and entitlement holders have made a lot of money, which has allowed them to hedge their risks in agriculture and commit a lot of money to water. The overall result has been a decline in broadacre farming in favour of permanent plantings – the exact reverse of what the key architects of the 2004 and 2007 water reforms envisaged for our dry continent. Vial has worked around the world in agricultural research and he told me the Murray-Darling Basin is 'exceedingly variable on a world standard and we are not honouring that truth.'

'There has been a creative element to the destruction so far,' Vial says. 'There have been opportunities even for broadacre irrigation. But the speed and magnitude of movement of entitlements and temporary transfers wasn't envisaged and it's testing the limits of river function and testing the limits of whole regions and societies that are going through the destruction process. I doubt whether the fathers of the reform process would have seen it come this far, particularly the spatial distribution of water use, and wealth from irrigation as a consequence.'

Bomm is a market kind of guy. He does not rule out that creative destruction was required. But his prediction of more permanent plantings will mean horticulturalists will try to bank more water for multiple dry years. When only so much water can be held over across seasons, there will ultimately be less available for everyone, except those crops that can pay the most for it. Bomm predicts the next to go after broadacre and dairy might be the small citrus and wine grape growers.

'Surely we have to work out whether that is good or not?' Bomm says. 'Surely we should ask, in this trend for government intervention, that perhaps highest value use solely driving markets is not the right way. I'm not convinced governments would make the right decisions, but it's worth having the discussion about what other approaches might look like and whether they are better or worse than where we are at. But it's not even on the table. And, you know, as much as we have seen upheaval, it hasn't totally flowed through. Do we wait and watch it fully play out or move to consider what else we want?'

This is the thing about this whole deregulation caper in agriculture over the past three decades. It started with cleaning out some of the hopeless, helpless and hapless bureaucracies and businesses, but eventually it reached a tipping point. Single farm failures are often put down to useless management, lack of scale, bad seasons and bad luck. You were not nimble enough for the marketing demands. You were not big enough at 500 hectares. You were not fast enough to buy the temporary water. Those high jumps keep creeping up. You are not big enough at 5000 hectares. You were not nimble enough to do the future trades. You didn't have the data to do the water trades. You don't have the technology to shave your production costs.

And then do we say to whole food-growing industries, sorry, dairy farmers, you weren't nimble enough. Milk doesn't earn enough. Sorry, wine grape growers, almonds make more money. Sorry, rice growers, we will buy from Vietnam (until they turn off the tap in a pandemic as they did in 2020). Sorry, citrus, we can buy cheaper oranges from Brazil. Eventually 80,000 farm businesses drop down to 800. Just as the supermarkets have settled into a duopoly over my lifetime. That's how it works. We turn around one day and the landscape has changed.

Chapter 13
ON SOIL

In 2020, the Nobel Peace Prize for Agriculture went to the soil scientist Rattan Lal, director of the Carbon Management and Sequestration Center at Ohio State University. Lal was raised on a small farm in India and sees air, water and soil as the 'trinity'. He argues the case for soil rights, because soil underpins the food system and is a living thing. His work has been used in the development of the UN's sustainable development goals. He has called out the useless either/or public debate that insists we have to choose between agriculture or addressing climate change. We need to do both.

'The problem is technology without wisdom. We have to use technology – wisely. We keep blaming agriculture for environmental problems. How can you blame agriculture as long as you like to eat food three times a day? We have an obligation to make agriculture a solution.'[1]

According to Lal's calculations, 135 gigatons of carbon has been lost from agricultural soils, and if you combine that with lost vegetation from clearing trees and draining wetlands, you get to a figure of 500 gigatons. Lal believes soil can sequester about 180 gigatons. Add vegetation and he calculates that we could sequester 330 in total. This would draw down 150 parts of carbon dioxide per million (ppm) in the atmosphere. In October 2020, the world CO_2 was tracking at 411 ppm.

Lal says he is driven by the need to achieve food and nutritional security while improving water and air quality to mitigate climate change. His life's work is to improve the soil and he is convinced it is part of the solution but it cannot be the whole solution. It is what he calls the 'most economic, natural, low-hanging fruit'.

To celebrate my birthday, I headed down the Hume Highway to a two-day soils workshop. It seemed necessary to brush up on my science if I were to understand this most fundamental of fundamentals – earth.

In the past, governments provided ongoing learning for farmers. These days, the diligent farmer can get up to date through industry-body research magazines, but government agricultural extension education that actively teaches farmers is difficult to find. Now, if you want to learn something about farming outside university, private training is pretty much the only option. If I want an ecologist to give some advice, or a soil scientist to tell me what's going on in the ground, I have to go down the private route. If a farmer is lucky, the courses might be part-funded by the state government, or she might hitch a ride with a university research program, but farmers can be wary of that option because it usually means quite a bit more work. The state soil conservation departments might be good to hire for a bit of offhand advice and earth works, like any other contractor, but that's about it. A drought workshop is the closest you'll likely get to the old government extension service.

That is important because without science-based courses how will the average farmer – currently in their late fifties – get up to date? The farmer needs to be across the latest science around agronomy, weeds, soil, stock management, and how to look after land or animals in a drought, and that's before you come to the business side. It's highly likely that the farmers in control of management decisions right now are at least thirty years out of formal education. If they have no training, their knowledge might be picked up from previous generations.

Still, this puts them way ahead of me. So I was heading to Bibbaringa, an Upper Murray property owned by farmer Gillian Sanbrook, to make mud pies and talk soil with agroecologist David Hardwick.

Sanbrook runs her place on regenerative principles, which seek to improve land across a range of verifiable measures like soil carbon, native habitat and tree cover. She runs beef cattle but the animals are simply a tool to serve the aim of regeneration. She began learning holistic management techniques with the Zimbabwean ecologist and farmer Allan Savory during his visits to Australia in the 1990s when she was living on a sheep stud in the New South Wales Riverina area. Savory, who is now eighty-five and splits his time between the US and Zimbabwe, rose to international prominence developing land management methods to combat desertification in grazing lands by using domestic livestock to mimic wild herd behaviour. He experimented with shepherding stock in larger concentrated herds while reducing their time in any particular location in order to let grassland recover and restore ecological function. The technique disturbs grassland and concentrates the herd's dung before the animals move off quickly, keeping hard feet off brittle landscapes for longer to allow regeneration. Savory's methods ensure land managers know their feed budgets intimately and plan thoroughly for changing weather patterns, so they are not caught short on feed. His method also seeks to align management with values. Will this decision serve my ultimate goal? Protection of landscape is a priority. Reducing drastically, or completely removing, livestock in times of droughts is common for holistic managers. Savory switched the mindset for land managers who follow his methods. For example, livestock managers might refer to themselves as cattle graziers because cattle are their priority. Holistic managers often refer to themselves as grass farmers because keeping ground cover to protect soil is their number one goal.

When Sanbrook moved to Bibbaringa, half an hour north of Albury, she and her former husband saw an opportunity to rehabilitate 990 hectares. The average rainfall was supposed to be a reliable 750 millimetres but is now averaging 500. It is hilly country, with big sweeping valleys. Sanbrook's place has swathes of tree corridors, planted along waterways like the posterior curves in a Brett Whiteley painting.

'I don't plant trees in straight lines,' she says as she takes me to the top of a hill to survey the landscape. She also uses the techniques of Natural Sequence Farming, most often associated with Australian farmer Peter Andrews and the Mulloon Institute, based at Bungendore just outside Canberra. As a result, the water is dispersed across the landscape rather than running in great gullies carving up the hills. It's a bit like the concept of a chain of ponds: allow water more time to sit and disperse, giving the soil the time to absorb moisture and cut down the chances of erosion. Sanbrook pulls out a photo album like a proud mother, revealing a detailed documentation of the growing ground and tree cover. She was breeding cattle for a time but decided to drop it for a more flexible agistment operation to better respond to the changing climate. When she has grass, she fattens other people's cattle. When there is none, the land can sit.

'I aim for 100 per cent ground cover 100 per cent of the time. That's my philosophy and I won't sacrifice that for anything. I feel that the only way to build soil is with minimum inputs and to use the animals as a tool. The last three or four years I've been trading [cattle] and I can offload when the water is low and the grass isn't growing. I can happily destock.'

Sanbrook also uses her place as a venue to share agricultural knowledge, extending farmers' interests in unexpected ways. For example, as an art lover, she has matched farmers with artists as a way of them exchanging information. The farmers taught the artists about their approach to land management and the artists taught farmers their approach to observation.

'We want to care for the land/country. In fact, we become land artists or land becomes our canvas of creativity. For every action we make there is a reaction, so we just have to make sure it is in the right direction,' says Sanbrook.

It required an opening up of minds, like tuning into a different channel. There was a nervousness among some of the farmers at first. But these are the intangibles. The sum of the whole was greater than the parts.

Agroecologist David Hardwick has travelled throughout Australia and Asia teaching people about soil and ecology through Landcare extension, technical education institutions (TAFE) and private consulting. He has worked with cane farmers in North Queensland, mango farmers in the Northern Territory, regenerative farmers, conventional farmers, graziers, croppers, permaculture enthusiasts and smallholders in Asia. He has explained the science thousands of times and studies adult education techniques to hone his skills to get maximum transfer of knowledge. He has a unique way of making the complex world of soil interesting, using role-play and boxes of wrapped lollies to represent the elements - nitrogen, carbon and phosphorus as well as bacteria, protozoa and exudates or sugars.

As the workshop began, it was both amazing and frightening to consider how little I remembered about basic biology. Dave peppered the group with questions. He drew out answers and expanded on people's knowledge. There we were, farmers and wannabes, and we had difficulty answering the most basic questions. What do plants need to grow? What do they create? How much carbon is in the air? What proportion of the air is nitrogen? What do plants give to the soil? Here were rudimentary questions of science that many people across the country – some in the business of growing stuff – cannot answer. This is not a criticism. I don't remember much biology. So for those who know this stuff, bear with me. Let me give you a taste of David's soil 101 explainer, focusing on carbon, nitrogen and phosphorus.

Plants need four essential things to grow. Sunlight for photosynthesis. Water via their roots. Carbon from the air. Nutrients from the soil. They grab those four elements to create oxygen for the air and sugars or exudates for the soil. In the process, they create lovely vegetation or plant biomass, whether it's grass, timber or herbage and their roots. Those plants cycle, whether they be a single wheat plant or a tree, eventually breaking down to feed the bacteria and the fungi.

Carbon is currently tracking at around 0.04 per cent of the Earth's atmosphere. Carbon is a trace element in the air. Even though that amount seems small, we know it is too high and is causing climate change. That's why we thank the harvest gods for the brilliant technology called a plant, which is busy grabbing that carbon, fixing it and turning it into sugars, or carbon dribble as Hardwick called it.

'We all need carbs as energy except Pete Evans,' he jokes. 'The deal is the plant gives carbon energy to soil in return for nutrients.'

Increasing organic carbon is good for soil and good for productivity because it makes soil healthy, more fertile and more absorbent.

The other thing in the air is nitrogen – 78 per cent of the air, in fact.

'Nitrogen is like Donald Trump's Twitter account,' says Hardwick. 'It's volatile. It doesn't tie up like other nutrients. It's such a hard nutrient to manage. It likes to live as a gas so the challenge is to keep it in the topsoil. The best way is to attach the nitrogen to carbon.'

That's why it's beneficial for farmers to build carbon in their soils by increasing the humus layer – the lovely black stuff that television gardeners rave about. Farmers have traditionally used legumes such as lupins or soybeans or clover as part of their crop rotation to increase nitrogen. The reason is legumes have developed with a symbiotic bacteria called rhizobium in nodules in the roots. Rhizobium exchange nitrogen from the air for sugars from the root zone. In the process they break the bonds of nitrogen and carbon, which provides the nitrogen in a more plant-accessible form. If soil is functioning well, Hardwick says no sales docket from your local global agribusiness is required.

There are many other free-living bacteria and fungi in soil. The big question is, how much are they contributing to the process? And what does the addition of a lot of inputs do to that bacteria and soil life? The other way for farmers to add elements like nitrogen is to buy it into the system to put back the good stuff shipped out every time a wheat crop is sold for our bread, or a lamb is sold for our chops.

This self-organising system, soil, is the key to the whole show. That is why conventional farmers in Australia, particularly, have moved towards the no-till systems that drill the seed directly into the soil without the plough. Old-fashioned ploughing mucks up soil's capacity to lay down the good stuff, like carbon and nitrogen. It upsets the whole nutrient cycle. But, while no-till farming gets big ticks for keeping ground cover, it does use chemicals like glyphosate to kill plants before sowing, precisely so that farmers don't need to get out the plough.

Hardwick uses the Queensland cane farmers as an example of a self-perpetuating cycle in the farm economy. Sugar-cane yield was declining, compaction of soils was a big issue and the industry wanted to find out why. Low yield means low incomes. So a bunch of scientists got together from the CSIRO and the Queensland Department of Primary Industries, among other bodies, and produced a report on ten years of research, which was given the catchy title 'Sugar Yield Decline Joint Venture'.[2]

'They found the reasons, nationally, sugar yields were going like that was poor soil health,' said Hardwick. 'The three specifics were compaction, low soil carbon and soil-borne diseases. While that research was going on, guess what the cane farmers were advised to do to keep soil yields? More fertiliser. So while research was saying it's a soil-functioning issue, the guys were told to put on more fertiliser.

'There is only so far that putting fuel in the tank will fix the missing wheel. At some point, it ain't going to solve the problem. Now the cane farmers are all regulated and legislated and we all think they are wrecking the reef. It's not their fault. They were told to put on more fertiliser. The industry told them to solve the yield problem by loading up with more.'

David explains that when soil loses structure and organic matter, and root systems are stressed, it loses a balanced diet because the self-organised nutrient cycle is no longer functioning and its complex food is not providing the trace elements it needs to have.

'I can solve it by buying a spray, all good. We get to the point where we literally flood this system with solubility. That's a pollutant but it still gives you a result, but there's so many side effects from that result – agronomically in that paddock alone, apart from the wider ones. You have no more structure and larger year-to-year variability. You can get away with this and you can even make it pay, but the problem is, over time, you start to get secondary side effects in soil function.

'There is more to nutrient management than having nutrients there. This system is not one way, it is driven by diverse plant communities, which drive a high level of nutrient cycling in the landscape. The whole show has to self-organise or no one can reproduce. That's the bottom line. Why has the earth got the right level of oxygen? There's a level of self-organisation going on.'

David teaches farmers to take a more integrated approach. He uses the example of integrated pest management. That is, rather than reaching for the drum of pesticide first up, you consider all of the factors in the ecological system. Chemicals are not forbidden but are minimised. 'Integrated pest management doesn't focus on a chemical to kill the insect in its habitat. It looks at the beneficial insects, looks at the time of the year, the insect's life cycle. That's ecology – considering an animal interacting with its environment. As soon as you bring that field of science into ag science, it changes the way you do ag science. Most conventional agronomists and ag scientists don't have any ecological training at all.

'This is an inherent problem that the skill set of the scientists involved in industrial ag excludes in the main ecological thinking. You do get good conventional agronomists that have been around the ridges and done stuff and they always think ecologically. They don't know it but they are always looking at things interacting.'

The farmer we met in 'On the middle', Pete Mailler, studied ag science and he is quite sceptical of the marketing around regenerative agriculture. But to him there's no question that agriculture in its current form is mining the system. This much is clear in the observable run-down in natural productivity and biodiversity.

'We are not putting it on at the rate we are taking it out. Add up all of the micronutrients, trace elements, macronutrients that we pull out of the paddock, then look at two things: 1. What would it cost me to put all of that back in?'

He rattles off a list of elements in the natural ecosystem that contribute to your food and fibre – potassium, phosphorus, copper, sulphur, zinc, iron, among others – and then considers what it would mean for the farmer to replace all of those things in some form.

'We don't get paid enough in the produce to be able to put it all back in. What we have systematically done is run it down until we need to put some on.'

In his words, the potential of the model is determined by the most limiting factor. Or the system is only as strong as its weakest link. For a long time, water has been our most limiting factor. National Party agriculture ministers are particularly fond of saying that agriculture is ready to take off – 'just add water'. But soil is also a limiting factor. Soil needs balance.

'You need this much nitrogen, this much phosphorus, this much potassium, this much sulphur, and if you're deficient in one of those, it doesn't matter if you've got all the phosphorus in the world. If you're deficient in sulphur, that's the thing that limits it. We keep running around saying "What have we got to add? What have we got to add?" But we're never replacing everything, we're only just putting in what we need to keep the system pushing.

'In order to keep producing, we are going to need to put these things back in, but at the moment we don't. For example, I don't apply a lot of potassium. But every time we send something off the farm, we're sending out potassium. So by definition we are mining. If you send something away from the farm, it has a certain nutrient load. That is the most basic measurement of it.'

This much becomes obvious when you compare farmed country to country that has had less disturbance. Mailler describes a common conversation among farmers who talk about the benefit of going on to 'new country'. New country is country that hasn't been farmed before 1788. 'Well, if that doesn't tell you instantly that you're mining the country, nothing ever will.'

'A lot of regen ag conversations, they seem to think magically the soil biota can fix and address all these problems, and it's just not true, but certainly there are biological responses that we can't explain in a traditional scientific way. Those responses aren't consistent or even general and farmers need more certainty. The work being done on soil biology and health is really important and hasn't been prioritised enough.'

These arguments between conventional and regenerative farmers take place in the main because soil science is so complex. In the noughties drought, many paddocks blew away. In the most recent drought, farmers were taking much more care to keep their ground cover as armour for their soil. No one argues about the goal of keeping ground cover anymore, but still, you do see soil that is bare and blowing away in a drought. What a soil needs and how it self-organises, however, is much more opaque. It is hidden and it's harder to go to scientific umpires and come away with a firm conclusion. We can get soil tests that tell some of the story but not the whole story. When Mailler was studying agricultural science at university thirty years ago, students were taught plant nutrition in a contained chemistry model so they could control the system. They were taught soil biology, but it was hard to manage, so they used a hydroponic system that allowed students to see exactly what they fed the plant and how it reacted. That chemistry model is the basis of what many current farmers know about growing stuff.

'You learn a lot from the chemistry model, but soil biology is important too. We know soils with higher organic carbon can store more water and exchangeable nutrients. We know we can do better things with soil. People with veggie gardens mulch. Mulching does wonderful things for the soil. From an ag perspective, farmers are trying to do that on a massive scale as best we can. It is rewarding when we find earthworms in our fields, but we can't afford to go and put thousands of tonnes of mulch on the paddock. But if you think about it, by bringing in straw to your garden you are actually importing all of those things. We can't do it on this scale on the landscape, and the bigger you get, the harder it is to do and in the end the farm business must export more than it imports to survive.'

The science has come a long way since Tony Abbott first talked up the prospect of soil sequestration in 2010. Then, it was dubbed 'soil magic'. A decade later, the major limitations remain – carbon is hard to consistently sequester particularly with a lack of rainfall and it is expensive to measure accurately. The government wants to fund the technology to make it cheaper for farmers to measure soil carbon. The Coalition government's goal is to reduce the cost of its measurement to under $3 per hectare per year, with a view to farmers getting paid to build it under their feet. Many farmers consider measuring soil carbon across the breadth of a farm is not worth it in an economic sense because there are no price signals to improve soil carbon. Yet.

The head of the Soil Cooperative Research Centre (Soil CRC), Dr Michael Crawford, thinks the major hurdle for farmers is not so much the cost of measurement but finding out how to sequester carbon in a reliable and profitable way, given farmers have to improve land and make a living. Right now, it is proving hard to build carbon in many Australian soils and keep it there. It is seasonal and it takes a long time.

'Reducing soil carbon measurement costs and saying it will increase soil carbon sequestration is like saying, get a better stopwatch and you will run faster. Reducing soil carbon measurement costs to (hopefully) encourage more farmers to participate in the Emissions Reduction Fund is goal displacement – it doesn't necessarily mean that more carbon is being sequestered.'

If governments are serious about relying on building soil carbon, more research funding is needed. (In the 2021 budget, the federal government committed almost $200 million over four years, the vast majority of which will be used to assess the holes in our national soil data, plug them up with some funded soil tests from individual farms and provide a little farmer training for soil education. The details remain sketchy at time of publication. While it sounds like a lot of money, more than half of the funding, which will cover the Soil Monitoring and Extension Pilot Program, comes out of the existing National Landcare Program, which means other things miss out.

This is an ongoing pea and thimble budgeting trick consistently played on Landcare, where the federal government makes a flashy announcement to make new money with dry-cleaned old money look like new money.)[3]

The other big thing holding back more soil carbon sequestration, according to Crawford, is the need for local context in soil research. It is hard to apply something in one part of the country to another part across a broad range of seasons. The Soil CRC works with twenty grower groups across Australia, and more are clamouring to be involved because they know local context is everything to understand what is best for farming in their place. But the CRC doesn't have enough funds to do the trials with the existing groups, let alone more farmer groups.

So place-based research is required to really understand how to get better results out of farming by building soil health and laying down carbon. One of Crawford's researchers, associate professor Vaughan Higgins, calls it 'softening the science and hardening the local knowledge'. That is, make the best science more accessible and relevant to the average farmer and back up local anecdotes and experience with science in a local landscape.

We need to find a way to help more independent extension advisors into paddocks to teach for their area. Increasingly, the Australian government has subcontracted extension and research out to agribusiness companies and their retail agronomists. As good as some of those agronomists may be, the business model is conflicted – many of them also have a sales imperative. This is not just an issue for companies involved in selling conventional chemicals and fertiliser products; it will equally be a problem for those selling 'biologicals' used in self-described regenerative systems.

The Rural Research and Development Corporations and CRCs are good at top-down research into how to get better at growing stuff nationally, or knowing more about soil, but they are remote from the average farmer. If you are part of a cutting-edge grower group, which exist in some areas, great. But if you are head down, bum up, as a small to medium grower, you might not get much contact. That remoteness has exacerbated farmers' isolation from research unless they are personally inclined to seek out the best advice.

The dearth of independent advice has caused a great fracturing in consensus about farming systems, causing the high-profile shouting matches. Regenerative agriculture versus conventional. Subsidies versus no support. Government doesn't need to play a paternal role but if society wants the best, healthiest food-growing systems, where does the diligent farmer go for the most independent, forthright advice?

Former governor-general the late Michael Jeffery was the first patron of Soils for Life and the first national soils advocate in Australia. He grew up in Wiluna, a little outback town known as the gateway to the Canning Stock Route, nearly 1000 kilometres northeast of Perth. The traditional owners of the extraordinary red soil around Wiluna are the Martu people.

Jeffery became passionate about soil in the latter part of his career. In his first report to the Australian government, in 2017, he urged government to consider soil, water and vegetation as key national natural strategic assets and to better support farmers, given they were managing up to 60 per cent of the continent. As a former soldier, he recommended an annual assessment on the current state of global food, soil and water in conjunction with the government's security agency, the Office of National Intelligence.

Jeffery also recommended much better funding of agricultural research and farmer education, independent of companies with vested interests. He used the debate over glyphosate as an example. Jeffery told me in an interview in 2018 that research needed to be conducted independent of chemical companies. (In October 2020, Richard Dickmann, the then head of public and government affairs at Bayer, was appointed to the board of the Grains Research and Development Corporation. The GRDC is funded by government and grower levies for independent research. Bayer is the manufacturer of glyphosate. Dickmann has since left Bayer and at publication remains on the GRDC board.)

'That's why you need government-run research stations, in my opinion, with properly trained agricultural scientists,' Jeffery told me. 'We ought to know if [glyphosate] is good, bad, indifferent or okay in little bits. If it is causing problems and people are being dishonest, then there should be all hell to pay. It is a little like the banks doing things improperly while knowing it. I suspect, in part, if there are companies who do this, they may have to be held accountable for what they have done.'[4]

Michael Crawford believes farm extension will never go back to a broadly government-funded model for two reasons. First, speaking with the experience of a former Victorian agriculture extension officer, he says a lot of people still missed out in that system. Second, the role of the public and private sector has moved on and why should farmers get free advice when other businesses do not? He hears the concerns about fertiliser and chemical company representatives but counters that there are still independent advisors who work for a fee.

In his role as head of the Soil CRC, Crawford speaks with many shareholders with an interest in soil. He says that in 2018, five out of ten of his conversations were about regenerative agriculture. By 2020, nine out of ten of them were. These are conversations with everyone. Farmers, investors, government, consumers. Australia's raging summer of bushfires in 2019–20 amplified the conversations exponentially, as did the pandemic, and concerns about food sovereignty and personal health. Regenerative agriculture is crowding conversations in agriculture among farmers, at barbecues, field days and on social media, because it is indisputable that eaters are developing very strong opinions about what they put in their bodies.

'My take on it is that after last summer – when effectively people in Canberra, Sydney and Melbourne lost their summer because of bushfires, or smoke from bushfires – they tied that back to climate change. It was made real for them. And in turn they said, "The government is not doing anything about it, so what can we do?" They started saying, "We can have an impact by the choices we make, by the things we buy and consume." And that's when you started hearing a lot more noise about food. Where it comes from. And they said, "Wouldn't it be good if all farmers did regenerative agriculture?" But without knowing what it means and what farmers are doing already.'

Food companies are looking to demonstrate their credentials by using their often massive buying power to shift market practices. General Mills, the sixth-largest food company in the world, which owns Häagen-Dazs, Old El Paso and Betty Crocker, to name a few of their brands, has committed to 'advance regenerative agriculture on one million acres' by 2030. Given the size of the US – 2.4 billion acres – this is a sliver. But you can see where their marketing is headed. They have supported farmer pilots in soil, wheat and dairy, committing to measure the outcome. Their global director of sourcing and operations sustainability, Kevin O'Donnell, told *Successful Farming*: 'We don't simply want to have a "tick the box" approach for the practices being implemented. We want to prove the business case by actually measuring outcomes in the places that matter most. In addition to improving farmer profitability, we also want to measure increases in soil organic carbon, because we believe that climate volatility is a real issue and a real threat to our business AND that farmers can be a major part of the solution for climate change through their ability to sequester carbon in soil.

'We also want to measure things like above-ground biodiversity, which again is a key unlock for getting Mother Nature to do some of the things farmers traditionally invest a lot of money in trying to get synthetic inputs to do for pests and disease. Water stewardship is another area where we want to measure outcomes.'[5]

General Mills' definition remains fuzzy and would fit most diligent Australian farmers I know. Understand the context of your farm operation. Minimise soil disturbance with low tillage or ideally no tillage. Maximise crop diversity. Keep the soil covered year round. Maintain a living root system in the ground year round. Integrate livestock.

Crawford largely agrees. He nominates five principles: reduced tillage; keeping soil covered, maintaining living roots for as long as possible; increased diversity in time (paddock rotation); space (multispecies crops); and integrating livestock. This takes us back to a more mixed farming system that acknowledges animals have an important function in the landscape (which also means the push by some climate activists to remove all livestock from the planet is simplistic).

'I would argue all farmers are trying to reduce inputs because no farmer wants to spend money for the hell of it. I would argue that 90 per cent of those principles are good ag practice. Not all farmers are doing it but it's what the science is saying is delivering the best outcomes. In a lot of discussions there are barriers being put up and there is an "us and them" situation. It's not helped by language such as "if you're not regenerative then you are industrial". Or "if you're not regenerative, then you are degenerative".'

Crawford says that while there are opportunities, he spends a bit of time tempering the wild expectations that we can offset all greenhouse gas emissions by building soil carbon in Australia. In Australian agricultural regions, many areas are generally lower rainfall, with poorer soils that often don't have the clay content for moisture retention. In those parts that do have higher rainfall and higher biomass, there are often also high temperatures and higher decomposition rates.

'Building organic matter, because of all the benefits organic matter brings to soil, will bring you greater sustainability and resilience and potentially higher productivity through improved soil structure, water holding capacity and water retention, biological activity and fertility etc.,' says Crawford.

He can already see investors – from the big superannuation companies to private equity firms – holding a greater stake in agriculture because of the potential for long-term profitability, a reflection of the trends we looked at in 'On corporatisation'. Those companies have to report to their members and their shareholders that the agriculture assets are well managed for good long-term outcomes. 'Therefore, we should be doing regenerative agriculture.'

'But if you are doing it to make some money out of being paid for sequestering soil carbon, it's a goal displacement. Farmers in the foreseeable future will still make the majority of their money out of growing crops, livestock, meat and wool, not being paid for carbon.'

Of course, the rules set by governments make a big difference to how farmers can transition and adapt to the new landscape. Someone who has been intimately connected and persistently disappointed in the roundabout of carbon policies is economist, government advisor, sometime ambassador and polymath Ross Garnaut. He completed his first Australian government climate change policy review in 2008 and three years later updated it.[6] Labor and the Greens implemented a carbon price based on his work and while the carbon price was dumped in 2014 by Tony Abbott's government, the Coalition hung on to the Gillard government's Carbon Farming Initiative, which also came out of Garnaut's report.

Garnaut has influenced many debates that affect all parts of the economy, but he has a particular affection for agriculture. He is a prolific writer: at last count more than forty books. You can find a chapter on agricultural economics in most of them, a fact Garnaut puts down to growing up in Perth when it was like a small town. In those days, everyone had relatives in the bush. He spent school holidays either in the wheatbelt or dairy country. His interest in farming was sparked, and, with wife Jayne, he owned a farm for two decades. (In the interests of disclosure, it neighboured ours.) He was chairman of the Australian Centre for International Agricultural Research for six years, and for seven years was the director and chairman of the International Food Policy Research Institute, the world's leading institution for research on rural development, based in Washington, DC.

He has consistently made the point that Australia is exceptionally well endowed with land and sea to absorb carbon and grow biomass. The mountain ash forests in Victoria contain the most dense carbon stocks in the world. It is not just the fertile areas that offer potential, but semi-arid ones as well. 'Large areas of slow-growing plants add up to large quantities of carbon,' he writes in his latest book, *Reset*.[7] Garnaut sees these as not only opportunities for climate mitigation and zero emissions industries but also substantial job creation that could lead to full employment by 2025.

But unlocking Australia's rich potential for sequestering landscape carbon through soil or vegetation would be a whole lot easier if there were a carbon market. With a reinstated market, he reckons rural Australia would have a large new source of income. If the Australian carbon market were still in operation, the nation would have been part of the European Emissions Trading Scheme and farmers would have been selling carbon credits into the EU at $60 a tonne.[8] Instead, our farmers are left a system that requires a lot of upfront personal investment with the hope of winning an auction in a very limited carbon market within a small budget of $2 billion. If the enthusiastic farmer is willing to do all that, they can receive $17 a tonne.

'It's as if anyone selling wool or mutton or beef was told, "Do your best and grow stuff, but you may or may not be able to sell it, and if you sell it, we will give you a quarter of the world price,"' Garnaut says.

Garnaut has suggested that the federal government expand funding for its Emissions Reduction Fund to cover more eligible reductions from the land sector. Alternatively, governments – federal or state – could require coal and natural gas companies to offset their fugitive emissions by buying carbon credits from land managers. This would effectively turbocharge the carbon farming industry.[9] So far, his suggestions have fallen on deaf ears because of the intractable politics.

He considers it 'very strange' that climate-change politics remain a partisan issue in Australia and the US, unlike other developed countries, including those of Europe, and in Japan, Korea, New Zealand or Canada. He puts it down to two reasons: the influence of Rupert Murdoch's News Corp, which has consistently attacked the science of climate change and action to mitigate it, in particular the carbon pricing scheme. And, second, the fossil fuel industry. By way of example, he names mining magnate and former politician

Clive Palmer's political intervention, funding political advertisements against Labor at the 2019 election. Palmer actually personally claimed credit for the Coalition victory.[10]

'I think the influence in News Corp is quite important. It's the dominant source of information in the US through Sky News, and in Australia through its domination of the print media. But it's just one of lots of voices in other places. That's probably the biggest single reason,' he says.

'Second, the fossil energy industry is very big in Australia and we've got fewer constraints on funding of political parties and campaigns. What Clive Palmer's done would be illegal in most democracies and all the money in the fossil energy fuel industry and the country National Party is funded heavily from the fossil energy industry so I think you have to go to some of those political economy issues to explain why it's partisan and divisive in Australia and not other countries.'

Garnaut makes the point that the world is moving on regardless of Australian carbon politics, and farmers will be impacted with or without a change in domestic policy. Europe is backing carbon border taxes already, while many companies have changed their supply chains to support zero emissions products for a market edge or to align with their values.

Garnaut also called for a big research effort to drill down into the science of regenerative agriculture. Any new area of economic activity requires that knowledge to maximise the value of land when carbon is part of the 'value stack'. He echoes Crawford's and Jeffery's advice that government needs to spend the research dollars to reap the benefits.

'One problem we've got is we have gutted Australia's capacity for agricultural research. We used to be the world leader through state departments of agriculture, the universities and the CSIRO. They all had very strong research efforts – it was the main thing CSIRO did. Well, we have gutted that. We only have European-style farming in Australia because we based it on a huge amount of research in the first 180 years of white settlement. But we have run down that capacity. So we are losing our leading position and that's a pity.'

In the days before the soil workshop, the Australian government named soil carbon as one of the five technologies in which it would invest to reduce emissions.

In 2020 soil tests are expensive and only give an indicative guide. We know the NFF has a goal to increase farming output from $61 billion to $100 billion by 2030, and net zero emissions by 2050. Western Australian farmers already have a more ambitious target of net zero emissions by 2030. Meat and Livestock was the first major industry body to set a goal that by 2030 'Australian beef, lamb and goat production, including lot feeding and meat processing, will make no net release of greenhouse gas (GHG) emissions into the atmosphere.'[11]

Goals are important. But a lot of farmers look at these goals and wonder how they will achieve them. Inherent in the goals is the acknowledgement that the way we grow food has a) an effect on the natural world; and b) we can improve the way it is having that effect. The message these goals send is that farmers want to do better. But how? One senior public servant and scientist quipped to me, 'Apologies to Matt Damon, but they are going to have to science the shit out of that.'

Soil carbon levels have declined and to raise them is a slow climb in all but the rarest cases, unless you have irrigated water. It is harder to improve carbon in hotter, drier and warming climates. Acidity and soil compaction make it more difficult. Some farmers have arrested a portion, but not all, of the carbon decline. Some have built their carbon slowly but surely. A landmark CSIRO study concluded that, 'Although the implementation of more conservative land management practices may lead to a reduced rate of loss of, or indeed a relative gain in [Soil Organic Carbon], absolute SOC stocks may still be slowly declining.'[12]

When I spoke to Mike Grundy, he had just retired as research director of soil and landscapes in the Agriculture and Food Business unit of CSIRO. He was involved in the conversations on the National Outlook report covered in 'On risk'. In 2019 Grundy gave a lecture in which he delivered a stark message. Whether Australia continues on the 'slow decline' pathway or whether we get our act together and develop an 'outlook vision', soil has to remain at the heart of both futures.

'Our growers, our farmers, our graziers are key players in this choice, and the soil in many ways is the frontline, and they need to be better armed to cope with this, and I actually don't think they are currently armed sufficiently,' he said in the lecture. 'You could make the case that the soil knowledge on the scale that we need to give them has been the limiting step.'

Grundy said that he was more confident we had the answer to unlocking a better future for Australia through soil improvement than he had been ten or twenty years ago. Over the last five years, many exciting things have happened. So where are we up to? Grundy sees the need for farmers to move from precision agriculture to a more responsive agriculture, which is possible because technology allows people to manage more finely what they are putting into the system. So tractors not only drive themselves but talk to farmers. Soil probes tell you the level of water in the soil. Knowing the levels of elements like nitrogen combined with finer-grained detail about the climate and the season ahead will help the farmer pick a way through their complex system.

'The farmer and the farm can have conversations with each other, then have tools to respond to opportunities that arrive, such as the varieties to use for short or long season, or the flexibility to understand useful livestock genetics. That is all part of a package and we are very close to achieving it if we take the view of highly responsive real-time farming. Some of the hardest bits of doing that are in the soil. New ways of understanding what's happening in soils using sensor networks, and intelligent machines and devices, mean the enigma that is soil might be close to being solved.

'That could be seen by some as reductionist. I'm not talking about a recipe. Recipes work when we can control the environment. I'm arguing for farmers to play what's in front of them because they have better knowledge of the dynamics of the farm environment. I don't think that's traditional farming or regenerative farming. Some of the profits and the promoters tend to promote recipes. Do this and you will have the solution. Everything we've learnt about agriculture and the environment punishes those who stick slavishly to a recipe. We can find a way through.'

Pivoting the practice of agriculture is increasingly being seen as one of a suite of solutions to global warming. Settling on the best way to farm creates angst among farmers because the answer depends on the place and the context. Strip away all the shouting and arguments about whether it is regenerative, conventional, biodynamic or organic and come back to soil.

'It doesn't matter whether I'm organic or conventional, as long as I am working with my soil biology,' says Hardwick.

My political instincts tell me straight soil science is a culturally safe space no matter what the farming system. That is because regenerative versus conventional has taken on the hue of a political culture war and we need to avoid that at all costs. The beauty of talking about farming through the soil is that you can leave your baggage at the door. You can argue about whether to use chemical or biological or zero inputs, but you can't argue about where nitrogen comes from, or whether mycorrhizal fungi exist, or the fact that increased carbon levels make for healthier soil.

Neither can you deny that global soils are in danger, nor the contribution of that soil loss to global warming. If eaters think healthy soil is a goal worth chasing, land managers need time and support to work on their soil. Rattan Lal reminds us how 'each scientific and innovative idea undergoes three stages: (a) I don't believe it, it can't be true; (b) I don't have time, I am too busy; and (c) I told you so. This has been the case ever since the debate that the Earth is flat and the sun rotates around it.'

Writing in the *European Journal of Soil Science* in 2019, Lal thinks we are at stage c when it comes to soil: 'Humanity must wake up to the fact that soil degradation by land misuse and soil mismanagement is intricately interconnected with global warming, food insecurity, the drought–flood syndrome, eutrophication of water and dwindling of biodiversity. Thus, soil scientists must work towards reconciling the need for advancing the United Nations (UN) Sustainable Development Goals (SDGs) with the absolute necessity of minimizing the conflict between agriculture and nature. In addition to advancing the frontiers of knowledge, soil scientists must also translate their data into a language that policymakers can understand and civic society and land managers can relate to. This is especially true regarding the importance of sustainable soil management for adaptation and mitigation of anthropogenic global warming.'[13]

Translating science into a language that land managers can understand, to its application on farms, is not always easy. That's what those skilled and government-funded extension officers were for. Land managers are often very smart, but earth science is incredibly complex and new developments in soil are happening rapidly.

I want a simple recipe for the perfect soil. David Hardwick tells me it depends on the locality. Mike Grundy says there is no recipe. Michael Crawford says it's not a tick-a-box exercise.

Lal distils his broad principles in his *Soil Science* paper. His basic principles for sustainable management of soils of agroecosystems are:

(a) keep the soil always covered and protected
(b) eliminate or minimise mechanical perturbation
(c) replace whatever is harvested/removed (e.g. nutrients, soil organic carbon)
(d) enhance activity and species diversity of soil biota (e.g. microorganisms, mycorrhizal fungi and earthworms)
(e) integrate crops with livestock and trees in complex farming systems, and
(f) recycle all of the byproducts back into the soil.

I can hear farmers from varied systems saying, 'Hey, I already do some/all of that stuff.' But for me, Lal's key message comes with an important rider. Avoid or minimise herbicides. And, by the way, you will not get the same yields.

Lal says that while 'conservation agriculture' in conjunction with cover cropping is promising, the 'use of tillage and herbicides must be avoided or minimized'. But understand that conservation agriculture 'may neither produce the maximum agronomic yield under specific situations nor sequester enough Soil Organic Carbon to mitigate climate change by itself'. Still, he says, 'it is an effective strategy to conserve soil and water, set in motion soil regenerative processes, and reverse the degradation trends'. But that may mean sacrificing 'some crop yield for the short-term', for the higher priority of long-term sustainability of agroecosystems, especially for fragile ecoregions.[14]

That is, farmers will have to 'sacrifice some crop yield for the long-term goal of sustainability'. Which means farmers will not get the same income they can from using current chemical reliant systems. This is a problem not only for many farmers but for governments, and for all eaters. Bottom line: farmers cannot maintain current incomes or keep producing such cheap food if you want a sustainable or regenerating soil system. The end.

Chapter 14

ON NATURAL VALUE

Except it is not the end. Since Norman Borlaug's Green Revolution, farmers have become so successful at feeding the world and its growing population that apparently we can now afford to live with a distribution system that wastes a third of what they produce.

Enter climate change. Add to it flatlining economic growth and wages. As we have seen, some economists now question the wisdom of our current path. Economic growth as it is currently framed is the never-ending story: in theory, we just keep growing ad infinitum, even if that means producing more with less. Except in Australia agricultural productivity has flatlined too. And arguably we are using balance sheets that only show part of the picture. One large part of the assets has always been left off the accounts of the food producer. The natural assets. The natural capital. We are not accounting for our spending in the natural world.

Humanity's connection to nature has been exercising thinkers since ancient times. The farming mindset is often about control of nature, yet it regularly yields to forces beyond its control. I have meditated for the last twenty years but it's The Farmer who has more equanimity. Seasons start with promise and then die. Crops flourish and wither. Prices rise and then fall. Prize rams find a new way to die. A cold snap and torrential rain arrive in the lambing season, as they did in 2020, leaving paddocks like a battlefield. Water pipes burst, trade wars flare, rain doesn't fall. Better luck next year, The Farmer says.

The contradictory impulses around the control fantasy come from living within the natural world but also making an income from it. The control is reflected in agricultural products marketed as weapons of war against nature. At the same time, the observation and yielding to nature are also a part of the farming instinct. The Farmer notices well before me that there are no bees in the Paterson's curse. Or that the ironbarks are flowering at the wrong time. Or that shingleback lizards are having a good season. Funny, he says, I haven't heard the sound of frogs in the back ramp for a few years.

These personal experiences ground him in the landscape. The detail of nature becomes imprinted on many. Those experiences have emotional roots, which form a filament to the natural world, even for those who might be regarded as bad land managers. This is not to excuse bad farming, but rather is an observation on why you might raise a farmer's hackles by saying they fail to understand or are destroying nature. When the political debate strays towards climate, or water, or biodiversity, or native vegetation, they feel unheard and under-appreciated, even if their actions are at odds with the wider goal of preservation.

Land managers balance two imperatives: looking after the landscape and making a living. Planting trees, setting aside habitat or fencing off a creek appeals to the landscape imperative. Finding a way to grow a decent crop with all the conventional inputs appeals to the economic imperative. If eaters are unhappy with some practices and want farmers to change, they have to understand that a farmer cannot be all for landscape regeneration without making a living – unless someone is paying for that regeneration.

Ken Henry's father was a timber cutter, making railway sleepers from felling trees. The Henrys sprang from a long line of 'cedar getters', working long days, from dawn until dusk. One afternoon when Ken was about thirteen, John Henry drove his three sons to the sawmill. On the ground was the biggest log Ken had ever seen. It lay there 'like the vanquished party in Jack and the Beanstalk', 2 metres in diameter and 12 metres in length, which was about all a truck could carry.[1] His father was proud to show his boys, proud of his work, given he'd had to climb so far up to get to a point where felling such a tree was possible. The monster log was just a portion of a much larger tree.

Henry and his brothers were, in turn, proud of their dad and like kids everywhere they were ready with questions.

'Dad, how old do you reckon the tree must have been?'

'Oh, very old. At least a hundred years. Anywhere up to five hundred.'

'Wow! How many houses do you reckon you could build out of that log?'

'It would make the framing for at least three houses.'

'Wow! So how much would that log be worth?'

'I'm not sure, but certainly thousands of dollars.'

'How much do you get?'

Henry credits that question, that moment, with sparking his career. His father told them that he would only get a couple of hours' wages. The sawmill would get the majority and the state government would get some royalties. The whole scene troubled young Ken. And he sensed his father and brothers were troubled too.[2]

'Our sense of unease only grew as our father told us that he had cut down hundreds of trees just like the one from which this log had come, but had had to leave them lying in the bush.' Old hardwoods typically have hollow cores and a sawmill didn't consider it economic to pay the transport costs for a log with less than one foot of solid timber around the hollow core. 'The problem was that you couldn't tell how hollow a tree was until you brought it down. That didn't trouble the sawmill, because it paid royalties only on what it took out of the forest. The Forestry Department didn't get a cent for what was left behind on the forest floor. Hundreds of trees, hundreds of years old, torn down, their carcasses left to rot where they fell.

'I don't know if I managed, at the age of thirteen, to discover the source of the sense of unease I felt at the time. But if I did, I hope that as I looked at that enormous hardwood log, I found entirely unacceptable the fact that somebody could legally appropriate, for only a few dollars, this extraordinary asset of the people of New South Wales – an asset that would take perhaps hundreds of years to replace. I hope that this smacked to me of highway robbery. I hope that I was less than impressed that the elected representatives of the people of New South Wales appeared to be demonstrating such disregard for the protection of their citizens' property. I hope I wondered about the ability of governments – and not just the venal – to redistribute wealth so arbitrarily, and to disenfranchise future generations. And I hope I vowed that one day I would do something about it.'

Henry's family story reminds me of the Cornthwaite brothers of Victoria. Bill was a farmer and George was a government surveyor.

In 1884, they were convinced that a particular mountain ash (*Eucalyptus regnans*) in Gippsland was the world's tallest tree. They figured the only way they could prove it was to cut it down and measure it. Down it came. They were proved right. The tree was 114.3 metres tall and they claimed a record.[3] A rusty plaque stands where the tree once stood.

Cultures, laws and economic signals change. Behaviour can be altered by leadership, or regulation, law or market forces. In conversations long after the felling of that tree, John Henry told his son of his remorse over the way he earnt a living and the effect of logging on the soil and the ecosystems, though he was simply providing for his family as his father had done for him. John's father, Ken's grandfather, had been given a 600-acre 'soldier-settler' block. The deal with the government meant he had to clear a certain number of acres each year to remain there. But the block was rainforest timber standing on the other side of Mount Comboyne. Ken Henry's grandfather cleared and watched as the place degraded.

'The trees were replaced by bracken fern and lantana, and the soil washed into the creeks and gullies, replacing the native fish that had long since been exploited to extinction. And I remember too that as the weeds spread and farming became too difficult, so my grandfather turned to more facile means of making a quid – stripping the native orchids out of what was left of his rainforest property. Years later I learnt that he had never had any interest in farming anyway.'

It's not impossible to imagine his grandfather, like many farmers, operating on conventional wisdom and bound by the rules of the system. And then gutted by his apparent failure. The whole story becomes an allegory for the interaction of humans and landscape. Business behaviour is driven by a mix of external influence and internal navigation. Internal navigation is harder to change, but a measure of it comes when the mob moves. As it is with sheep, so it is with humans. There is safety in numbers and change comes when it is culturally and economically safe to allow it.

Tall trees throw a long shadow. The shadow of John Henry's tree followed his son into university. Ken learnt lots of things along the way. That property rights were important. That free markets might fail. That people in commerce could benefit from exchanges that might impose costs on others, including future generations. That prices guide resource allocation. He also learnt that governments might manage the common wealth in the common interest.

'I came to the view that people's behaviours had a lot to do with their pursuit of self-interest, and that a lot of what I might have found objectionable about the things humans did could have something to do with the opportunities and incentives established by governments.'

Henry was secretary of Treasury from 2001 to 2011. His 2010 analysis of Australia's tax system came up with 138 policy recommendations to streamline the nation's overly complex processes. The Rudd government implemented just one: the resource super profits tax, known as the mining tax – a complete change in the way Australia would account for natural resources to future generations. It was swiftly killed by the incoming Abbott government after the mining industry bankrolled a political campaign that would hone its skills to defend the coal industry for another decade or more.

After Henry retired from Treasury, he was still working for that tree. Despite a lifetime reporting on the current economic measures, he has a problem with one of the biggest staples of government budgeting and economic performance: the Gross Domestic Product (GDP), used to measure the health of the economy.

When you get intimate with one piece of land, the world shrinks. It reinforces that the system is limited. Only so much grass. Only so many trees. Only so much soil carbon. Only so much water. It becomes obvious, particularly in a drought, how quickly things can turn. For the longest time, parts of farming culture reinforced a more circular economy, and in some places still do. Animal manure was used in fields. Sheds held the recycled detritus of years gone by. It is obvious on our farm. Baby formula tins hold nuts. Jam jars hold bolts. Pallets have been made into storage cupboards, timber boxes into bedside tables. Strict accounts are kept to measure the flows of products. When the wool, wheat and lambs are shipped to market, they have to be accounted for. So many sheep, this much wool. So many acres of crop, this much wheat. All accounted for.

The way countries account for resources is different in the GDP. If you look at it more plainly, it sounds like a conjuring trick. It is better than the rabbit pulled out of the hat. It is as if the resources come from nowhere.

Many people look at the national economic accounts and are seduced by the notion that GDP provides a pretty good measure of material living standards as well as a basis for considering how living standards change over time. It also forms a basis for international comparisons. Henry argues that the people who came up with GDP and the system of national accounts developed it as a way to keep track of the peaks and troughs in aggregate demand within Keynesian macro-economic policy. It was never intended to be used as an indicator of the standard of living.

The most spectacular problem with the national accounts, according to Henry, is that they make no allowance at all for the loss of natural value, the loss of raw materials and all the stuff that goes into production processes. If somebody digs a tonne of iron ore out of the ground, the national accounts regard that tonne of iron ore as having been created the moment it was extracted from the ground. It simply didn't previously exist.

If it's exported, then that full tonne of iron ore contributes to Australia's GDP in the quarter in which it is extracted and exported. There is, however, no recognition that it is now unavailable for future generations, or even the present generation.

'If it was a tonne of iron ore sitting in your backyard, you would certainly want some recognition for that. You would regard it not as income in the quarter in which you sold it; you would regard it as a sale of an asset. But that's not how the national accounts treat it.'

When economists realised this, they asked the wrong question. They sought to modify the existing system. Is there some way of adjusting the national accounts to address these problems, so we are left with a more accurate metric of what is happening to the standard of living? Henry thought for a long time that would be possible but realised he had to take a step back.

The bottom line, he says, is that the human brain is simply not that good at placing a dollar value on the condition of an environmental asset. Numerous and classic studies prove this. One involved asking three classes of students to value seabirds trapped in an oil slick. How much would students personally be prepared to pay to save 2000, 20,000, or 200,000 birds? The numbers came in at between $80 and $88, irrespective of the quantity. The students took no account of scale or scope.

'When you ask a human to process that sort of question, the brain uses a mental heuristic, a short cut,' Henry says. Incapable of imagining 2000 seabirds, let alone 200,000, it is 'most likely producing an image of one bird trapped in an oil slick'. In the same way, he says, 'You can't really ask people questions like "What value do you put on the Tarkine forests?" Or any bit of wilderness. Because the human brain is at best going to imagine one tree.'

Henry decided it would be good to start with the scientists who already have measures of condition, species, water and air quality. They won't fall into the short-cut trap.

Now, a not-for-profit called Accounting for Nature (ACN), on whose board Henry sits, has come up with a system of assessing the environment relative to, in his words, 'a pristine benchmark'. The Wentworth Group of Concerned Scientists began in 2002 to drive science on land and within water reform to protect critical environments. They have developed and accredited an Econd unit to describe the current biophysical condition of an environmental asset as a number between 0 and 100, where 100 is a measure of the asset in its undegraded state.

Once you start measuring, you are left with tables of figures that show whether the environmental asset is going up or down, whether it is trees, or a fish stock, or a riparian habitat, or the number of macroinvertebrates. Each asset is categorised in a balance sheet of sorts so you can see, year on year, the stock's movement, just as a farmer might do with sheep numbers or tonnes of grain or cherries or cauliflowers. The environmental account becomes a barometer for the land and water assets.

The big and very contentious question is whether we should place a dollar figure on the environment in the national accounts. Some environmental activists are against such accounting. George Monbiot says, 'Everything will be fungible, nothing will be valued for its own sake, place and past and love and enchantment will have no meaning. The natural world will be reduced to a column of figures.'[4]

Around the world, governments are struggling with this issue. Monbiot was reacting to the UK government's initiative to assess natural capital. The risk is that governments will allow people to inflict even more degradation, provided they can demonstrate that the commercial value of the alternative land use exceeds the assessed environmental value. Henry agrees that is a risk.

Nor do some scientists – including Peter Cosier, Henry's fellow ACN board member and a member of the Wentworth Group – want a dollar value placed on the environment; and they don't buy into the idea that you can monetise everything. Cosier just wants things measured so we know if we are doing well or badly.

Henry shares a concern about putting a monetary value on environmental amenity to use it as a basis for making commercial decisions about various land uses – with one very important exception.

'The natural capital initiatives I have had something to do with simply couldn't be applied in the way Monbiot imagines. They would necessarily give a farmer an incentive to avoid further environmental damage. Right now, the farmer loses no revenue based on environmental amenity but gains an income from cropping or grazing. And Australia's history of land clearing and mining approvals provides pretty convincing evidence that policy makers carry in their heads a valuation of environmental amenity that is not much above zero.'

When the UN's working group settled the rule book for a standardised system of national environmental accounts ten years ago, Henry had a little mental celebration, but the Australian government decided not to fund the system. So the impetus for ACN was 'to start from the ground up. Literally to build it up, paddock by paddock by paddock.' One day, Henry thinks, a future Australian government will find the approach interesting; they'll send in the

ABS to take responsibility for the measurement of environmental condition. 'Yeah, I do think that will happen,' he says.

Consider how much the debate over our natural world changes if we have a simple, standardised measure of our environmental condition. It would be the ultimate feedback loop. The Australian public can then decide what to do when the dashboard is showing that petrol in the tank is low. Is the resource renewable or not? If not, can we afford to use more of those resources? We can determine how much we are willing to blow and how much we are willing to save. Hopefully we think about our grandchildren when we are doing it.

It's a bit like the decline of coal or the rise of carbon prices. Private markets are heading in the direction of valuing natural capital whether or not governments have a consistent measure of environmental value. As a former chairman of NAB, Henry is confident that banks and their products – including the average farm loan – will soon start measuring environmental condition. This will have implications for land managers across the country and the globe. Not only are eaters demanding more environmentally sustainable ways of farming but banks will use assessments of land condition to calculate interest rates. In the same way that banks look at assets and investments when lending money, they will look at paddocks and, potentially, other big measures – vegetation, ground cover, soil and water – to determine what farmers pay from month to month.

Any farmer with a loan will have had the annual visit from the banker for a cup of coffee and a chat to take the temperature of the business. The bank already knows every physical asset on the place and how much money is coming in and going out. Sometimes the banker might have a poke around in the cropping program or ask about the livestock program for the year ahead.

Our poor banker has to put up with more questions from me than he asks us.

But there is a conundrum. One farmer might be pushing harder to get maximum productivity in the short term. Growing more. Making more money. Another farmer might be operating more lightly, ensuring maximum ground cover, balancing inputs more carefully, planting trees and understocking in case the season turns. Possibly making less money.

Who is the bank going to favour? I would have thought the first farmer, because ultimately the bank wants to see the money paid back.

Henry disagrees. The bank will have a less risky loan book by favouring the second. 'Putting my former banker's hat on,' he says, 'the worst thing that can happen for the bank is that the farm is completely degraded by the time it's forced to take possession of it . . . That is what the whole field of regenerative agriculture is, literally, about. It is regenerating.'

There are arguments over the definition of regenerative agriculture. Henry's definition is simple. 'It is something that improves the condition of the environment and increases the returns for farmers. It doesn't matter where the revenue comes from.'

I have met enough farmers to know that the idea of farm loans determined by environmental condition might send up some red flags. First, more work would be required to provide the information and open up the landscape and farm books to greater scrutiny. Second, what is the information used for? Open the gate; the measurement is taken; new rules are imposed: that's how it goes in the farmer's imagination. Often the farmer's instinct is correct. But the flipside of measuring is gathering evidence that shows how improvements in land condition – regeneration, if you like – might boost your bottom line. That would add income for the land manager and a better environmental outcome as well.

I started researching natural capital after I met Stephen Lacey. He was working for the Queensland agricultural advocacy group AgForce at the time. A farmer, ex-soldier and native of the UK, he grew up on the edge of the New Forest, William the Conqueror's hunting ground in the eleventh century. The commoner rights of the New Forest allowed pigs and ponies to graze for hundreds of years. The pigs ate the acorns, and the cattle and ponies chewed down the gorse and the heathland. Those animals are protected but are also used as a tool to manage the asset. This has shaped Lacey's view of the natural world as being woven into the human community and vice versa.

When Steve and his family came to Australia, he discovered many farming policies were based on farm activity while not considering the outcome of the activity. Holding sheep through a drought might attract government assistance but will it be good for the land? Influenced by the Oxford University professor of economics Dieter Helm, he became convinced that accounting for the natural capital in any farming system – the water, the air, the vegetation, the soil that nature provides for free – would be a way of setting policies for the next generation.

'When you have a massive asset, you tend not to measure it until it's too late,' Lacey says. 'Some policies were about agricultural growth and productivity as opposed to profitability. By bringing the extra layer of natural capital into the accounts line, you could actually show you were working within a safe limit of your asset base and determine whether it was renewable or non-renewable.'

Lacey likens a farm to his own body. As a young man, 'I flogged my body,' he says, 'but when it went wrong, it's never been the same machine since. I have seen that in the grazing industry. The time it takes to rest country once it's gone past a certain point, that's the bit that's so hard on a grazier who has to produce income. That can push people to work the country harder than they need to because they need turnover. We often hear farmers are the true environmentalists. Well, some are and some aren't fantastic at it. State and federal policy tended to support landholders to stay on the land rather than allow them to exit and get someone else to manage it.'

He worries that government and industry too often focus on exports and dollars to the exclusion of other things, which renders food production unsustainable. If we thought about what is best for the landscape, land managers, banks, governments and whole economies, Lacey argues, we would be in a far better position.

This means governments also need to pull the right policy levers. For the past thirty years, the government policy signal has been to push harder. The only way to get a pay rise if you are under pressure is by pushing your country as hard as you can.

Yet now, in countries around the world, lightbulbs are turning on. People are questioning that rationalist approach – not just in agricultural policy but in finance, in industry and in communities. The time has come for more balance. The simple productivity solution that has reigned from the 1970s onwards is so last century. Farming is entering the next phase and it will require a thinking shift to integrate the natural world more fully for both our farming systems and our eaters.

Once you account for natural capital in the nation's or the farm books, 'ecosystem services' are the most discussed method of paying to address things like soil health, species habitat and vegetation. You will hear a lot more of terms such as this as governments around the world scramble to mitigate carbon emissions and put back some of the natural capital that farmers and eaters have collectively blown.

Western Australian farmer Sue Middleton, whom you met in 'On families', has worked hard to diversify a traditional sheep and cropping farm into pigs and citrus. Middleton can see the debate moving from a productivity-based paradigm to a natural capital paradigm. 'One of the things that's come out of COVID is we don't want an economy at all costs. What we want is to be able to look after some of the elements that are life-giving. Nature is life-giving. Some of these values we have to pay for. A beautiful landscape. We want to have functioning ecosystems. We want species maintenance. Those things can't come from a tonne of wheat because we don't get paid for them in the price of wheat. Those values have to be paid for by a separate market system. And "efficient" markets do not pay for those things.

'We could mandate that landscape is important. Or ecosystem services are important and there's a public good to that and we could pay for that out of the Australian budget because Australians value having functioning ecosystems. We don't want to have extinction of species . . . [and] we also want things that have local or regional character or flavour.'

Take manuka honey. Honey is food+; food as medicine. People understand the intimate connection between nature and good, unadulterated honey. Manuka is produced in Western Australia (as well as the southeastern states and New Zealand), and the Western Australian jarrah forests it requires are dying, dwindling under the weight of human impact.

'If we don't maintain our jarrah resources in WA, we could actually lose the capacity to produce our high-quality honey,' Middleton says. 'We have this opportunity to be a disease-free, high health status, high medicinal property honey producer. But to do that, we have to look after our jarrah resource. There is no policy that says you have to maintain your biodiversity in Australia so that you can maintain the pollinators that maintain the ag resource that maintains biosecurity. But there should be, because that is critical.'

The NFF and groups like the AFI are pushing for similar ecosystem service payments whether the money comes from governments or private markets. Australia currently has a range of ecosystem or biodiversity programs but they are neither uniform nor strategic.

This is a live policy debate, not just in Australia but around the world. The future of British agriculture, for example, is one of the key political and social choices facing the UK as a result of its withdrawal from the EU. Farming districts largely supported Brexit, a phenomenon *The Economist* dubbed as 'turkeys voting for Christmas'.[5] The result of Brexit is that UK farmers have moved away from the Common Agricultural Policy (CAP) system, which paid them based on the amount of land they managed. Critics said that the system pumped up land prices, kept farmers on marginal areas, locked young farmers out of land and gave no incentive for good practice. Instead, future payments will be for provision of 'public goods' in the form of environmental land management. The pot of public money remains on par with the EU's CAP contribution, in the vicinity of £3 billion a year.

One of the key questions is whether eco services payments come from governments or private companies. If the dollars come from government, there may be trade implications for what might be argued as a subsidy rather than a service. Framing it as 'payment for services' rather than 'subsidy' would see Australia continue to berate others in the world to lower their trade barriers. But such payments could also come from the private market, from companies who want to invest in people 'doing the right thing' – however that is defined.

Ken Henry says there will be billions amassing in private markets in the next few years. Ultimately, too, he thinks there will be a dollar value on the environment by default. He points to Queensland's $500 million Land Restoration Fund (LRF), a state government-run program that funds farmers and land managers for biodiversity values and carbon. Ross Garnaut also believes Queensland's LRF is a good model for the Commonwealth to use. Programs like the LRF will allow people to figure out a dollar value for environmental services.

Wilderness Society's Tim Beshara is still hoping for eucatastrophe for Australia's environment. He reckons a national set of accounts that tracks environmental condition would be good, but he points out that Australia already has a lot of data on environmental degradation. The problem is that information never gets to the decision-making circles of government.

'I don't recall any time in my lifetime an Australian Treasury that has ever given a shit about the Australian environment, whether they have had the information to hand or not. So I think providing a Treasury secretary with more information is kind of moot unless the Treasury secretary is given a remit to care about it.'

For Beshara, the incredible uniqueness of Australian flora and fauna provides a stark contrast with the limp government accountability on decisions affecting that environment. Environment ministers are rarely held to account for their decisions or lack of action. They are more likely to face a no-confidence motion for travel expenses than for failing to implement a species recovery plan.

He also worries about how a natural capital account could rate the sheer value of these incredible places. Take a Gondwanan rainforest that has evolved over 100 million years and once covered Antarctica, South America, Australia and New Zealand. 'It's now left on a few hilltops in Australia. How do you account for a few hundred million years of evolution in one place?'

Australia's break away from Gondwanaland meant our biodiversity evolved without the rest of the planet. As a result, the continent has songbirds with ancient lineages and the richest reptile life on Earth. In world environmental contests, Brazil might beat us on numbers of frogs but we have an entire limb of frogs that no one else has. The mammal family tree has three branches. They are monotremes (like platypus and echidna), marsupials and the placentals, but Australia has the most of two of those entire branches (monotremes and marsupials).

'Environmental reporting will talk about loss of condition in Australian biodiversity but they won't say this particular place is not like anywhere else on the planet. It's like saying we are losing condition in our ten Van Goghs, and then trying to compare them with degradation of kindergarten paintings in other countries. It is like comparing a masterpiece with an amateur work.'

The sheer specialness of our environment, which might swell the chest with nationalistic pride if it were a sporting team or an opera house, is hard to comprehend.

While Beshara's expectations of government action to save environmental values have been clipped, environmental accounts with detailed information on biodiversity impacts would allow banks and big institutional investors to make better decisions. Then, there is the very real prospect of holding large institutional investors responsible for where they put their money. We already see that happening on climate change, for example, with Australian banks ruling out funding the Adani coalmine. There are moves afoot in Europe for finance sectors to take an interest in biodiversity values.

Farm advocates and National Party ministers are fond of saying farmers are the best environmental stewards.[6] Beshara says that is simply not true on the evidence. He points to Australia's extinction records for mammals: 'The worst on the planet.'

'The line that farmers are the best environmentalists in the world is complete and utter bullshit. If they were, things wouldn't be going backwards.'

But he knows, no matter what system we use, it will cost money. So Beshara is absolutely prepared to entertain the idea of direct payments to farmers for eco-services as long as there is an appropriate quid pro quo.

'The most important thing we need to see is a net improvement in the amount of damage that's being done and a net improvement in the amount of restoration that's being done. If we achieve that via payments to farmers for a national quid pro quo, in exchange for a European-style handout, it would be a win-win for all.

'Because, seriously, how much more land do we need to bulldoze to grow our cropping industry? There are other pathways to growth that are not bulldozing native vegetation.'

Equally, he thinks those payments should be extended for land restoration and management of natural areas on Indigenous-owned land, on parity with national parks funding.

'Indigenous funding for land restoration is not sitting on a level playing field for the efforts of the benefits to the country they are delivering.

'And if the wider ag industry stopped the bulldozing, and game-playing with water, I think the environment movement would back a large and ongoing transfer of funds in perpetuity. I am certain the public would back it. In fact, the public would back it anyway.'

As we have seen, there are plenty of critics of the natural capital approach. British economist Kate Raworth is the most notable, and her book *Doughnut Economics* is a favourite among some policy wonks, environmentalists and general readers alike. The doughnut defines the boundaries – illustrated by concentric rings like a doughnut – that humanity has to live within to create a balance between overshooting our natural resources and not having sufficient resources to maintain our population base.

She dislikes the very term 'ecosystem services' because it changes nature from being man's material means to being an asset on a balance sheet. It appropriates nature for human usage, unlike the Indigenous view of the world, which sees nature, earth, rivers, landscape as a family, rather than something to be used. Raworth told me that setting money as the measure is relying on a fickle and mercurial metric.

'Why don't we start with the metrics that belong on the planet? Let's start with the metrics of a stable climate, let's start with the metric of recharging water . . . Let's start with the metrics of human life and the metrics of how much is sufficient nutritious food in a day,' Raworth says.

The point of doughnut economics is to set all those measures up to create a dashboard of indicators to compare countries' performance, which you can see at the University of Leeds.[7] From that, we can see that, per person, Australia is overshooting the planet's biophysical boundaries on CO_2 emissions, phosphorus, nitrogen, land use change as well as its ecological and material footprints. These overshoots are coloured red.

'These are the metrics. I don't need to put a price on it. You can see the red. You can feel the alarm, you know there's a need for transformation. So I believe the twenty-first century of big data is the century when we are going to create a dashboard of metrics. We are going to measure well-being in terms of the Earth and her people, and we are going to do it so much better than in the past. I don't think everything needs to be priced. I don't use the term "natural capital" because I don't think the Earth is a piece of capital to be put on the balance sheet of an economist. I think the living world is our home.'

Nature is not, of course, here for human use alone. It has an intrinsic value. So I get how the idea of natural capital, as if it is one big new form of wealth that can be potentially traded, is offensive to its critics. But there is an urgency to this debate. In 2014, the Food and Agriculture Organization warned that the world's topsoil could be gone in sixty years. Sixty harvests. Around 2080 – when my grandchildren will be about my age. While that date has been contested, no one is suggesting conditions of soil, water or biodiversity are improving. We are already facing water shortages. Whichever system the economists settle on, humans need to live and eat in a way that improves the planet. We are all going to have to accept change in order to achieve this.

ON BALANCE

I began this book because it's not clear what Australians and their governments expect from farming. I think that's a problem. It's a strategic problem. It's a problem for the communities that grow food. It is, in many ways, a problem for eaters. And for me, it's a very personal problem.

When a government thinks about an issue in contradictory ways – as it does with farming and land management, or in unsettled ways that drift, as it does with climate change – it becomes a political problem. Lack of strategic thinking on something as fundamental as growing food in a warming climate transforms outcomes as much as active policy does. The result can warp the chain in surprising places.

So, let's end where we began – by looking forward. The near future is often framed up to 2050. Henry and Lily, my first two grandchildren, will be around thirty. All things being equal, at eighty-five I will be able to look back and survey the past five decades from a farming vantage point. The world's population is projected at ten billion people by then. The global climate aspiration – laggards aside – is zero emissions, but, remember, the experts say carbon neutrality has to happen much earlier than that.

The only goals I can see on the horizon for eaters, farmers and our land relate to dollars.

There is plenty of talk in government and advocacy about feeding the world. The question is not how we feed the world. The question is how we feed the world without harming the planet. That is the existential challenge so that should be the goal. My hope is that the economics of farming catches up with that goal.

This goal is starting, finally, to galvanise global governments. Governments are acting because of imperative, or leadership coupled with the demands of their voters. That will have implications for our trade agreements. As the global market has done for centuries, it will lay its invisible hand on our farms and our food.

I begin and end this book with the unerring belief that farming is an exceptional industry. We must eat; farming grows food. I have come across no research that changes my mind on that point. I have argued against some of the structural changes happening to farmers, such as the influx of large and sometimes foreign-owned corporations that are increasingly getting a hold on our landscape. I accept that a well-run, long-term corporate agribusiness could have a positive effect on the landscape, to improve its ecosystems with the advantage of deep pockets and patient capital. When a global food processor demands changes to a system, suppliers attuned to the global market have no choice but to react. The problem is that so much of the big movement in corporate farming right now is akin to renovation shows like *The Block*: capital gain, rather than sustainable production or long-term landscape management, is the main game.

When competition reforms began in earnest thirty years ago, Australian farming was filleted. Right along the food chain, competition policy has created less competition. In food retailing, the Australian supermarkets have whittled down to a few players. Will the number of farm businesses keep shrinking and eventually be dominated by a smaller number of big players? If so, does that matter?

I think it does. I think more than half of the country being owned by a smaller number of large food growers, whether they are dynastic families or global corporations, will decimate our country communities. Farming is about people and we are losing people with the structural changes driven by higgledy-piggledy policy. As Richard Heath of the Australian Farm Institute said, 'Productivity growth means hollowing out the middle. That's what it means.'

Farmers are fragmented, frayed into thousands of versions. There are big and small, families and corporates, bulk commodity producers and niche growers, tech heads and Luddites and everyone in between.

Eaters too are fragmented. Carnivores, vegetarians, flexitarians, pescatarians, vegans, paleos, locavores, gluten-frees. The list is endless.

In between the farmers and eaters are some big players whose influence reaches down the food chain to the farmers, and up the chain to the eaters. They have the most power in the supply chains. They are big agribusiness, big commodity traders, big processors and big retailers. These businesses increasingly dominate the food manufacturing and retailing system. Food chain analysts refer to the hourglass, with farmers and eaters representing the wide ends and a concentration of companies in the middle. That leaves eaters with little choice when it comes to buying food unless they actively seek it out.

Yet experts in risk are warning we have holes in our food production system. The Bartos report into resilience in our food supply chain described our system as vulnerable to disasters, particularly when they are combined. Think of the floods that followed the fires in 2020. Or, hypothetically, a bushfire with a pandemic. Or a pandemic and floods. It is true to say that we produce and export a lot of food, but our economic structures and our ecosystems are stretched.

The increasing concentration in the food chain of farmers, manufacturers and retailers will be further challenged by the impacts of climate change, with its accompanying droughts, fires and floods. The pandemic and China's trade restrictions added extra complications in 2020, with effects that will linger on into the next few years at least.

We have long supply chains. Supermarkets' supply systems cannot bring the food in fast enough to meet demand when it spikes unexpectedly. And yet then we see growers such as Perth's Luciano Monte plough 100,000 iceberg lettuces into the paddock because he could not get labour to pick them with a $30 per hour labour rate.[1] Usually young backpackers or overseas seasonal workers fill the gap. Some farmers are fantasising about robot pickers, and why wouldn't they? But that will strip more people from those communities.

We have arrived at a fork in the road. The Australian government has acknowledged the hole in the supply chains by making food one of the six areas for funding under its 2020 Modern Manufacturing Strategy.[2] After three decades of waving goodbye to manufacturing businesses and their equipment, our leaders have decided 'manufacturing is critical to a modern Australian economy'. It is an implicit recognition that the structural changes that removed a measure of diversity and capability from our economy were a mistake. Allowing too much control of our landscapes and our food-production capacity by single entities is also a mistake. Worship of *Farmer economicus* alone has left us and will continue to leave us exposed.

If the Modern Manufacturing Strategy is pulled off, we will return to making some stuff. But governments have yet to recognise that economic diversity – of business size, scope and produce – in farming might be a sensible strategy.[3] This equates to diversity of people looking after the land. Our regulatory frameworks still favour size and our government agricultural departments still push scale and capital above all else. We continue to excel at growing two or three food stuffs for export without ever wondering whether we could produce a more diverse basket of foods to supply local markets as well. The dynamics I have covered will change not just the landscape and your dinner, but the local communities who currently produce that food.

If major political parties are not alert to the national strategic implications of these changes, perhaps they might consider the political implications. The most recent political disruptions in the 2019 election in rural seats have been due to water management and land usage, while in the cities we have seen independents campaigning on climate change. These are all issues of critical importance to farmers. They are also issues that divide farmers into those with or without the resources and capacity to change their systems to suit the wild swings and roundabouts of global warming.

The people managing land – Indigenous or non – are the ultimate ground truthers. They need to be trusted and they need to trust those imposing the rules. That means we need a political feedback loop that functions better than it currently does. Governments need to listen and trust land managers, and land managers need to have faith in governments. That requires better feedback machinery.

We need to acknowledge that good land management has

positive benefits outside farm fences in the same way as poor land management has a negative effect. Economic signals have not factored in the environmental effects of pushing the ecology to its limits. Australian farmers have got better at producing more with less water and less labour on less fertile land. Strides have been made in better farming practice, no doubt. There has been a sharper focus on soil, water efficiency and vegetation management. Australian rice is grown with 50 per cent less water than the global average. Australian farmers have had to be better than those in other places because their soils were less forgiving.

But we are entering a new paradigm that acknowledges farmers and food production exists within landscape. That means farmers, eaters and governments have to change their mindset. The new model must combine verifiable land stewardship with growing healthier, better quality food. We have to look after land as if our lives depend on it, because they do.

We need what sustainable agriculture expert Professor Andrew Campbell has described as an 'intrinsically Australian food and farming system', which honours the landscape and the people who grow food. Much of the work designing the principles for a more Australian system has been done.[4] The framework is indisputable. Campbell outlines a system that would be resilient under increasing variability, miserly with water, careful to keep ground cover, kind to soil, profitable in good seasons and capable of withstanding bad seasons. It would build nature, people and profit, attracting the best to farm and manage landscape in rural, peri-urban and even urban places.

It has some foundational principles in Indigenous history. Farmer Oral McGuire told me about the threat of serious desertification due to the ravages of farming, a threat he described as 'just years away'. His work to replant his farm to create a more endemic grazing system for animals and humans is one way forward. He remains committed to working on how fellow Noongar families make an income within the many government constraints on Indigenous business. And he urges people to look to Indigenous ways of managing land. As a former firefighter, he has underlined that the threats of climate change, fire, flood or plague would not affect Indigenous structures: 'It's not Noongar assets that's going to burn.'

He goes on to urge: 'Put our culture into context and acknowledge we are the oldest living culture. Understand what we have done and compare 60,000 years to 190 years. We have longevity and we lived with sustainability.'

Noisy farm advocates fight over the way we should grow food. We often get tangled in the weeds of definition. Regenerative, conventional, low input, high tech. Farmers are as fractured as eaters with their various dictates. But there is value to being the wedgetail eagle of farming. It is useful to sail over the top every so often and get a view of the whole country. There are commonalities across different landscapes.

McGuire, with his 60,000-plus-year lineage, explains to his kids the complexity of the Noongar spiritual knowledge system that connects the sun and the sky and the clouds down to the bottom of the root system of the trees. If reinvigorating Indigenous farming through a cooperative model doesn't work, he will simply return to sacred places with his kids. 'I don't want to be a burnt-out blackfella.'

Brad and Kate Jones use high tech and big machinery to farm on soil type in Western Australia, but still muster their kids in the school holidays to plant trees for a beautiful landscape. The Jones family is realistic that their large farm may end up being run by a corporate, but they look after their land as if it won't. They are the modern agricultural version of the Burkean 'temporary possessor'.

Or consider the people in the little outfit Acres & Acres, hoping to become more self-sufficient with their local fruit and veggies. Having control of some of their food source is worth more than the food itself. It is worth community, therapy and security. And Emma Germano, whose passion for growing good cauliflowers is only surpassed by the need to tell the complex story of food and how it fits into human society. Or Vince Heffernan, trying to integrate good healthy food production within the larger agroecosystem while avoiding being screwed economically.

An accommodation has to come between farmers and eaters. This is not a battle. We all have positive and negative effects on our environment. Our actions flow on to everyone else. One end of the equation cannot bear all the costs.

Sometimes the writing gods send you a gift to reward the daily grind. Late in this process, *Griffith Review* invited me to chair a panel on natural capital with Ken Henry, writer and economist Jane Gleeson-White and businessman cum philanthropist Alan Schwarz. You met Ken in the previous chapter. Gleeson-White literally wrote the book on natural capital, *Six Capitals*. Alan Schwarz set up the Universal Commons Project, to bring about 'Mutualistic Capitalism that genuinely advances human wellbeing while preserving the planet that sustains us'. Travelling via different routes, all three question why profit and value have become so out of whack in the modern economy. It gave me comfort that people with many more qualifications than me were struggling with flaws in the current economic system.

Takeaway 1: contrary to popular opinion, government is doing too little rather than too much.

As a non-economist, I had been struggling with Milton Friedman's arguments that a corporation's only responsibility is to maximise its profit (see 'On the middle'). I never understood how economists, as humans, could rule out the intangible stuff like nature and social benefit. Henry underlined the historical context. Friedman's *Capitalism and Freedom* was published in 1962, the year of the Cuban Missile Crisis. He was worried about government intervention in the form of socialism, not government leaving the playing field altogether.

'Believe it or not, government's role is not to support business. It's to do the opposite. Government's role is to control business,' said Henry.

'Is it the responsibility of business to stay within the rules of the game itself? Friedman says no, it's not. Business should maximise profit, subject to the laws of the land. It is our responsibility, the rest of us, to elect people to a democratic process to frame the laws and fund the regulatory agencies to ensure consumers are protected from fraud and deception.

'[Friedman's] big concern was that government would do too much, that government would become a Frankenstein . . . I am sure it never occurred to him that government might do too little. But I reckon if he was in this room tonight, he would have to admit that's what's happened. It's not that government has done too much, it's that government has done too little.'

All my working lifetime I had heard many politicians saying governments should support business and should get out of its way – often in the name of Milton Friedman and other economists. Farmers in particular love this argument when it suits them. Yet Friedman himself said that governments have a clear role in a healthy economy to regulate business.

Farmers have an awesome responsibility as land stewards

because their impact travels far beyond the boundary fence. The non-farming population has the right to expect farmers will look after landscape within the laws set by democratically elected governments, but eaters need to pay a fair price for the food farmers produce.

Takeaway 2: business has a right to make profits as long as they're aligned with the value created for society.

Schwarz's insight was to think of business minds as 'reptilian optimisers'.

'We are relatively amoral. We take the world as it is and we try to maximise outputs from inputs. We are like a machine. You get a bunch of inputs, you get a bunch of rules, you get a bunch of restraints, and you're an optimiser. The right businessperson is the person who says, "I'm a reptilian optimiser, [but] I think we should have as many rules as we possibly can to make sure my profit is aligned with value I create for society. I am happy to accept that."'

And for Schwarz, that is where business fails. Businesses complain about red tape getting in the way of profit. But as science shows the natural world is straining, Schwarz recognises the rules that guide business must change from the current 'extractive system'.

'It's a political struggle, for mutualism and cooperation, which we as human beings have done for a long time, incredibly well. We keep developing larger and more complex systems of cooperation than have ever existed, which is why we dominate the earth. I'm an optimist but I think occasionally we screw things up really badly and I'm terrified with what is happening with climate.'

Like some of the farmers you have met, Schwarz is already seeing ways to continue making money while being part of the solution. But he believes governments also need to provide guidance. 'A business deserves every cent of profit it makes, as long as it obeys the rules, it supports good rules and doesn't oppose good rules.

If you asked me tomorrow for all my investments to go to net zero because it was really important, I would say, "I can't do that, give me some time." That's where you need government guidance.'

Takeaway 3: accountants may still save the world but they need to recognise the right of nature to exist for its own sake.

I was immediately drawn to the notion of natural capital because here was a way to express the value of nature in the language that policy wonks and politicians would understand. Having watched politics for so long, I knew that in order to change the ground rules, we had to change the minds of politicians.

Jane Gleeson-White was way ahead of me. She knew accountants had been instrumental in every moment in history, from the invention of writing to the Renaissance to the Industrial Revolution and the reconstruction of the postwar economy. She discovered accountants are gatekeepers of capitalism and even they could see their system was broken.

After she wrote *Six Capitals*, Gleeson-White found herself at a Wall Street sustainability conference for billion-dollar-wielding hedge funds. It was 2016 and she pricked up her ears because they were talking about 'blue gold'. But her heart sank when she realised they were talking about cornering the market for water.

'They were already geo-mapping the world to find out where the new supplies of fresh water were, all in the name of sustainable development. That is, sustainable for Pepsi Cola and Coke to ensure . . . their supply for the next forty years. I just saw hell, actually. That's what sent me looking for new ways of articulating value for the natural world.'

So Gleeson-White no longer speaks of valuing 'society and nature' via capital. She considers the economic terms are 'too small for all that we are as humans and the Earth's living systems'. She is heartened that the UN System of Environmental Economic

Accounting is also considering nature's value in its own right, not just as a value to humans.

Like the scientist Helen Macdonald and Oral McGuire, Gleeson-White reminded us that humans are part of the natural world, not separate from it. And her fellow panellists agreed.

'I think it's incredibly important that humans face up to the reality that humans are part of a system,' said Henry. 'They are probably the only natural being that thinks they should be in control of the entire system. But with that comes huge responsibility. It's not obvious as a species that we are comfortable with that responsibility. We seem to want to shirk it.'

I left that evening convinced that the ground was shifting underneath me. I was also convinced that if these three people, who had had influence via government, business and writing, were all coming to similar conclusions, perhaps there was room for change. As Schwarz reminded us, 'Institutions are not set in stone. They are not the natural order, nor a divine right; they are not ordained by God, and they are not discovered by science. They are ours to create and they are ours to change.'[5]

And that change in rules might make a material difference to farmers, land managers and Indigenous land stewards in good ways, if farmers are prepared to consider new ways of looking at their job description. And if they lean into their role as food producers and environmental stewards, they need support from all those who care about the state of nature.

It is November and we have had a bumper season, with rain coming in sheets almost every week. This is La Niña and she favours above-average rainfall. The wheat stands tall, as high as I have seen it.

Sporadic heads stand taller still, like sentinels, pushed on by the moisture. They are big crops and we are wracked with the anxious anticipation of a good harvest that could turn to shit in a heartbeat. The storms have increased. We get sudden downpours and lightning strikes, which have already taken out the power twice. A farmer just west at Junee lost a massive 6-tonne canola crop to hail a few months ago.

We have had this happen before. The year that ended the noughties drought was wet as a shag. Remember the time we lost that wheat crop to hail in the 1990s? Or when the frost knocked us out a few years ago? But these are not cycles. Or rather, if they are cycles, the cycle is blowing badly out of shape in one direction.

Climate change lays over the top of the other structural pressures on farming, including corporatisation, power imbalances, the influence of financial markets, trade spats; the control of big agribusiness, big food and big supermarkets throughout the chain. Farming is also limited by the space between the ears, the need for knowledge, the family culture and the capacity to ask for help. Farmers, like everyone else, exist in a rapidly changing economy. After decades of a relatively stable international economy, growth is stagnant. The manifest rise of China and the weakness of the US at the end of the Trump era is pulling farmers in two different directions. Climate change engorges these factors. Loading a heavier weight on all horses, it makes the race harder to run. Climate change is the effective globalisation of natural systems. The filaments of our eight billion lives are interconnecting like the roots of one of our wheat plants.

Yuval Noah Harari argues that humans didn't domesticate wheat, wheat domesticated humans. It was just one of many wild grasses 10,000 years ago. Yet wheat manipulated humans to clear fields and plant. Wheat influenced us to break our backs and lug water and protect it from pests and diseases. Then we harvested it and ground it and ate it and spread it all over the world. Wheat is now one of the four biggest crops in the world, along with soybeans, corn and rice.

Nature shapes us and we shape nature. In the past few decades I think we have been getting ahead of ourselves, telling ourselves we can be the ones in charge of nature. But, as it always will, nature is giving full and frank feedback to our behaviour in ways that will change our lives forever. Nature has forced governments to act in ways their constituents cannot. It seems Wendell Berry was right. Nature does have more votes.

So if we are to come to an accommodation, if we are not to lead this dance of food production, then perhaps it's time for a truce. No more wars against nature from farmers. No more expectations from eaters that we can produce food for next to nothing. We need food systems that seek nature's permission and work in conjunction with the natural world.

NOTES

Introduction

1 'Irrigation in Australia: Facts and figures', National Program for Sustainable Irrigation, undated; www.nswic.org.au/pdf/irrigation_statistics/Facts%20Figures.pdf

Chapter 1: On the big picture

1 Food and Agriculture Organization of the United Nations; www.fao.org/hunger/en/
2 IPCC, 'Special report on climate change and land: Summary for policymakers', 2019; ipcc.ch/srccl/chapter/summary-for-policymakers/
3 'The Green Revolution: Norman Borlaug and the Race to Fight Global Hunger', PBS, 3 April 2020; pbs.org/wgbh/americanexperience/features/green-revolution-norman-borlaug-race-to-fight-global-hunger/

Chapter 2: On history

1 Rural Industries Research and Development Corporation, 'Native grasses make new products – a review of current and past uses and assessment of potential', June 2015, agrifutures.com.au/wp-content/uploads/publications/15-056.pdf
2 Michael Symons, *One Continuous Picnic*, Melbourne University Press, Melbourne, 2007 (ebook accessed)

3 C. J. King, *The First Fifty Years of Agriculture in New South Wales*, 'Extracts from review of marketing and agricultural economics', August 1948 – December 1949, Government Printer, p. 549
4 Carter Goodrich, 'The Australian and American Labor Movements', *Economic Record*, November 1928, pp. 206–7
5 Wendell Berry, 'The Unsettling of America', *The World-Ending Fire: The Essential Wendell Berry*, Penguin Books, London, 2017

Chapter 3: On risk

1 CSIRO (chaired Ken Henry and David Thodey), 'Australia's National Outlook', 2019; csiro.au/en/Research/Major-initiatives/Australian-National-Outlook
2 Ibid., p. 2
3 Ibid., p. 60
4 Ibid., p. 39
5 Ibid., p. 62
6 Ibid.
7 Ibid., p. 63
8 Ibid., p. 62
9 Ibid.
10 David Littleproud, 'Our food security among the world's best', media release, 16 March 2020; minister.awe.gov.au/littleproud/media-releases/food-security
11 Agvet Chemicals, 'Market Drivers and Barriers', Department of Agriculture, July 2019, p. 23
12 Australian Government, Department of Agriculture Fisheries and Forestry, Stephen Bartos et al., Resilience in the Australian food supply chain, p. vii
13 Ibid., p. viii
14 Kim Berry, 'The rise of ready meals', *Food and Drink Business*, 26 August 2020
15 Bartos, op cit, p. vii
16 Ibid., p. viii
17 Ibid.
18 Ibid., p. ix
19 Ibid.
20 Ibid.
21 'Food Insecurity in the Time of Covid-19', Foodbank Hunger Report, 2020; foodbank.org.au/wp-content/uploads/2020/10/FB-HR20.pdf

22 Calla Wahlquist, 'Australia's severe bushfire season was predicted and will be repeated, inquiry told', *Guardian*, 25 May 2020

Chapter 4: On farming culture

1 'Food sovereignty', La Via Campesina, International Peasants' Movement, 15 January 2003; viacampesina.org/en/food-sovereignty/
2 Alison Hewitt, 'The truth about cats' and dogs' environmental impact', UCLA newsroom, 2 August 2017; newsroom.ucla.edu/releases/the-truth-about-cats-and-dogs-environmental-impact
3 Dairy Australia, 'Bobby Calves', undated; dairyaustralia.com.au/animal-management-and-milk-quality/calf-rearing/bobby-calves#.YNJcAGgvNaR; Adele Ferguson, 'Chinese owner's "catastrophic failure" drives Australia's biggest dairy farm into the ground', *Sydney Morning Herald*, 9 April 2021

Chapter 5: On food tribes

1 OECD, Meat consumption (indicator), 2021; oecd-ilibrary.org/agriculture-and-food/meat-consumption/indicator/english_fa290fd0-en
2 Sarah Whitten, 'Teens would rather eat out than buy more clothes: Study', CNBC, 10 April 2018; cnbc.com/2018/04/10/teens-would-rather-dine-at-starbucks-than-buy-more-clothes.html

Chapter 6: On economics

1 'State of Nature report', RSPB, 2019; rspb.org.uk/our-work/state-of-nature-report/
2 Alan S. Blinder, 'The Free-Trade Paradox: The Bad Politics of a Good Idea', *Foreign Affairs*, January/February 2019; foreignaffairs.com/articles/2018-12-11/free-trade-paradox
3 Ibid.
4 Australian Government, Department of Agriculture, Water and the Environment, 'Farm Management Deposits Scheme Statistics', January 2021; agriculture.gov.au/sites/default/files/documents/jan-2021-fmd-statistics.pdf
5 Larry Schlesinger, 'Woolies plans giant fresh food warehouse as online demand soars', *Australian Financial Review*, 8 February 2021
6 Chanticleer, 'Ghosts of the past haunt Woolies' record year', *Australian Financial Review*, 23 June 2020

Chapter 7: On politics

1 Labor Party, 'A Fair Go for Australia', ALP National Platform, 2018; alp.org.au/media/1539/2018_alp_national_platform_constitution.pdf

2 Dan Conifer, 'China imposes 80pc tariff on Australian barley for next five years amid global push for coronavirus investigation', ABC News, 18 May 2020

3 Kath Sullivan, Bill Birtles, Emilia Terzon, 'China puts tariffs of up to 200 per cent on Australian wine', ABC News, 27 November 2020

4 Jonathan Kearsley, Eryk Bagshaw, Anthony Galloway, '"If you make China the enemy, China will be the enemy": Beijing's fresh threat to Australia', *Sydney Morning Herald*, 18 November 2020

5 Andrew Cameron, Charley Xia, Rohan Nelson, 'Agricultural overview: March quarter 2021', Australian Government, Department of Agriculture, Water and the Environment; agriculture.gov.au/abares/research-topics/agricultural-outlook/agriculture-overview

6 Scott Waldron, 'The Logic of China's Economic Coercion on Australian Agriculture', Future Directions International, December 2020; futuredirections.org.au/publication/the-logic-of-chinas-economic-coercion-on-australian-agriculture/

7 Ibid.

8 George Christensen, 'The China Problem', blog, undated; georgechristensen.com.au/chinainquiry/#the-china-problem

9 Osmond Chui, 'I was born in Australia. Why do I need to renounce the Chinese Communist Party?', *Sydney Morning Herald*, 14 October 2020

10 Inspector-General of the Australian Defence Force, 'The Afghanistan Inquiry', Australian Government, Department of Defence, 2020; afghanistaninquiry.defence.gov.au/

11 Reuters, 'Chinese official's "repugnant" tweet of Australia soldier likely amplified by fake accounts, experts say', *Guardian*, 5 December 2020

12 Peter Somerville, Jane McNaughton, Kellie Lazzaro, 'Vegetable growers forced to dump $150,000 worth of celery crops due to picker shortage', ABC News, 14 January 2021

13 Adam Jeffery, Emma Newburger, 'Wasted milk, euthanized livestock: Photos show how coronavirus has devastated US agriculture', CNBC, 2 May 2020; cnbc.com/2020/05/02/coronavirus-devastates-agriculture-dumped-milk-euthanized-livestock.html

14 Australian Government, Department of Agriculture, Water and the Environment, 'Agricultural Production Employment is Trending

Downwards; agriculture.gov.au/abares/research-topics/labour/australian-agricultural-workforce-trends#agricultural-production-employment-is-trending-downwards

15 Food and Agriculture Organization of the United Nations, 'Migrant workers and the COVID-19 pandemic', 7 April 2020; fao.org/3/ca8559en/CA8559EN.pdf

16 'Global Forecast to 2023', Food and Agriculture Technology and Products Market by Industry and Region, report, March 2019; researchandmarkets.com/reports/4758470/food-and-agriculture-technology-and-products#src-pos-1

17 Luke Housego, 'Brown Brothers and CSIRO look to climate-proof grapes', *Australian Financial Review*, 14 April 2019

18 Lorena Allam, 'From 40C heat to -36C snow: NT Indigenous rangers share expertise in Canada', *Guardian*, 18 February 2019

19 Christine Slade, Angela Wardell-Johnson, 'Creating a climate for food security: Governance and policy in Australia', National Climate Change Adaptation Research Facility, 2013; nccarf.edu.au/creating-climate-food-security-governance-and-policy-australia/

20 Ibid., p. 1

21 Ibid., p. 28

Chapter 8: On the middle

1 Kenneth Clements, Jiawei Si, 'Engel's Law, Diet Diversity, and the Quality of Food Consumption', *American Journal of Agricultural Economics*, vol. 100, issue 1, January 2018, pp. 1–22; onlinelibrary.wiley.com/doi/epdf/10.1093/ajae/aax053

2 Our World in Data, 'Share of consumer expenditure spent on food', 2016; ourworldindata.org/grapher/share-of-consumer-expenditure-spent-on-food?time=2016

3 Rural Bank, 'Australian Farmland Values', 2021; ruralbank.com.au/siteassets/knowledgeandinsights/publications/farmlandvalues/national/afv-national-2021.pdf

4 Australian Government, Department of Agriculture, Water and the Environment, 'Snapshot of Australian Agriculture', 2021; agriculture.gov.au/abares/products/insights/snapshot-of-australian-agriculture-2020

5 ClimateWorks Australia, 'Land Use Futures: Australia's Land Use', Deakin University and CSIRO, undated; climateworksaustralia.org/land-use-futures/australias-land-use/

6 Milton Friedman, 'A Friedman doctrine – The Social Responsibility Of Business Is to Increase Its Profits', *New York Times*, 13 September 1970; nytimes.com/1970/09/13/archives/a-friedman-doctrine-the-social-responsibility-of-business-is-to.html
7 Bill Pritchard, 'Implementing and Maintaining Neoliberal Agriculture in Australia – Part I: Construction Neoliberalism as a Vision for Agricultural Policy', *International Journal of Sociology of Agriculture and Food*, no. 13, January 2005, pp. 1–12
8 Alan Lloyd, 'Some Current Policy Issues', *Australian Journal of Agricultural Economics*, 1970, p. 106
9 Stuart F. Harris, 'Change in Agriculture: The Relevance of Agricultural Economics', *Australian Journal of Agricultural Economics*, 15(3), 1971, p. 129
10 John L. Dillon, 'The Outlook for Agricultural Economics', *Australian Journal of Agricultural* Economics, 16(2), 1972, p. 79
11 Parliament of Australia, *Hansard*, 26 August 1970; parlinfo.aph.gov.au/parlInfo/search/display/display.w3p;query=Id%3A%22hansard80%2Fhansardr80%2F1970-08-26%2F0114%22
12 Jess Davis, 'How the AWB oil-for-food scandal changed Australia's wheat industry: 10 years since deregulation', ABC News, 3 July 2018
13 ACCC, 'Big gains to consumers from dairy deregulation', 9 April 2001; accc.gov.au/media-release/big-gains-to-consumers-from-dairy-deregulation
14 ACCC, 'Dairy inquiry, final report', April 2018; accc.gov.au/system/files/1395_Dairy%20inquiry%20final%20report.pdf
15 Andrew Marshall, 'Landmark-Ruralco merger unrest – farmers doubt value in deal', Farm Online, 24 June 2019; farmonline.com.au/story/6235027/rural-resistance-rising-against-landmark-ruralco-merger/
16 ABS, 'Agricultural Commodities, Australia', 14 May 2021; abs.gov.au/ausstats/abs@.nsf/mf/7121.0
17 Large farms are those with annual receipts above $1 million. Medium farms are those with receipts between $200,000 and $1 million; and small farms are those with receipts below $200,000. (The ABS only counts those with an Estimated Value of Agricultural Operations over $40,000 and that number has jumped from $5000 in 2014–15. These figures are adjusted for inflation.)
18 'Snapshot of Australian agriculture', ABARES, 2020
19 Yu Sheng et al., 'Productivity and farm size in Australian agriculture: reinvestigating the returns to scale', *Australian Journal of Agriculture and*

Resource Economics, 27 May 2014; onlinelibrary.wiley.com/doi/full/10.1111/1467-8489.12063

20 Penny Vandenbroek, 'Snapshot of employment by industry, 2019', Parliament of Australia; aph.gov.au/About_Parliament/Parliamentary_Departments/Parliamentary_Library/FlagPost/2019/April/Employment-by-industry-2019

21 Australian Competition and Consumer Commission, 'Dairy Inquiry, Farmers Guide to the Final Report', April 2018

Chapter 9: On families

1 WA Country Hour, 'Lawson Grains farmland parcels hit the market, sale predictions to truly eclipse $500 million'. ABC News, 15 March 2020

2 Lawson Grain, 'Our values', website; lawsongrains.com/about/ (accessed 25 May 2021)

3 ABC Rural, 'Gina Rinehart's Hancock Agriculture to sell northern cattle stations with herd', ABC News, 8 March 2021

Chapter 10: On corporatisation

1 Felicity Lawrence, 'Barclays face protests over role in global food crisis', *Guardian*, 26 April 2011; Geoffrey Lawrence and Kiah Smith, 'Neoliberal Globalization and Beyond: Food, Farming and the Environment', *Cambridge Handbook of Environmental Sociology*, Cambridge University Press, Melbourne, 2020, pp. 411–28

2 Australian Government, Department of Health, 'Genetically modified crops in Australia', 2018; ogtr.gov.au/internet/ogtr/publishing.nsf/content/9AA09BB4515EBAA2CA257D6B00155C53/$File/11%20-%20Genetically%20modified%20(GM)%20crops%20in%20Australia.pdf

3 Larry Schlesinger, 'Prime farmland smashes equities with 15pc total return', *Australian Financial Review*, 19 July 2020

4 Frank Delahunty, 'Australian Farmland Index registers a strengthening to 14.91 per cent annualised total return for year to 31 March 2020 by increased income', Australian Farmland Index press release, March quarter 2020, 10 July 2020

5 Australian Government, Department of Agriculture, Water and the Environment, 'Disaggregating farm performance statistics by size'; agriculture.gov.au/abares/research-topics/surveys/disaggregating-farm-size#statistical-tables

6 'Water supply and demand in the southern Murray-Darling Basin: An assessment of future water availability and permanent horticulture irrigation water demand', Aither, 7 June 2019, p. vii

7 Mike Foley, 'Irrigators urge states, MDBA to follow Victoria's lead on water', *Queensland Country Life*, 15 July 2019; queenslandcountrylife.com.au/story/6274714/irrigators-urge-states-mdba-to-follow-victorias-lead-on-water/?cs=1496

8 'Aussie almonds continue to rise', Good Fruit and Vegetables, 3 September 2020; goodfruitandvegetables.com.au/story/6897769/almonds-the-juggernut-of-aussie-hort/

9 Peter Hunt, 'Duxton Water's Sales Surge', *Weekly Times*, 28 February 2020; weeklytimesnow.com.au/news/national/duxton-water-sold-879m-temp-water-in-2019-compared-with-235m-in-2018/news-story/872690d7f0ed96d0daf9ea6b8afcc082

10 Fortune 500: TIAA, 2020; fortune.com/fortune500/2019/tiaa/

11 Geoffrey Lawrence, Sarah Ruth Sippel, Nicolette Larder, 'State-Led and Finance-Backed Farming Endeavours: Changing contours of Investment in Australian Agriculture', *Finance or Food?: The Role of Cultures, Values, and Ethics in Land Use*, Hilde Bjorkhaug, Philip McMichael, Bruce Muirhead (eds), University of Toronto Press, Toronto, 2020, pp. 125–52

12 'Why farmland now? Amidst unprecedented market volatility, a durable and consistent investment with compelling upside', Nuveen, 17 April 2020; nuveen.com/global/thinking/alternatives/why-farmland-now

13 Josh Nicholas, Calla Wahlquist, Andy Ball, Nick Evershed, 'Who owns Australia? Complex web of data reveals large swathes of country controlled by small number of billionaires and large companies', *Guardian*, undated

14 Register of Foreign Ownership of Water Entitlements, report of registrations, 30 June 2020; firb.gov.au/sites/firb.gov.au/files/2020-05/2019-rfo-water-entitlements.pdf

15 Colin Bettles, 'Howes has a point: Fitzgibbon', Farm Online, 6 December 2013; farmonline.com.au/story/3582897/howes-has-a-point-fitzgibbon/

16 Quoted in Jennifer Clapp, *Food*, Polity Press, Oxford, 2020

Chapter 11: On disruption

1 Lisa Richards and Nigel Brew, '2019–20 Australian bushfires—frequently asked questions: a quick guide', Parliament of Australia, Foreign Affairs, Defence and Security, 12 March 2020, aph.gov.au/About_Parliament/Parliamentary_Departments/Parliamentary_Library/pubs/rp/rp1920/Quick_Guides/AustralianBushfires
2 Tim Beshara, 'Tolkien's inspiration for climate advocates', *Eureka Street*, 29 June 2017; eurekastreet.com.au/article/tolkien-s-inspiration-for-climate-advocates
3 The most obvious example is glyphosate, which has attracted multimillion-dollar legal challenges in the US and fierce discussion in Europe. Germany was looking to ban its use completely by 2024 and, at publication, draft legislation was being considered. Vietnam banned its use in 2019 and no longer allows imports. Europe is already imposing regulations on chemical usage for Australian farmers exporting into EU countries. See also Alex McBratney, '4 reasons agriculture needs to phase out reliance on glyphosate', University of Sydney, 9 October 2018; sydney.edu.au/news-opinion/news/2018/10/09/4-reasons-agriculture-needs-to-phase-out-reliance-on-glyphosate.html
4 George Levantis and James Fell, 'Non-tariff measures affecting Australian agriculture', Australian Government, Department of Agriculture, Water and the Environment; agriculture.gov.au/abares/research-topics/trade/non-tariff-measures
5 Michael Greshko, 'Amphibian "apocalypse" caused by most destructive pathogen ever', *National Geographic*, 29 March 2019; nationalgeographic.com/animals/2019/03/amphibian-apocalypse-frogs-salamanders-worst-chytrid-fungus/#close
6 Laura Dalrymple and Grant Hilliard, *The Ethical Omnivore*, Murdoch Books, Sydney, 2020, p. 20
7 Ibid., p. 13
8 See Haidt's book, *The Righteous Mind: Why Good People are Divided by Politics and Religion*, Pantheon, New York, 2013

Chapter 12: On water

1 World Economic Forum, 'Global Risks Report 2020', 15th edition
2 Oliver Gordon, 'Fortune Agribusiness bid for NT water licence challenged by native title holders', ABC News, 25 February 2021

3 'Singleton Station groundwater licence application Fortune Agribusiness Fund Management', Central Land Council, undated; clc.org.au/wp-content/uploads/2021/03/Singleton_water_license_application_fact_sheet_.pdf
4 Daniel Fitzgerald, 'Singleton Station granted 40,000 megalitre water licence in staged approval', ABC News, 8 April 2021
5 Courtney Fowler, 'National parks and water management plan for heritage-listed Fitzroy River sparks tension', ABC News, 29 July 2020
6 Calla Wahlquist, 'Fitzroy River: the push to prevent a repeat of the Murray-Darling basin "disaster"', *Guardian*, 5 September 2020
7 Lana Hartwig and Professor Sue Jackson, 'Submission to ACCC's Murray-Darling Basin Water Markets Inquiry: Interim Report', 28 October 2020, pp. 44–56
8 For a good understanding of cultural water rights, see Lana Hartwig, Sue Jackson and Natalie Osborne, 'Recognition of Barkandji Water Rights in Australian Settler-Colonial Water Regimes', *Resources*, 2018; mdpi.com/2079-9276/7/1/16/htm
9 National Water Commission, 'Water markets in Australia: a short history', Canberra, 2011, p. 20
10 Daniel Connell, *Water Politics in the Murray-Darling Basin*, Federation Press, Leichhardt, quoted in National Water Commission, op cit., p. 22
11 National Water Commission, op cit.
12 Ibid., p. 40
13 Clint Jasper and Kath Sullivan, 'Water for Fodder's second round of funding abandoned by Federal Government', ABC News, 7 August 2020
14 Murray-Darling Basin Authority, 'Guide to the proposed Basin plan', p. xix; mdba.gov.au/publications/archived-information/basin-plan-archives/guide-proposed-basin-plan
15 Anne Davies, 'New South Wales told to go back and try again on Murray-Darling Basin plan submissions', *Guardian*, 6 May 2021
16 Clint Jasper, 'Murray-Darling Basin Plan under serious pressure from states who want out, but what will it mean if they bail?', ABC News, 15 December 2019
17 Peter Cullen, 'Adapting to Water Scarcity: A Global Challenge for the 21st Century', New Zealand Freshwater Sciences Society, Australian Society of Limnology, December 2007; wentworthgroup.org/docs/Adapting_to_Water_Scarcity1.pdf

18 Interim Inspector-General of Murray-Darling Basin Water Resources, 'Impact of lower inflows on state shares under the Murray–Darling Basin Agreement', Australian Government, 2020; igwc.gov.au/sites/default/files/2020-09/iig_final_report.pdf
19 Figures for the Murray River alone below the Barmah Choke, where the river narrows at the Barmah Forest in Victoria, show the total area planted across the three states increased from 140,000 to 155,000 hectares between 2003 and 2018.
20 Lauren Day, 'Australia's dairy farmers issue warning as mass exodus continues', ABC News, 26 June 2017
21 Murray Darling Basin water markets inquiry, final report, February 2021; accc.gov.au/system/files/Murray-Darling%20Basin%20-%20water%20markets%20inquiry%20-%20Final%20report_0.pdf
22 Ibid., p. 7
23 The Commonwealth Environmental Water Holder Jody Swirepik acknowledged as much in Margaret Simon's excellent *Quarterly Essay* 'Cry Me A River', 2020
24 'Updated estimate of water supply and horticulture demand in the southern Basin', Victorian Water Register, 27 June 2020; waterregister.vic.gov.au/about/news/321-updated-estimate-of-water-supply-and-horticulture-demand-in-the-southern-basin
25 Ibid.
26 Walgett was surviving on bore water during the 2019 drought. Stanthorpe in Queensland was trucking in bottled water for its population of 5000 in the summer of 2019–20. At the same time, a foreign-owned company was given approval by the local council to run a water mining operation from a bore near Stanthorpe to sell it as bottled water; Ben Smee, 'Chinese company approved to run water mining operation in drought-stricken Queensland', *Guardian*, 28 December 2019
27 Lucy Barbour, Caitlyn Gribbin, Emma Machan, 'How long until drought-stricken towns run out of water?', ABC News, 27 January 2020
28 Bret Walker SC, 'Murray Darling Royal Commission' report, 29 January 2019, p. 32
29 Ibid.
30 Dr Leigh Vial and Andrew Bomm, 'Creative destruction in Australian water markets', Australian Farm Institute, February 2021; farminstitute.org.au/wp-content/uploads/2021/02/Creative-destruction-in-Australian-water-markets_AFI-Feb-2021_Vial-and-Bomm.pdf

Chapter 13: On soil

1 Virginia Gewin, 'The World Food Prize Winner Says Soil Should Have Rights', Civil Eats, 15 July 2020; civileats.com/2020/07/15/the-world-food-prize-winner-says-soil-should-have-rights/

2 A. L. Garside et al., 'Managing yield decline in sugarcane cropping systems', CSIRO Laboratory Labs, undated; daf.qld.gov.au/__data/assets/pdf_file/0004/76954/Monoculture-in-sugarcane.pdf

3 Australian Government, Department of Agriculture, Water and the Environment, 'National Soil Strategy', 2021–2; awe.gov.au/sites/default/files/2021-05/national-soil-strategy-factsheet.pdf

4 Gabrielle Chan, 'Look after the soil, save the Earth: farming in Australia's unrelenting climate', *Guardian*, 21 October 2018

5 Laurie Bedord, 'General Mills Believes Farmers Have a Massive Role to Play in Solving Climate Change', *Successful Farming*, 21 August 2020; agriculture.com/news/crops/general-mills-believes-farmers-have-a-massive-role-to-play-in-solving-climate-change

6 Ross Garnaut, *Climate Change Review*, Cambridge University Press, Melbourne, 2008; and *Australia and the Global Response to Climate Change*, Cambridge University Press, Melbourne, 2011

7 Ross Garnaut, *Reset*, La Trobe University Press, Melbourne, 2021

8 As at April 2021

9 Ross Garnaut, *Superpower*, La Trobe University Press, Melbourne, 2019

10 'Election 2019: Clive Palmer says Scott Morrison can thank UAP's anti-Labor ads for result', ABC News, 29 May 2019

11 'CN30 overview', Meat and Livestock Australia; mla.com.au/cn30/#

12 'Soil: carbon dynamics', Australia, State of the Environment, 2016; soe.environment.gov.au/theme/land/topic/soil-carbon-dynamics

13 Rattan Lal, 'Managing soils for resolving the conflict between agriculture and nature: The hard talk', *European Journal of Soil Science*, 24 June 2019; onlinelibrary.wiley.com/doi/full/10.1111/ejss.12857

14 Ibid.

Chapter 14: On natural value

1 Ken Henry, 'Ken Henry: "The memory of that afternoon has troubled me for all of the last 30 years", Master of Economics 30-year reunion', Speakola, commencement and graduation speeches, ANU, 2001; speakola.com/grad/ken-henry-30-year-reunion-anu-2001

2 Ibid.
3 Richard Allen, Kimbal Baker, *Australia's Remarkable Trees*, Melbourne University Press, Melbourne, 2009
4 George Monbiot, 'Can you put a price on the beauty of the natural world?', *Guardian*, 22 April 2014
5 'British farmers fret about losing their protection and their subsidies', *The Economist*, 27 February 2017; economist.com/britain/2020/02/27/british-farmers-fret-about-losing-their-protection-and-their-subsidies
6 E.g. Fiona Simson as president of the NSW Farmers Association: Michael Condon and Sally Bryant, 'NSW Farmers welcome change in native veg policy', ABC News, 14 June 2013; and federal agriculture minister David Littleproud, 'Media conference at ABARES Outlook Conference, Canberra', 3 March 2020; and, 'Smart Farming Partnerships gives money to get farms more environmental', Good Fruit and Vegetables, 20 March 2020, goodfruitandvegetables.com.au/story/6673219/horticulture-given-bucks-to-get-greener/
7 'A Good Life for All within Planetary Boundaries: Country Comparisons', University of Leeds, 2021; goodlife.leeds.ac.uk/countries/#Australia

On balance

1 Anita McInnes, 'Grower desperate for pickers to get vegetable crops to market', Yanchep News Online, 17 September 2017; yanchepnewsonline.com.au/grower-desperate-for-pickers-to-get-vegetable-crops-to-market/
2 Australian Government, Department of Industry, Science, Energy and Resources, 'Manufacturing a new future for Australia', 6 October 2020; industry.gov.au/news/manufacturing-a-new-future-for-australia
3 Australian Government, 'Modern Manufacturing Initiative and National Manufacturing Priorities announced', 1 October 2020; industry.gov.au/news/modern-manufacturing-initiative-and-national-manufacturing-priorities-announced
4 Andrew Campbell, Jason Alexandra, David Curtis, 'Reflections on four decades of land restoration in Australia', *Rangeland Journal*, 39, 405–16, 2017; publish.csiro.au/rj/RJ17056
5 Alan Schwarz, 'Returning Value to Profit: My late onset political awakening', *Griffith Review, Remaking the Balance*, 71, February 2021; griffithreview.com/articles/returning-value-to-profit

ACKNOWLEDGEMENTS

It remains an act of folly, I think, to try to present a picture of Australian agriculture and land management as it is now. Neverthe-less, I have done it, not without a large measure of teeth-gnashing in the privacy of my little sleep-out office. I was possessed by the story because I think it's important to meditate on how we live in and off the landscape. It was like standing in the middle of a paddock and choosing which way to go. You will see I have travelled into some mad terrain but I hope you can see the point of the journey.

Over the course of the writing process, there were so many conversations and only a small proportion made it into the final manuscript. The ground was changing so quickly, in so many policy areas: trade, natural capital, food processing, water projec-tions. A lot happened between the time I began interviews, in late 2019, and going to press in mid-2021. The story changed from its first concept, partly because of pandemic and partly because of the discovery process. But every conversation filled a little piece of the whole, so thanks to all of you who took my calls and opened your front gate.

I checked in semi-regularly with a range of people because they had a broad, constructive perspective, or were devil's advocates, or just natural-born shit-stirrers who forced me to think of other points of view. Some were a mix of all three. Sue Middleton has been a wise head in farming and life; Pete Mailler kept me questioning; and Kate Burke tested my assumptions; thanks also to Lyndon Frearson. Steve Lacey's cross-fertilisation of agriculture and the environmental space was invaluable. Likewise, Tim Beshara. I am loath to name them all, though, because if there are six degrees of separation in the world, there are one and a half in country Australia. Guilt by association is a thing in rural political circles. You know who you are and I am eternally grateful.

As to the writing process, the book would not have been possible without my publisher, Meredith Curnow, and managing editor Catherine Hill, and all the good people at Penguin Random House. I remain in awe of their talent. Meredith could see the concept where many wouldn't. Catherine's eye for fine detail while holding the whole damn thing in her head has made it a much better book. Reliable sounding boards always include Lucy Clark, George Megalogenis and Katharine Murphy. Bee Robinson sent constant messages of writerly support across locked-down international borders.

My family put up with my distracted self, so thanks to Harry, Alexandra, Genevra and Louis. The Farmer had to watch as the entrails of his culture, occupation and business were pulled apart and sewn back together. There was blood on the floor. Those closest to writers must suffer.

Mostly, though, I kept pushing this topic for my grandchildren, Henry and Lily, and all to follow, because I want them to inherit a healthy, thriving, bounteous planet that can feed its inhabitants. And they won't, unless we think more deeply.

FURTHER READING

Books

Richard Beasley, *Dead in the Water: A very angry book about our greatest environmental catastrophe, the death of the Murray Darling*, Allen & Unwin, Sydney, 2021

Wendell Berry, *The World-Ending Fire: The Essential Wendell Berry*, Penguin Books, London, 2017

Gabrielle Chan, *Rusted Off: Why country Australia is fed up*, Penguin Books, Sydney, 2018

Jennifer Clapp, *Food*, Polity Press, Oxford, 2020

Julian Cribb, *Food or War*, Cambridge University Press, Cambridge, 2019

Laura Dalrymple and Grant Hilliard, *The Ethical Omnivore: A practical guide and 60 nose-to-tail recipes for sustainable meat eating*, Murdoch Books, Sydney, 2020

Matthew Evans, *On Eating Meat: The truth about its production and the ethics of eating it*, Murdoch Books, Sydney, 2019

——, *Soil: The incredible story of what keeps the earth, and us, healthy*, Murdoch Books, Sydney, 2021

Bill Gammage, *The Biggest Estate on Earth: How Aborigines Made Australia*, Allen & Unwin, Sydney, 2012

Ross Garnaut, *Reset: Restoring Australian after the Great Crash of 2020*, LaTrobe University Press with Black Inc., Melbourne, 2021

—, *Superpower: Australia's low carbon opportunity*, LaTrobe University Press with Black Inc., Melbourne, 2019

Jane Gleeson-White, *Six Capitals: Capitalism, climate change and the accounting revolution that can save the planet*, Allen & Unwin, Sydney, 2014, 2020

Yuval Noah Harari, *Homo Deus: A brief history of tomorrow*, HarperCollins, New York, 2018

—, *Sapiens: A brief history of humankind*, HarperCollins, New York, 2015

Dieter Helm, *Natural Capital: Valuing the planet*, Yale University Press, Connecticut, 2016

—, *Green and Prosperous Land: A blueprint for rescuing the British countryside*, William Collins, London, 2019

Tim Lang, *Feeding Britain: Our Food Problems and How to Fix Them*, Pelican, London, 2020

Aldo Leopold, *A Sand Country Almanac: And sketches here and there*, Oxford University Press, New York, 1968

Charles Massy, *Call of the Reed Warbler: A new agriculture, a new earth*, University of Queensland Press, Brisbane, 2017

Helen Mcdonald, *Vesper Flights*, Jonathan Cape, London, 2020

Donella Meadows, *Thinking in Systems: A primer*, Chelsea Green Publishing, Vermont, 2008

Patrice Newell, *Who's Minding the Farm? In this climate emergency*, Penguin Books, Sydney, 2020

Bruce Pascoe, *Dark Emu*, Magabala Books, Broome, 2018

Michael Pollan, *In Defense of Food: An Eater's Manifesto*, Penguin Books, New York, 2008

Richard Powers, *The Overstory*, Penguin Books, New York, 2019

David Raubenheimer and Stephen J. Simpson, *Eat Like the Animals: What nature teaches us about the science of healthy eating*, HarperCollins, New York, 2020

Kate Raworth, *Doughnut Economics: Seven Ways to Think Like a 21st-Century Economist*, Random House, London, 2017

James Rebanks, *English Pastoral: An Inheritance*, Penguin Books, London, 2020

Jonathan Safran Foer, *Eating Animals*, Penguin Books, New York, 2013

Michael Symons, *One Continuous Picnic: A History of Australian Eating*, Penguin Books, Melbourne, 1984

—, *Meals Matter: A Radical Economics through Gastronomy*, Columbia University Press, New York, 2020

Watkin Tench, *1788*, Text Publishing, Melbourne, 2012 edition

Isabella Tree, *Wilding: The Return of Nature to a British Farm*, Pan Macmillan, London, 2019
Don Watson, *The Bush*, Penguin Books, Melbourne, 2017
—, *A Single Tree: Voice from the bush*, Penguin Books, Melbourne, 2016
Tara June Winch, *The Yield*, Penguin Books, Sydney, 2020
Tyson Yunkaporta, *Sand Talk: How Indigenous Thinking Can Save the World*, Text Publishing, 2019

Essays

Alan Blinder, 'The Bad Politics of a Good Idea', *Foreign Policy*, 2019
Judith Brett, 'The Coal Curse', *Quarterly Essay*, 78, June 2020
—, 'Fair Share: Country and City in Australia', *Quarterly Essay*, 42, 2011
Alan Schwarz, 'Returning Value to Profit: My late onset political awakening', *Griffith Review, Remaking the Balance*, 71, February 2021; griffithreview.com/articles/returning-value-to-profit

Academic papers, speeches and reports

Kym Anderson, Ernesto Valenzuela, 'International agricultural subsidies and their impact on Australian agriculture', *Agrifutures* National Rural Issues, April 2020
Stephen Bartos et al., 'Resilience in the Australian food supply chain', Australian Government, Department of Agriculture Fisheries and Forestry, 2013
Andrew Campbell, Jason Alexandra, David Curtis, 'Reflections on four decades of land restoration in Australia', *Rangeland Journal* 39(6), 22 August 2017, pp. 405–16; doi.org/10.1071/RJ17056
—, 'Paddock to Plate: Policy propositions for sustaining food and farming systems', Australian Conservation Foundation, 2009
Peter Cullen, 'Adapting to Water Scarcity: A Global Challenge for the 21st Century, New Zealand Freshwater Sciences Society, Australian Society of Limnology, December 2007
CSIRO (chaired by Ken Henry and David Thodey), 'Australia's National Outlook', 2019; csiro.au/en/Research/Major-initiatives/Australian-National-Outlook
Sue Jackson, Lesley Head, 'Australia's mass fish kills as a crisis of modern water: Understanding hydrosocial change in the Murray Darling Basin', *Geoforum* 109, 2020
Rattan Lal, 'Managing soils for resolving the conflict between agriculture and nature: The hard talk', *European Journal of Soil Science*, 24 June 2019

Geoffrey Lawrence, Sarah Sippel, Nicolette Larder, 'State-Led and Finance-Backed Farming Endeavours: Changing Contours of Investment in Australian Agriculture', *Finance or Food: The Role of Cultures, Values, and Ethics in Land Use Negotiations*, Hilde Bjorkhaug, Philip McMichael and Bruce Muirhead (eds), University of Toronto Press, Toronto, 2020

Mark McGovern, 'Subprime Agriculture and Australia', *Economic Analysis and Policy*, 2014, pp. 243–58

Bill Pritchard, 'Implementing and Maintaining Neoliberal Agriculture in Australia – Part I: Construction Neoliberalism as a Vision for Agricultural Policy', *International Journal of Sociology of Agriculture and Food*, 13, January 2005, 1–12; ijsaf.org/index.php/ijsaf/article/view/311

——, 'Implementing and Maintaining Neoliberal Agriculture in Australia – Part II: Strategies for Securing Neoliberalism', *International Journal of Sociology of Agriculture and Food*, 13, June 2005; ijsaf.org/index.php/ijsaf/article/view/306

Erin Smith and Bill Pritchard, 'Australian Agricultural Policy: The Pursuit of Agricultural Efficiency', *Rural and Regional Futures*, 2015, pp. 58–70

Kiah Smith, Geoffrey Lawrence, Carol Richards, 'Supermarkets' governance of the agri-food supply chain: Is the "corporate-environmental" food regime evident in Australia?' *International Journal of Sociology of Agriculture and Food*, 17(2), 2010, pp. 140–61

Angela Wardell-Johnson et al., 'Creating a climate for food security: The businesses, people and landscapes in food production', National Climate Change Adaption Research Facility, 2013

Podcasts

Agtech So What?
agtechsowhat.com

EvokeAg
evokeag.com/news/tag/podcast

FarmGate
faifarms.com/podcasts

Feed
tabledebates.org/podcast

Talking Politics: A history of ideas
talkingpoliticspodcast.com/history-of-ideas